NOT ON MY
PATCH, LAD

Also by Mike Pannett

Now Then, Lad

You're Coming With Me, Lad

Mike Pannett was born in York and served nearly twenty years in the police. After starring in the BBC's *Country Cops* he was inspired to write about his adventures in the North Yorkshire force. Mike now lives in a small village in the shadow of the North Yorkshire moors.

NOT ON MY PATCH, LAD

MIKE PANNETT

HODDER

First published in Great Britain in 2010 by Hodder & Stoughton
An Hachette UK company

First published in paperback in 2011

7

Copyright © Mike Pannett and Alan Wilkinson 2010
Map © Ulla Saar

The right of Mike Pannett and Alan Wilkinson to be identified as the Authors of
the Work has been asserted by them in accordance with the Copyright, Designs
and Patents Act 1988.

A CIP catalogue record for this title is available from the British Library.

ISBN 978 0 340 91879 1

Typeset in Sabon MT by Palimpsest Book Production Limited,
Falkirk, Stirlingshire

Printed and bound in the UK by CPI Group (UK) Ltd, Croydon, CR0 4YY

Hodder & Stoughton policy is to use papers that are natural, renewable and
recyclable products and made from wood grown in sustainable forests.
The logging and manufacturing processes are expected to conform to the
environmental regulations of the country of origin.

Hodder & Stoughton Ltd
338 Euston Road
London NW1 3BH

www.hodder.co.uk

For my dear mother, Shirley, and in
memory of my father, Jeff – he would
have been very proud.

With special thanks to Alan Wilkinson
and my wife, Ann.

As in my first two books, *Now Then, Lad* and *You're Coming With Me, Lad*, all of the cases I deal with actually happened. I have changed the names of the characters – police as well as villains – and altered the locations only when absolutely necessary to protect people's identities.

Policing procedures are always being updated; what you read here accurately reflects the way we operated at the time each event took place – which in every case is within the last ten years.

Mike Pannett
North Yorkshire
June 2010

Contents

Chapter 1 **First Sunset** 1

Chapter 2 **Winner Takes it All** 27

Chapter 3 **The Ultimate Potting Shed** 51

Chapter 4 **The Fast and the Furious** 77

Chapter 5 **It's a Bullseye** 112

Chapter 6 **Naked Truth** 135

Chapter 7 **The Sun Goes Down** 167

Chapter 8 **A Dark Night** 195

Chapter 9 **Dig a Little Deeper** 218

Chapter 10 **We'll Meet Again** 246

Chapter 11 **Tracked Down** 271

Chapter 12 **Count Your Blessings** 307

Acknowledgements 339

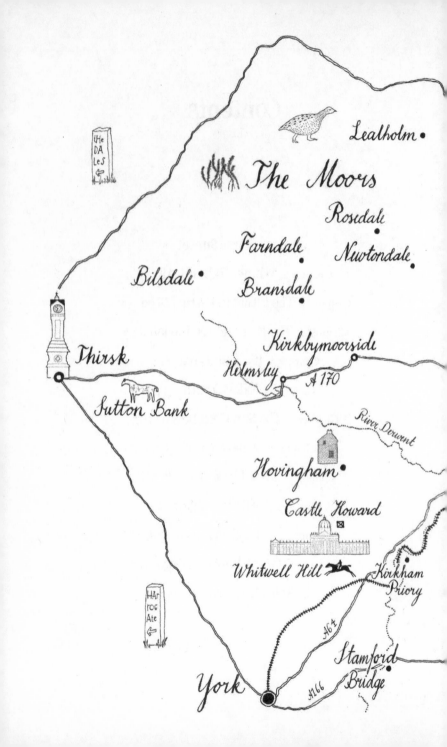

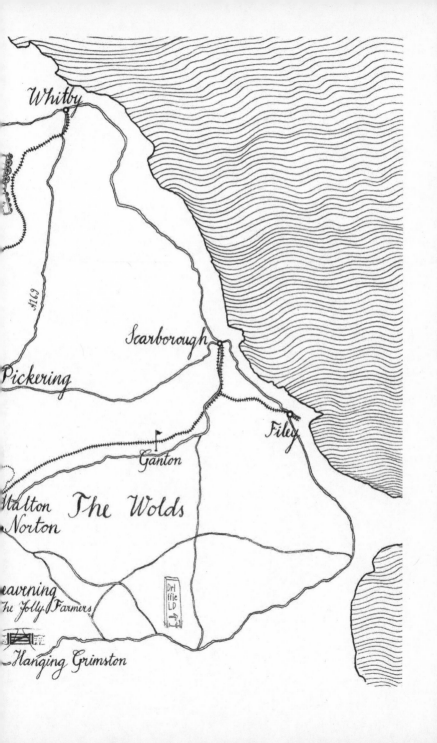

Whitby

A169

Pickering

Scarborough

Filey

Ganton

Malton
Norton

The Wolds

Leavening
The Jolly Farmers

Driffield

Hanging Grimston

Chapter 1

First Sunset

'Been a few changes since I was last here.' Walt had gone ahead of me into the living room and dropped one last armful of logs into the large wicker basket by the hearth.

'The woman's touch,' I said, kicking off my wellies in the kitchen and following him inside with two brand-new, matching mugs filled to the brim with dark, strong tea.

'Wouldn't suit me, mind.' He pulled a piece of bark off his coat sleeve and threw it into the fireplace, then leaned forward to sniff the stubby red candle on the mantelpiece. 'Couldn't be doing with all this scented going-on for one thing,' he added, wrinkling his nose.

'Why, you're stuck in the past, mate. Everyone burns them these days. Hey, and take a look at the window. See that? Proper curtains. Not like them old castoffs at your place. Even got matching cushions on the settee there. I tell you what, mate, it's all the comforts of home.' I passed him his drink, stepped into my new slippers – neatly lined up beside the brass fire-irons – and plonked myself down in the chair. 'Connubial bliss, that's what it is. You won't catch me going back to bachelor life.'

Walt shoved his old cap back and scratched his head. 'Aye, but you want to beware of that there tender trap, mate, that's what I say.'

'Tender trap? What you on about?'

'Why, it's all very well getting your laundry done and your slippers laid out and all these here knick-knacks, but if she's owt like most of 'em she'll soften you up with her home cooking and fancy frills and next thing she'll have you painting and decorating every spare minute and – why, you'll never have no time for yourself, lad.'

I eased myself back in my recliner and sipped at my tea. May as well let him ramble on, I thought. Walter had made his mind up many years ago. Women were best kept at arm's length. He was going to see out his days in splendid isolation. 'Why give half your food away to get the other half cooked?' and all that. I'd heard it before, and to tell the truth it made me laugh. Good luck to him. But as far as I was concerned, the day Ann moved into Keeper's Cottage marked a turning point in my life. It had pulled me out of a dive; and here I was, heading for the sunlit heights. Okay, so I'd had to give up the wardrobe and hang my one suit and two or three decent shirts on the back of the door, but, as she pointed out, the rest of my clothes were only fit for the Oxfam shop. As for her collection of shoes, all laid out on the bedroom floor and tripping me up on a dark morning, well, girls will be girls I say – and that's the way I like 'em. Of course, my sister had to get in on the act and bring us a housewarming gift in the shape of Henry, the manic springer spaniel, and he was already proving a bit of a handful – but hey, I like dogs; and I like a challenge. And Henry was certainly that.

No, I wasn't having any of Walter's doom and gloom. I didn't feel cramped in any way, even though I was now sharing the

house. With Ann working her shifts in York there was no chance
of us getting bored with each other's company. There were times
when we hardly saw each other all week, and communicated
by notes and text messages. Here was I, due to start a late turn,
just before she was due back from her early turn. We might
pass on the drive, and we might not; and we might have half
an hour together when I got home – if she hadn't crashed out.
You never knew.

'Aye well, I s'pose I'd best be off up that hill.' Walt had said
his piece about entanglement with womankind, supped his tea,
and was in the kitchen putting his boots on.

'And I'd best be getting ready for work.' I looked at my watch.
'Hell-fire! Twenty to two?' I leapt out of my seat and headed
for the door. 'They'll have my guts for garters.'

'I shouldn't worry, lad.'

'No, cos you don't have to face the inspector's wrath.' I
grabbed my packed lunch, tapped my trouser pocket for the car
keys, and bustled him out through the door.

'Why, you've no worries now,' Walt said as I locked up and
checked that the dog was in his kennel and his bowl full of
water. Henry had worn himself out, dismantling the logpile as
fast as we built it up, and now he lay there, half asleep, looking
as if butter wouldn't melt in his mouth. 'Aye,' Walt continued,
'no worries at all now that you're a kept man.'

'You what?' I was in the car now, winding the window down.
'You talk in riddles, you do.'

He grinned and pulled his cap down over his forehead. 'Why,
her on a sergeant's pay and you a humble beat bobby. Wouldn't
do for me, lad.'

'You're only jealous, Walt.'

He ignored my remark. 'Aye, and another thing, that there

Henry of yours . . . Tell you what, lad, when you've had enough of chasing him up hill and down dale, you come and see me.'

I laughed as I drove off down the lane. It was a cracking April day, and nothing Walt said was going to spoil it. As the hedgerows flashed by, tinted with green, and here and there the white splash of a blackthorn in bloom, I thought yet again about what a good move I'd made, returning to North Yorkshire. I reminded myself that it wasn't just the coming home to friends, family and fishing. It was about quality of life. Up here we had space, and we felt free to enjoy it – in safety. In fact, if I thought about it I'd say that our part of the world is as safe a place to live as you can find. Yes, there's crime, same as there is every-where. Whatever you read about happening in Leeds or Manchester or even London, sure, the same sort of stuff goes on here, but it's all on a much lower scale – and a lower frequency. The only thing is, as a working copper, you never know what's around the corner.

The inspector, Birdie, was just about to start his briefing as I hurried into the parade room. 'Sorry, sir. Crossing gates,' I said. He took his hand out of his pocket and looked at his watch. 'There's no train due at this hour, Mike, and you know it as well as I do. Now, take a seat. We've a bit to get through.'

It was the usual crew on my shift that afternoon. There was Ed, fresh from a spot of overtime on nights and stifling a yawn; Jayne, just back from her first-aid refresher course; Thommo – who'd been off sick the last fortnight and had his arm stretched out on the desk with a big white bandage for everyone to see; young Fordy, looking his usual eager self, pen poised over his notebook; and there was Chris Cocks, our regular desk sergeant, grinning at me as I stumbled over his legs and grabbed a seat.

'I'll start again,' Birdie said, as I pulled out my notebook.

4

'We've had some intelligence from our friends up north. Cleveland Police, and Northumbria, have been plagued by a gang – at least, they're pretty sure it's all the same gang – who've been committing a series of' – Birdie was measuring his words – 'relatively high-value non-residential burglaries. Shops, warehouses, supermarkets, those sorts of premises. They plan well, get in fast, and get away faster. They're disabling alarms, and putting out the CCTV. So they're not idiots. They're well organised. And we've very little information on them as yet. However, what intelligence we have got leads us to think they consist of four or five members, all male, all white, all of them hardened criminals, all known to their local forces.' He looked around the room. 'And all of them willing to assault police officers.'

Thommo stirred in his seat and pursed his lips. If there was one thing that brought out the old beat bobby in him it was any sort of threat to the uniformed officer. He may be an idle, skiving so-and-so, I thought, but if some gang of burglars fancied having a go at me, he's the man I'd want by my side.

'Now,' Birdie continued, 'the point of all this is that we've reason to suspect that they're planning to move into our area. Their *modus operandi* suggests that the sort of retail premises and warehouses we have in Ryedale might be attractive to them.'

'You mean places that are isolated, sir?' Fordy asked.

'Isolated, not very well protected, certainly unattended at night. And of course they'll be well aware that our resources are stretched to the absolute limit.' He pulled out a sheaf of papers and passed them around. 'You'll see we have photographs of some of the suspects.'

I glanced at the pictures as Fordy passed them on to me. I saw that each suspect had a CRO number by his photograph, indicating that they had been in previous trouble with the police.

Otherwise there was nothing remarkable about them. You see pictures like these on a daily basis and it's virtually impossible to remember them all. You try to look for something distinctive, like a scar or a tattoo, a misshapen nose or a missing tooth, but as a rule they're much of a muchness. These characters, however, did make one strong general impression on me. They looked nasty. Frightening, if you want the truth. Not the sort of people you want to meet when you're on your own on a night shift.

'Anyway.' The inspector was wrapping it up now. 'It seems that they're pulling a job every week or two, generally at night. Oh, and they have a name. The Sunset Gang. Don't ask me, but the Geordies came up with it. Something to do with them going out to work after dark.'

'It was an advertisement, sir.'

'I beg your pardon, Thompson?'

'An advert. Used to be on the telly. There was a woman, washing her hair in a river, and lots of birds singing.'

Jayne was shoving her notebook in a kit-bag. 'That was Sunsilk, you plonker,' she muttered. 'Even I remember that.'

'Yes. Thank you, WPC Maddocks.'

As I went on my rounds that day I thought about how vulnerable we were to the sort of crime Birdie had outlined. It only took a couple of road traffic accidents, a punch-up outside a pub and a domestic incident of some sort, and that was our entire shift accounted for, leaving six hundred square miles of God's own country to the mercy of thieves and burglars. And what if we were on our own, single-crewed, and got a call to say that this Sunset lot were in a warehouse somewhere and the alarm was going off? Would you want to confront them on your own?

The dangers were brought into sharp focus just a few days

later. I'd come in for an early turn and the first person I bumped into was the sergeant off the night shift just ending. Pete was a tall, powerfully built lad, very capable of looking after himself, and always willing to take on the hard cases. But he'd come off second best this time. No doubt about that.

'Christ,' I said, 'what happened to you, mate?' He was sitting in a chair with a mug of coffee in one hand. The other was heavily taped, and he held it to his midriff as if protecting it. He had his tie off, his hair was all over the place, his uniform trousers were out at the knee, and his eyes were red and swollen.

'Looks like I've established contact with that Sunset mob,' he mumbled through swollen lips. 'Bastards.'

'What, were you on your own?'

'No, I was with a WPC. From Scarborough. We were short-handed, so they sent her across to double up with me.'

What Pete went on to say brought home to me just how vulnerable we all are. It seemed they had got a call about two in the morning. The alarm had gone off at a warehouse just outside town. We all knew the place. One or two people had had a go at it over the years. It was known to store confectionery, cigarettes, booze – in large quantities. A natural target.

'We were in town, just handy, so we rushed over and – bingo. Or so we thought. Side door open, van parked outside. Well, you know me . . .'

'Oh yes, don't we just.'

'What was I going to do? Stand there and watch them take off with the loot? I had backup on the way and . . . well, you know how it is.' He sipped his coffee, closing his eyes as the hot brew touched his lips, then carefully stretched his left leg out in front of him, wincing as he did so. 'All I did was poke my torch inside . . .'

'Don't tell me . . .'

'Aye, the buggers came swarming out.' He dabbed at his eyes. 'Frigging gassed me too. Knocked me flat and sprayed me right in the face.'

'CS gas?'

He nodded.

'That's well out of order. I've never known that in this neck of the woods. Bloody outrageous.'

'That's what the Scarborough lass said. She got a faceful too.'

'I take it the buggers got away?'

'Oh hell, aye. We were in no fit state to give chase. It disorientates you. Totally. Plus the fact that they slammed us into the side of the building. By the time I could see anything they'd long gone.'

We were all shocked at Pete's story. Shocked and angry. It struck me as a particularly audacious assault – and one that wouldn't have been perpetrated by your run-of-the-mill local villains. And the realisation that this was probably the work of outsiders really stuck in the throat. Maybe we were jumping to conclusions, but the general consensus was that this was the Sunset Gang that Birdie had briefed us about.

They say it never rains but it pours. Hard on the heels of this incident came reports of a sudden rash of armed robberies around the area. I mean the wider area: Scarborough, Teesside and Humberside. But this wasn't the work of a gang. This was an individual who carried a sawn-off shotgun. So far, he'd attacked two service stations and a small supermarket. And he was about to show his face on my patch.

I was back on nights. I got into work at a quarter to ten to find the station buzzing.

'Have you heard?'

'Heard what, Fordy?'

'Armed robbery, mate. Out at Staxton. Your Country Watch bloke.'

'Jack? At the all-night place?'

'That's the one. By the roundabout there.'

'He's not been hurt, has he?'

'No, he's okay; but he was held up. Early hours this morning. Sawn-off shotgun.'

'Shit, I was there last night – on my two-to-ten shift. Sat there supping tea and saying how quiet it was. What time did it happen?'

'About two, according to Cocksy. Sounds like that mad bastard we've been hearing about.'

'Has to be. You're with me tonight, aren't you?'

'Yeah.'

'Right, I'll give Jack a bell. Soon as things quieten down we'll get ourselves across there.'

Before we set off I had a word with Chris on the desk. 'What have we got on this armed robber?'

'Nothing concrete, but what information there is points to a lad from the Sunderland area. He's well-known up there. History of violence. CID and the Intelligence Unit are trying to build a clearer picture. Sounds like a bit of a loose cannon.'

'You mean crazy.'

'Unpredictable, Mike.'

'Well, let's hope the ARV boys are around if we need them.'

It was an odd feeling, walking across the yard with Fordy, wearing my body armour. A lot of officers wear it routinely. I don't. I find it uncomfortable – restrictive – and generally leave it in the back of the car. But with a nutter like this on the loose I wasn't going to take any chances, even though I doubted how effective it was. The body armour we had at that time was stab-resistant, but not a lot else. The best you could say was that if a shotgun was fired at you from a distance it might offer limited protection. Mind, it was an improvement on the ballistic clipboard we were issued with in our early days in the Met. That was about as much use as a chocolate fireguard. This stuff – well, whatever I thought about it, I had little choice but to put it on and hope for the best: we'd just had a letter from on high, reminding us that failure to wear our protective equipment on duty could reduce any insurance claim in the event of death or injury.

'Times like this I wouldn't mind carrying a gun,' Fordy said as we drove out onto Old Maltongate. He was waiting for a response. 'I mean, to protect myself.'

It's a divisive issue, the arming of the ordinary police officer on the beat. Some are for it, some are rigidly opposed. Personally, I wouldn't have a problem, but by and large I don't feel it's necessary to my personal safety on a day-to-day basis. Not in our neck of the woods anyway. There have certainly been situations when I wished I'd had one, sure there have, but then of course you have to ask yourself the question: How would you feel about using it? About actually having to shoot somebody? It's not a thing you'd do lightly.

'I know how you feel,' I said, and left it at that. Then I handed him the car keys. 'Here, you can drive. I've got a call to make on the mobile.'

Jack picked up right away. 'Now then,' I said. 'Where are you?'

'Behind the counter, Mike. Where else?'

'Bloody hell, mate. I thought you'd be at home. You all right?'

'Oh, not so bad. Bit jumpy, like.'

'Couldn't you have taken the night off?'

'Come on, Mike. That ain't my style. You fall off your bike, you get straight back on it, don't you?'

'Okay, we'll be over in an hour or two.' I switched the phone off and turned to Fordy, who was just taking us out onto Old Maltongate. 'Always a good idea to fly the flag.'

'What d'you mean?'

'You know, show your face. Give your support. And who knows, if any villains are watching for an opportunity to do a follow-up raid, at least we've let 'em know we're about.'

I think we both felt edgy. Once you know that you've got an armed robber on the loose you're never going to relax. And of course, lurking in the background, or so it seemed, was this Sunset lot. They could break cover at any point. At times like these you're on full alert, totally focused and switched on.

We were fortunate that evening. Town was quiet, as indeed were we. Neither of us was saying a lot. I don't know what was going through young Fordy's mind but I kept thinking about Jack. He was one of my most loyal and diligent Country Watch members. Always willing to turn out on patrol. He'd spent many a night parked up in some layby watching the 'crime corridor' as our senior management team liked to call it – it's the A64 to you and me – and suddenly he finds himself, dead of night, on his own, staring down the barrel of a gun. It's frightening enough when you're trained for it. First time it happened to me was when I kicked down a door in South London and found myself face to face with a youth, high as a kite on crack cocaine, pointing a sawn-off shotgun in my face. Not a nice feeling. Not a nice weapon. And not a very nice youth either. When they take a gun like that and saw the barrel off they only have one thing on their mind. It's not just what you'd think – to make the weapon easier to conceal; it's also to make it more lethal. At a distance, a shotgun will hurt you but you've a good chance of surviving. Up close, with the barrel cut back to nothing, they'll kill you. Simple as that. The pellets have no time to spread out. They just punch a large hole, straight through you.

As we made a final turn through the deserted streets of town, Fordy turned on the windscreen wipers. 'Just what we need,' I said. 'A nice drop of rain. That'll send any miscreants scuttling for cover. Come on, let's get ourselves over to Jack's place.'

Jack was, as he put it, shaken not stirred. 'Didn't see any point in staying off,' he said. 'Mind, this time last night I was wondering whether I'd ever see home again. Like a bloody horror movie, it was.'

'I bet.'

'He come in wearing a baseball cap and a scarf round his face. All I could see was his eyes. I knew it was trouble, but Christ – it happened so fast. I was just sat at the till here, reading my paper. Saw this car come in, but instead of filling up he drove straight through, into the Little Chef there. I never thought owt of it. Next thing he's leaned across the counter pointing the gun at me. "Get the money out the till. Now! Don't f***ing mess with me or you're f***ing dead!"'

Fordy was shaking his head. 'You must've been frightened half to death.'

'I tell you what, mate, I was angry, that's what I was. Handing over cash to a piece of scum like that? He was only a little bugger too. If he hadn't had his gun, why, I'd have taken him out with one punch. No, mate, I got frightened afterwards, when I rang the wife. Then I started thinking about what could've happened. That's when I felt the fear, mate. That's when the old hand started shaking.'

'But how did he get in in the first place?' I said.

'Through t'door, what else?'

'Thought you locked it at night. Served 'em through the little hatch there.'

'I do now, Mike. But to tell you the truth I like a bit of company. They're more likely to stop and chat if they can come inside. Kills a bit of time. I mean, it gets pretty deadly here after about midnight. You're always hoping somebody'll call in.'

'Careful what you wish for, eh?' Fordy said.

'Anyway, go on,' I said, 'you gave this fellow the cash, then what?'

'Well, I only had a hundred quid or so. I hand that over, then he starts shouting at me for cigs. I gave him a few packs, maybe a dozen. He grabs 'em, and next thing he's backing out the door pointing the bloody weapon at me. Trust me, if he'd lowered that gun I would've been at him. I could feel it rising in me. Cheeky little sod. Anyway, he shot off to the car and I dashed to the door. Got the number. Then I called your lot. Course, by the time the traffic car got here he was well away.'

We called back on Jack a couple more times during the night. He never asked us to, but somehow it didn't seem right to leave him there on his own. We even got the traffic lads to drop by, plus a Filey crew. So when we called in at five o'clock for a last check there were six of us all stood around supping coffee, and the first customers of the day were coming in wondering what the hell was going off.

I got back home about six thirty that morning. Ann was still in bed. I took Henry for a walk down through the woods and around the fields. At least I went for a walk; he hared about like a mad thing. I had him on the long lead, but he still managed to get into the little beck and cover his legs in mud as he came crashing through the undergrowth. By the time I'd untangled him and got back home, Ann was up and dressed and eating toast. I told her the tale about Jack.

And that's another thing I'd been enjoying since she moved in – having someone to unload to. Many a time I've driven home exhausted, emotionally wrung out after attending a nasty accident, perhaps a fatality, or dealing with a violent offender, and having nobody to talk to. It's the sort of scenario that drives some officers to the bottle. So even though Ann was on her way out, it was a relief to be able to give her the bare outline of what had happened. She was shocked. 'It's just not what people are used to,' she said. 'It's not the sort of thing that happens out in the country.'

When I went up to bed I was still thinking about the probable reverberations. Word would have spread like wildfire; any time now my Country Watch people would be calling me; the media would have a field day. And we would be under pressure, as a force, to 'do something about it' and 'get it sorted'.

I was awoken by the phone. It was the duty sergeant. 'Mike, hope I didn't get you out of bed?'

I looked at my watch. Just turned one. I'd had five hours, roughly. 'Go on,' I said. 'What can I do for you?'

'Look, I know you're still on nights, but can you get yourself down here for the late turn? We've had a tipoff. We think we've located that armed robber. The Staxton job.'

'Brilliant, mate.' I was out of bed and squirming into my T-shirt and shorts. 'Where is he?'

'The information is he's in a flat in Scarborough. We're getting a firearms team together. We, er – we need your door-opening skills.'

'Give me thirty minutes,' I said. 'No, make that twenty.' Breakfast could wait, but I needed to get showered before I hit the road.

People think that beating a door in is easy. It certainly is in the films. One good kick, or a shoulder-charge, and they're matchwood. Wouldn't it be nice? In reality there's a fair bit of science goes into gaining access through a locked door. It's one thing breaking a lock, but you'd be surprised how hard it can be to get the door actually to open – and quickly – so that you can gain access. Because speed is of the essence. If you've got an armed suspect on the other side you've got to be in like Flynn, before they have a chance to realise what's happening and grab their weapon. The element of surprise is crucial. So breaking the door in is a job for a trained officer, which was why they'd called me in. As part of my training for the TSG, the Met's riot police, I'd been taught a number of door-opening techniques, using various pieces of equipment.

I put my uniform on, slapped a piece of ham between two slices of bread, and drove into town. The team had gathered at Scarborough, but I had to call in at Malton to collect my gear, starting with my door opener. This was a piece of real high-tech equipment. Well, that's what I told the lads. Basically it was a solid metal cylinder about four or five inches in diameter, with a handle at each side so that it could be operated by a single person, or two working together. As I picked it up and heaved it into the back of the car, it reminded me of Algy's cannon, the one he'd fired off to see in the new year that time. It was the same size, but a bright, fire-engine red. I also packed my goggles and a pair of heavy-duty leather gauntlets to protect myself against splinters of wood or shards of broken glass – again, not the sort of thing you'd see a copper using in the movies. But then those actors, they're tougher than us. And better looking.

I was driving an unmarked car, standard practice for an operation like this. We keep a couple at Malton, both equipped with blue lights and a siren, and of course the police radio, but all of that's hidden from view. I was just loading up when one of the late-shift PCs drove into the yard in his patrol car. 'What's going off?' he asked.

'Can't tell you, mate. Sorry.'

'Not that armed robber, is it?'

'They never told me, bud.'

You don't like acting coy, but you expect your fellow officers to understand that some jobs can't be talked about, especially when you're liaising with personnel from another station. And he got the message. He wouldn't be offended. Loose lips sink ships, as the saying goes.

As I drove along the A64 I found myself going over the various possible scenarios. You always do when you're going to a job where you might be putting yourself in danger. You can't help it. This was going to be the first time I'd worked with the North Yorkshire Police Firearms Team. Part of me was excited. You can't help that either. This was, after all, why I joined the force: for excitement, to capture the bad guys and bring them to justice. But at the same time I was apprehensive. You never know how these things will go. And when firearms are involved the risks are high – for all of us. Back in the Met I'd been on numerous operations with SO19, their crack firearms team. Those guys were one hundred per cent professional. They dealt with armed suspects on a daily basis. Here in North Yorkshire a live firearms incident is a rarity. So how experienced were the team? How would they cope?

I arrived at Scarborough nick, parked in the covered station car park, left the battering ram in the boot, and took the lift to the top floor. I headed for what is now the conference room, but used to be a bar where officers could pop in and unwind after work. A dog handler sat in the corner with his German shepherd lying at his feet. A firearms team of six had been mustered, with a sergeant in charge. They had been pulled together from three different ARV units across the force. I recognised one or two of them. They were sitting round a large table with maps of the town spread out in front of them, and a plan of the building where the suspect was supposed to be. The mood was almost jovial, which took me by surprise at first; but then I thought back to my Met days, and the way we'd always have a bit of a laugh and a joke when we were about to go on a dangerous operation. You know you're not kidding anyone, least of all yourself, but it helps to relieve the tension. God knows what it was like for the firearms lads, all kitted up in their dark overalls and boots, with their gun belts around their hips. They were wearing their handguns but of course in the vehicle they'd have their stubby Heckler and Koch semi-automatics. I couldn't help making comparisons with the way it had been in the Met. Their teams worked together all the time on such operations. They knew each other inside out. They would unwind together after a day's work. They had the confidence you gain from that depth of experience, that close co-operation, that team spirit, built up over months and years. In a place like North Yorkshire, where a firearm incident is a rare and headline-grabbing event, the lads just wouldn't have bonded the way you do when you're training and working together every day.

Just as I was introducing myself the inspector arrived from Harrogate, and with him came the Tac advisor, a specialist who would advise on the tactics best suited to a given situation.

'Right,' said the inspector. 'I'll be taking charge on the ground, but I'll be liaising by phone with the force senior officer who is on the late turn at York.' He gave us a name, but it meant nothing to me. 'She'll be making the final decisions – because she'll be carrying the can if things go wrong.'

The question was, how best to achieve the desired outcome? 'Our information,' said the inspector, 'is that intelligence has linked a number of armed robberies over the past few weeks with one individual. You'll all be aware of him from your own local briefings. We have images, a possible ID, and we're satisfied that we have good information that this individual is now located in a top-floor flat at the building marked on the map there, close to the town centre. We also believe that the vehicle with which he has been linked is parked a couple of streets away. Also marked on the map.' He prodded at it with his pen. 'We currently have in place armed obs on both the vehicle and the front door.'

I looked around me. The firearms boys were quiet and still, concentrating on what the inspector was saying. He leaned over the map.

'Okay then, the building is a Victorian terraced house; three floors and a basement. You'll proceed to within a hundred yards of the premises in an unmarked van – the late-turn sergeant is getting one now – and then approach on foot. Late-turn officers will cordon off the area around the building – here.' He pointed to the spot with his forefinger. 'We've got keys to the main front door. You'll enter together, proceed to the top floor where PC Pannett' – he nodded at me – 'will force entry. Once he's done his stuff we'll aim to talk the suspect out. If that doesn't work we'll send a dog in.' He referred to his papers once more. 'Mike, the door is a normal wooden-panelled job with a single Yale lock.'

Yes, I was thinking, but what about bolts? I wasn't going to take anything for granted.

The inspector continued with his briefing. 'Just remember, everybody, this is an extremely violent individual. He could be facing twenty-five years inside. He may well be thinking that he has little to lose.'

He was silent for a moment. We knew what he was saying. Up on the wall the clock's hand ticked forward. I looked around the table again. No one was joking now, least of all the ARV boys. I say boys: they did look very young. A lot was resting on their shoulders. Not only had they got to ensure the safety of the public, their fellow officers and themselves in the face of an armed and potentially murderous criminal, but they also had at all times to maintain the strictest professional standards. Carrying a gun may give you a measure of security, but it doesn't give you licence to blast away the minute you come face to face with a villain. I've said it before: it's not like on the telly. If the worst comes to the worst and you have to discharge your weapon, for whatever reason and whatever the outcome, you will most likely be suspended from duty and put under investigation just as if you have committed a criminal act. These lads were well aware of that, and to me that was a measure of their courage; that they would go after an armed criminal knowing that if they got it wrong they could, in the worst-case scenario, end up in the dock, facing prison for unlawful killing. I didn't envy them.

'Are we all set then?' asked the inspector. We all nodded.

'Right, RVP in the car park in ten minutes.' Just time for a last visit to the toilet, then.

In the car park the firearms boys changed into their pro- tective outer clothing. Fighter pilot meets riot police: guns on hips, helmets with visors and built-in microphones. All I had on was my body armour and the usual uniform. Except today I wore my black rainproof jacket rather than the standard-issue fluorescent one. I took my trusty battering ram from the boot. 'Who's gonna carry this?' I asked.

'You're not in the Met now, Pannett,' one of the lads said. 'You carry your own tackle.'

'Bloody hell!' I said. 'We used to have a man assigned to t'job. I mean, I'm the star man, me. The striker. You don't want me staggering into the penalty area all out of breath, do you?' No answer. I picked the ram up and carried it across to the unmarked hire van, grinning as I heaved it into the back and climbed in with the others.

It only took three or four minutes to get to the rendezvous point, a street or two away from the target house. We parked up next to an ambulance that had been brought in on standby. Not far away I could see the uniformed shift officers, in place and ready to stop any vehicles or pedestrians from entering the area. We got out of the van and moved forward in a line, the firearms team first, then me with the door enforcer on my shoulder, and finally the dog handler. God knows what we looked like. There was a single onlooker, a middle-aged man at his open front door, holding a Tesco bag. He stood there frowning and watched us troop past.

We walked quickly along the side of the building, almost breaking into a trot. When we got to the front the lead man took out the key and opened the communal entrance, a big heavy door with panels and an old brass knocker. We followed him in, our rubber-soled boots squeaking on the tiled hallway floor. All the while I was thinking about the door to the flat. I was hoping that the intelligence was correct and it would go in easily. If we'd had more time to plan this I would have done a recce. I enjoy those. It's real cops-and-robbers stuff. Subterfuge. One time I got hold of an electricity company ID card, knocked on the door and had a good look around inside before telling the occupant I must have got the wrong address. A few days later when I broke the door in and arrested him for dealing in heroin he looked at me and said 'Don't I know you?'.

We were on the third floor now, moving forward quietly. The firearms boys had their guns at the ready as they glided smoothly around corners. My heart was thumping now – and not just from lugging the ram up those stairs. We were approaching the door of the flat, with just two more steps to mount. The lead guy gestured me to the front with his hand. I crept forward and inspected the lock. It looked easy enough. Bending down, I reached out a hand and pushed gently but firmly at the bottom to make sure there was no bolt on the other side, then did the same at the top. I closed one eye and checked down the crack between the door and the frame for any mortise locks. Nothing, just the Yale about a foot above the handle. I turned to look at the lead firearms man, raising an enquiring eyebrow. He nodded. I gestured for him to step back a foot or so, then lifted the ram up over my shoulder, leaned right back, took a deep breath and put everything into a huge swing. If this didn't work I'd be straight onto the hinges.

Wallop! I'd bust clean through the lock and removed the top half of the flimsy wooden panelling.

'POLICE! POLICE! Armed police! Show yourself with your hands in the air!'

As the remains of the door swung open I was bundled aside and almost thrown to the floor as the first two lads sprang forward, locking their shields to block the doorway. Two other firearms officers leaned across the top of the makeshift barricade, pointing their weapons into the flat.

A single lightbulb illuminated the little hallway and the opening into the living room. There was no movement, no sound, just a fridge humming in the background. We stood for a few seconds, listening, waiting, sweating.

'Armed police! Show yourself!' Still no response. The team held their position for what seemed like several minutes and repeated the challenge. Still nothing. Nobody moved; nobody said a word.

Finally we heard the firearms sergeant updating the inspector by radio. No, he was saying, we had not 'engaged the subject'.

'Right,' he said, 'let's have the dog in here.' The handler moved forward with the German shepherd. He knew what he had to do and he was clearly anxious about it. He was patting the back of the dog's head, reassuring it. This was his colleague, his friend, his oppo. And he was about to send it into a flat to confront a man armed with a gun. But to the dog this situation might as well have been just another game. It looked intelligent and alert, eyes fixed on the handler, ears pricked forward and its hind legs quivering with anticipation, waiting for the command. But first his handler gave out another warning.

'Police dog and handler. Show yourself or I'll send the dog in.'

Still no reply. People don't realise how deliberate and painstaking this kind of operation is. You give a suspect every chance – and you protect your team. All the way.

'Police dog and handler, show yourself.' At a sign from the handler the dog barked to reinforce the message.

Silence. The dog was now like a coiled spring, looking up at its handler, eager to do what it was trained to do.

The Armed Response officer nodded and the handler released the dog and whispered, 'Find him.'

The dog ran forward into the hallway and disappeared into the living room. Still there was nothing, just the sound of its paws click-clicking and slipping on the vinyl flooring as it sniffed into every corner. When an empty beer can clattered to the floor I braced myself, fully expecting a shot to ring out at any moment. But it was just the dog, nosing around. I was crouched low down, trying to relax the muscles in my leg, but failing.

The dog returned to the hallway and looked at the handler. He gestured with open hands for the dog to return to him, then turned to the firearms sergeant. 'It's clear,' he said.

'You sure?'

'Sure as I can be. No indication given. He's a reliable dog.' He moved back from the door a little way down the corridor, where he knelt and tousled the dog's head. Both of them then resumed a standby position, eyes fixed on the door. The handler was probably praying that the dog had got it right. If the dog had missed the suspect and he had wrongly given the all-clear, he would be putting his colleagues at risk when they entered. But that wasn't going to happen until the inspector had been consulted by radio.

The whole operation was tightly controlled, with the important decisions being made by the late-turn senior officer. Only when she gave the go-ahead did the firearms team move slowly into the flat to begin their search. The silence that followed made my heart pound as hard as if we'd been in action.

From the outside I could hear furniture being moved around, and the shouts of 'Clear' as each room was searched in turn. Eventually they returned to the hallway, beckoning me to come inside.

'The bird has flown – if he was ever here,' the sergeant said.

'He was here okay – or someone was.' I was in the kitchen with my hand on the kettle. 'This is still warm.'

In the living room a rising sash window was half open. I leaned out and looked around. 'Sarge?' I said. He came over to the window. I pointed across the garden to where a uniformed officer could be seen in his fluorescent jacket, just a street away.

The sergeant swore. 'Plain as bloody day. No wonder matey disappeared.'

'Christ. Thought we'd sorted those cordons out.'

'Might as well have sent him a bloody telegram telling him we were on our way,' someone said.

While we stood there, taking in what had happened, the CID arrived with a search warrant and went through the premises looking for anything connected with the armed robberies. I could feel the tension go out of my body. Disappointed we may have been, but the immediate danger was past. And my job was done – or should I say my involvement was over. The last thing I heard on the scene was the sergeant radioing all the officers we had around the area.

'Yeah, suspect believed to have escaped through the window and made off across the rooftops.' That meant there was a good chance he was still in the area. 'So we'll take no chances. We've got the Humberside police helicopter on its way. We'll continue the search when it gets here.'

I lugged the battering ram wearily back down the three flights of stairs, out the front, and along the road to the van.

You always go over these things afterwards. You ask yourself what lesson could be learned, what you would have done differently. There was only one answer in this case: be more discreet. If there was a single crumb of comfort to be taken from that cock-up, it was that nobody had got hurt. On the other hand, we still had an armed robber on the loose. That was not a good feeling.

Back at Scarborough nick we had the usual debriefing session. It was a sombre affair. You feel angry, frustrated, a little bit stupid. You can't wait for it to be wound up. The conclusion was that the firearms team had done a good job but had been let down by the uniformed officers being clearly visible – and of course the poor positioning of the cordons. There was no getting away from the fact that the local inspector had stationed them too close to the target address.

So – a painful lesson for him. But this is why you have debriefing sessions, to learn from your mistakes and iron things out for the future. The blessing in this case was that the cop I'd seen from the window hadn't been used as target practice by the suspect.

It was past midnight by the time I got back to Keeper's Cottage. Ann was fast asleep and due up at five for an early turn. I let Henry out and was soon kicking myself as he disappeared into the distance. It was a full half an hour later when I slipped into our nice warm bed – to be greeted by Ann grumbling sleepily about my cold feet.

She'd already left by the time I woke up next morning, so I didn't hang about. I wanted to get into work early. I was still on edge, still angry about that cock-up at Scarborough. I felt as if I had unfinished business. But the look on Chris Cocks's face when I walked into the station was a joy to behold. He was grinning from ear to ear, and he had his thumbs up. 'We've got him,' he said.

'What, here?' I said.

'No, no. Northumbria police. Sounds a bit hairy. He pulled another job, took off in his car, but they spotted him and gave chase. Reckless bastard, he took a pop at them.'

'Bloody hell. Anyone hurt?'

'No. Could've been nasty though. Thankfully, he crashed the car.'

'What happened to him?'

'Survived – unfortunately. Knocked unconscious and woke up to find four firearms boys pointing their guns at him.'

'I tell you what, Chris, it makes you wonder what he would have done – I mean, what if we'd cornered him in that flat?'

'Forget it, Mike. All that matters is he's banged up now.'

'Well, let's hope they throw the bloody book at 'im. I know what I'd give the little . . .'

'I know what you mean, Mike. Let's hope the court feels the same. We've done our bit. Now it's up to them.'

'Aye but sometimes the sentence doesn't quite seem to reflect the crime.'

'No. Don't even think about it. Just make yourself useful and get that kettle on.'

Chapter 2

Winner Takes it All

It was a glorious spring morning. With the exception of one last reluctant ash, the trees around Keeper's Cottage had all come into leaf and we were surrounded by greenery. A woodpecker was hammering away in the woods at the bottom of the lane, and I'd just spotted the first of the swallows scouting around for a place to build a nest.

'We'll have a decision to make there,' Ann said. We were sitting on the log, drinking tea and soaking up the sunshine. Well, Ann was sitting – in what used to be my seat – and I was perched on a nasty little knot at one end. A second bird was darting about under the eaves, flashing its white underbelly at us. 'I mean, lovely to see them and so on, but they'll make a right mess of the windows.'

'Leave 'em, I say. We can always wipe a few droppings away.'

She smiled at me. 'Glad you said that. Some people get in a total lather, putting up those strips of coloured plastic to scare them off. I mean, why? They're such beautiful things.'

'Ann,' I said, shifting position on the log, 'I don't mean to change the subject but . . . what would you say if someone told you I was a kept man?'

'I beg your pardon?'

'It's something Walt said the other day. He was just trying to wind me up. You know what he's like. But it got me thinking.'

'It's got me thinking too. What *are* you on about?'

'He meant you being on a sergeant's pay while I'm still a humble beat bobby.'

'Mike, you can't have everyone getting promoted or specialising or we wouldn't have any PCs left to pound the beat. We need experienced career PCs more than ever these days. And besides, what's wrong with being a beat bobby for thirty years? It's the foundation of the force, you're on the front line dealing with the public and doing what most of us joined up for.' She put a hand on my shoulder. 'Anyway, the way I see it we spend half our life at work, so why not stick at doing what you like best?'

'Aye, but . . .'

'But what?'

'You know how people are.'

'Yeah. Some people are fine. And some are prats. And if some of the prats choose to think badly of you because I got promoted . . . I mean, what would they say if you'd got promoted and I was still a WPC? Would I be a "kept woman"?'

'You know what they'd say. They'd say that's different.'

'And is it?'

'Well, no, not really.'

'End of conversation then. Tell you what though' – she nudged me in the ribs and handed me her empty mug – 'if you are a kept man, you may as well earn your board. Is there any more tea in that pot?'

When I returned with our mugs refilled I brought the calendar with me. Ann had marked all our shifts on it, mine in black and hers in red. When you work different turns you need to keep a track of where you both are and when you're likely to have time for the normal things in life. It's not just days off or evenings out; you need to grab the occasional morning when you're free to go into town – little things that most couples take for granted. For us they're a real treat.

We sat out there for another half-hour or so. It was the nearest we'd had to a bit of downtime together in a fortnight, and any time now she'd be off to Leeds for a court hearing. We were wondering when we could next manage a day out together.

'How about Sunday?' I said.

'Sounds good to me. I'm early start on Monday though, so we don't want to be out too late.'

'Right then. Let's make hay while the sun shines. What do you fancy doing?'

Ann closed her eyes, tilted her head back and let the sun caress her upturned face. 'I'd say breakfast in bed would be a good start.'

'Cooked by me, I suppose?'

'Mike, you do a fry-up like nobody I've ever known. And you know how you enjoy looking after me.'

'I spoil you rotten, that's the truth of it. Look at you.' I shoved up against her. 'I even let you sit on my special seat that I had custom-made to fit me.'

'Well, fetch Nick back with his chainsaw and get him to carve another one. There's plenty of room. Anyway, stop changing the subject. Are you going to bring me bacon and eggs in bed, that's what I want to know.'

'Aye, go on then. And mushrooms, I presume? Cos they'll have to go on the shopping list.'

She nodded, then turned her face back up to the sun.

'Any chance of some of those cherry tomatoes I saw in the fridge? On the vine?'

'I was saving those for my pack-up. But I tell you what – you promise to do the dishes and you can have them.'

'I always do the dishes.'

'True.'

'But why? Why do I always get lumbered with the washing up?'

'Cos I'm rubbish at it. And you're a natural. You have a tidy mind. Same as I have a natural talent for fry-ups. It's horses for courses.'

She was quiet for a moment, and I shuffled back along the log, waiting for the elbow in the ribs. But her mind was already elsewhere.

'Horses for courses, eh? Now that's an idea. How about point-to-pointing?'

'Eh?'

She sat up straight and turned to face me. 'For our day out. We'll have a nice cooked breakfast, then go point-to-pointing.'

'I thought the season was over.'

'No, it goes on till about the beginning of June. End of May anyway.'

'I wouldn't know. I've never been.'

'Well, you're in for a treat then,' Ann said. 'If my memory serves me, there's a meeting at Whitwell. We always used to go there when my dad was riding.'

'You mean he actually competed?'

'Competed? I'll have you know he won the Grimthorpe Gold Cup, the prestige event of the year.'

'You serious?'

'Course I am. You can look it up in the record books. 1976 it was. He rode Villa Court.'

'You never told me any of this,' I said.

'She belonged to my grandad. Then when he retired her she lived in our paddock and I got to ride her. We called her Mary. Lovely horse, she was. Really gentle.'

'1976, eh? I'm surprised you can remember back that far, young lady.'

'I was very young, Mike. Very young indeed.'

I saw Ann off to Leeds and got my things together. I wasn't due at work till two, but I wanted to prepare for a Country Watch meeting I'd arranged for later in the week. I'd been too busy the last month or so to get around to all my contacts. With forty-plus members involved in the scheme, there was always the odd one I missed out. As a rule we only had a meeting when there was something big on – like a spate of farm burglaries, or a gang of rustlers at work. Most of our members were farmers, gamekeepers and the like, and they were always busy. If it wasn't the harvest it was ploughing, and if it wasn't that it was drilling, lambing, fencing, or ditching; or the hunting season. There was always something. But from time to time, perhaps once a year, I liked to get them together to have a bit of a catch-up.

The first thing I did when I got into the parade room was to have a look at the last circular I'd sent out, which had gone to all the members just after New Year. It made interesting reading. There was the disappearance of twenty-three sheep from a farm at Thorpe Bassett – still not solved; and the theft of a dog kennel in the same village. Now, who would do that, and why? We never did find out. More satisfying was the case of the exploding phone boxes. Now that could've been a real head-scratcher if we hadn't got lucky one January night. It was a gang from Leeds. They were making their own bombs: emptying the gunpowder out of fireworks, taping it up in a plastic tube, and triggering it with blue touchpaper. I have to say I was surprised at how much damage they were able to do. Their misfortune was that they happened to be out at three o'clock one morning just as the traffic boys were test-driving a new car up and down the A64. They saw a man in a phone box with a car parked nearby. Thought nothing of it until half an hour later when they noticed the same vehicle beside another phone box several miles down the road. They radioed Malton and the duty sergeant went out to investigate in an unmarked car. He was just passing a third box at Scagglethorpe when there was a yellow flash and the door flew off its hinges, scattering debris right across the road. You don't often come across a crime in progress; even more rarely do you manage to round up the miscreants at the same time; but Pete did. He found the gang lurking in the parked car and had the cuffs on them before the smoke had cleared. At least, that's what he told us. He found three cash-boxes in the back of their vehicle, and a small mountain of coins. A highly satisfying outcome, which was why I'd put it in the newsletter. Along with the rundown of crimes, solved and unsolved, I'd also included the usual list of registration numbers of all the vehicles currently believed to be involved in some sort of crime. So that was my morning's work: preparing another handout for the meeting on Friday.

We convened at the usual place, the Dawnay Arms in West Heslerton. It was a popular spot, and easy to get to, being tucked away in the village just off the Scarborough Road. The landlord was always pleased to have us in and would put on a few trays of sandwiches in a back room where we could close the door and have a bit of privacy. If it was cold he'd bring us a pot of soup as well.

We had about thirty, maybe thirty-five by the time I kicked things off by thanking them all for turning out. There were the usual suspects. Pete Jowett, who'd helped me chase the last of the Barnsley Three the previous winter – or was it the winter before? Anyway, he showed up, as did the Colonel, still complaining about his arthritic knees but full of enthusiasm for the fight against crime. 'Because this was our brainchild, if you remember, Mike?'

'That's quite right, Colonel. The time you lost your balls.'

'Indeed,' he chuckled. 'Seems like yesterday. Geoffrey and Nick, yourself of course, sitting in my kitchen and plotting out the whole thing.'

'And then that planning meeting we had in the Gun Room. It was Churchill's bunker all over again, wasn't it? With tea and biscuits.'

'Ha ha ha, quite so, Mike, quite so. By the way, been meaning to ask you, did you ever track down the chappy who was stealing the milk off our doorsteps last autumn?'

'Oh, didn't I tell you about that?'

'No. Don't think I've seen you since you came by that time. The thefts just stopped as suddenly as they'd started. I presumed you'd "had a result", as the young people like to say.'

'We certainly did, Colonel.'

'So you got the blighters. Good show. Schoolchildren, I suppose?'

'Let's say the culprit was young at heart.' I wasn't going to spill the beans about Ronnie Leach. The last I'd heard, the lad was working and keeping his nose clean.

Two other veterans of Operation Bulldog were there, Stan and Pauline, as well as Nick the gamekeeper with his son and two former Special Constables. I addressed the multitude for a few minutes, filling them in on the latest crime scene in Ryedale, and then got onto the issue of confidentiality and security.

'I've been talking with two of our fellow organisations in Hambleton and Craven,' I said. 'Some of you will have heard of Vale Watch – and Sheep Watch. They work along the same lines as us: ordinary farmers and country people like yourselves, gathering intelligence for the fight against crime in their areas. Anyway, they both mentioned a disturbing trend. It seems that they're getting to be so successful – as we are, I should add – that they've both had a local villain trying to join up.'

'Not a mole, surely?' someone said from the back of the room.

'That's the word I was looking for. Thank you. You wouldn't have thought it, but people are trying to infiltrate organisations like ours to find out what we're up to, what we know, who we suspect, and so on. I'm not suggesting a witch hunt, but if you get anybody wanting to join us on our patrols, just ask yourself: who are they, and why are they doing it? We've also had a bit of media attention, sniffing around looking for a story. Now my advice is that we should keep well away from them. It's not like we're doing cloak-and-dagger stuff, but you'll all be far more effective as eyes and ears if nobody knows what you're up to.'

I handed out my updated newsletter. I'd spent some time preparing it, making sure there was nothing confidential or sensitive. Once you've handed out forty copies of that sort of thing you've no way of controlling who reads it. There was little other formal business, and of course the idea of a get-together like this is to talk to people, exchange ideas and information. There was no shortage of people wanting to chew my ear, especially when the perennial problem of poaching came up.

Bob Easton, who farmed up on the Wolds, was a bit of a hothead at the best of times, and just mentioning the word 'poachers' in his presence was like waving a red rag at a bull – especially when he had a pint in his hand. 'Why, we're too lenient wi' them,' he growled. 'Them old Wild Westerners had the right idea. Cattle rustlers and horse thieves, you hung 'em from t'nearest tree.'

'Now steady on, Bob. This is the twenty-first century.'

'Aye, but them buggers are committing a nineteenth-century crime. If they want to live like they did in olden times, that's fine by me. But maybe we should give 'em a taste of olden-time justice, that's what I say. I've been plagued with 'em this past winter, sniffing around with their dogs, and I'm telling you . . . Well, I hope they realise who they're dealing with, that's all. Mind, I've put paid to them once or twice already.'

'Oh hell, what have you done? Or don't I want to hear about it?'

'Nowt illegal, Mike. Just when they're out lamping I park myself in a nice quiet spot, maybe three or four hundred yards away, half a mile even. Then I wait till they've spotted sommat and shine my own lamps. Knackers the job completely.'

I knew what he was on about. A bright light will startle a hare or a deer and drive it away. And as to the poachers, they've no way of knowing whether it's us they're seeing, or a rival gang. I couldn't help laughing at first, but I had to say my piece. 'Bob,' I said, 'don't get me wrong now. I understand where you're coming from but . . .'

'I know, I know. You're worried I'll take the law into my own hands.'

'Or provoke a confrontation. By all means warn them,' I said. 'You've a perfect right to do that, but when it comes to action you call us in. Some of these people can be very unpredictable, not to mention violent.'

I worried about Bob. And as things turned out it wouldn't be long before my worries were justified. But I left it there for the moment, mainly because I could see Nick was wanting a quiet word.

'What's on your mind?' I asked him.

'Why, it might not be anything at all, Mike, but I was having a chat with a fellow over at Helperthorpe. You'll know him. Has a farm on the tops there. Used to be a big estate with cottages all over. Anyway, he runs it more or less on his own now; with his lads, I mean, and he rents out a couple of the old places. Jenks, they call him.'

'Can't say I remember the name – and I would, cos it's an odd one.'

'Big fellow, drives about in a Land Rover pick-up.'

'Ah, I know the one. Sort of beige coloured?'

'That's it. You don't see many of them around. Anyway, he was telling me about a couple who've taken over one of the old farmhouses. They have a youngster, goes to school in the village. He was out shooting there a few weeks back. They've a big old barn. Brick-built job. And he said they'd blacked out all the windows.'

'Hmm, why would they do that, d'you think?'

'Could be owt. Could have made it into a workshop, or a studio. Who knows? But to say they're only renting . . . I mean it's a lot of effort to go to.'

'Okay, Nick. I'll drop by some time when I'm out that way. Be interesting to find out what they're up to.'

People were already starting to drift off home by this time, but there was a handful wanting to make a night of it. Well, why not, with the weekend coming up? As for me, though, I needed an early start Saturday. I had a few chores to do around Keeper's Cottage, and with Ann at work I'd have the weekend shopping to do, then I'd be preparing for our day at the races.

When Sunday came we were blessed with the kind of weather you dream about: a blue sky dotted with white puffy clouds, and a balmy southerly breeze. I left Ann in bed half asleep, threw on a pair of shorts and a T-shirt and headed quietly downstairs. I put the kettle on and put a few rashers of bacon in the frying pan with the little tomatoes, set it on a low heat, then slipped on my wellies and went into the garden to let Henry out. I should have known better. As soon as I'd opened the kennel door he was off, like shit off a stick, over the dyke and across the field towards the rabbit warren.

By the time I got him back I was lathered in sweat, my feet were drenched, and the bacon was done to a crisp. I shoved the overdone tomatoes to one side, threw some eggs in the pan, put the toast on and made another pot of tea, then carried the lot upstairs and climbed back into bed next to Ann.

'God, you're freezing!' she shrieked. 'And wet! And look at your legs!'

'Have some sympathy,' I said, 'they're covered in nettle rash.'

'Mud, you mean! Look at the state of these sheets. What the hell have you been doing?'

'It's not me, it's that bloody dog. I tell you what though – by the time I get the little bugger trained up I'll be fit as a . . .'

'As a butcher's dog?'

We both laughed. 'Ah well, it's all in a morning's work – and at least he's had his run for the day,' I said.

'That dog gets more and more like you every day, Mike.'

37

'What do you mean?'

'Wayward – and in need of some training.'

'I'm not wayward. I just have boundless energy and enthusiasm for life.'

'Precisely. Just like Henry.'

'Never mind that – just eat up and let's go racing.'

The weather held up perfectly. By the time we got to Whitwell and joined the queue of cars waiting to turn into the fields, the temperature was nudging the twenty-degree mark. They had a whole lane coned off to help us across the dual carriageway. 'Looks like they'll have a fair old crowd,' I said as the stewards directed us in through a farm entrance.

'Including one or two familiar faces,' Ann said, waving to three figures hunched under a tree beside the gate.

'Is that Walter and his mates?'

She laughed. 'It is. The three wise monkeys. What are they doing there?'

Walt scuttled up to the car and poked his head through the window.

'Now then,' I said, 'you off to the races?'

'Course we are. Just hold it there while we pile in, will you?' He'd already opened the rear passenger door and was beckoning to his brother Cyril and his mate Ronny, grinning from ear to ear. 'What did I tell you, lads? You get here early enough, you're bound to bump into someone.' He was in the car already, squirming his way across the back seat to make room for the other two. 'Bit of a squeeze,' he grunted. 'You want to get yerself one of them whatsits, lad – them four-wheel jobs.'

'Walt, what is going on?'

'We need to ride wi' you, lad.'

'But you've only got to walk across that field and you're in. Where's your car anyway?'

'Never mind me car,' Walter said as the other two climbed in after him with their Thermos flasks and brown paper bags. 'You're holding up the queue, look.'

'Oh hell.' Behind us the traffic was backed up onto the near-side carriageway, and a very large steward in a fluorescent yellow jacket was making her way towards us, talking into a two-way radio. 'Shut the door then and mind them maps. Stick them on the shelf behind you.'

We bumped our way around the farmyard that led into the field. I was just about to ask Walt to explain himself when I felt his hand on my shoulder. 'Here,' he muttered, 'stick that in your pocket.'

'A fiver? What, for a fifty-yard drive? Tell you what, mate, at that rate we'll take you to the coast if you like.'

'You know how I am, Mike. I always reckon to pay me way.'

'That's very square of you, Walt, that's all I can say. Tell you what, I'll put it on the first race – and if I win I'll see you right for a drink later on.'

We were at the car-park entrance now, and there was a lady in a riding jacket holding her hand out. 'Twenty-five pounds per car,' she said as I pulled up at the gate.

'Here you are, love.' I handed her a twenty, plus Walt's five. That's when the penny dropped. 'Hang about!' I said. 'Ann, do you realise what these buggers have done?'

'I wondered when you'd twig. They've parked their car down the lane somewhere – haven't you, Walter?' Walt just chuckled and opened the door. 'Look at it this way, Mike. They've saved us five quid on our entry fee.'

'Aye, but they've saved themselves twenty,' I spluttered.

'Hey, Walt, how do you work that one out?' But Walt and his mates were off, melting into the crowds and heading for the beer tent, leaving me to get out and close the car door after them.

We parked up and walked across the sloping hillside. Away to the south the Vale of York was a shimmering, sunlit sea of green and yellow. Thirty miles away, on the horizon, the familiar puffs of white cloud marked the giant cooling towers at Drax and Eggborough. And there in the fields below us we could see the course marked out beside hedgerows splashed with may blossom, the brush fences all neat and erect. As we wove our way through the crowd to the refreshment area, we passed stalls selling everything from fresh coffee to meat pies to homemade jam and bottles of sloe gin. To one side the bookies were setting up under their umbrellas. Some had the modern electronic displays with the names and prices all up in orange lights, but plenty of them were still chalking them up the old-fashioned way, on blackboards.

'They're a bit keen,' I said. 'The first race isn't till two o'clock, is it?'

Ann flipped through the programme we'd been given at the entrance. 'That'll be for the pony races,' she started, before she was drowned out by a voice coming over the PA system, confirming what she'd just said.

With over an hour to wait until the first proper race, we went and grabbed a bite to eat and sat on the grass with our race cards. 'What's the budget, then?' I asked. 'How much are we going to risk?'

'How about a fiver each race – between us?'

'Sounds fair enough to me.'

'I mean we have two fifty each – separate bets – and whoever wins the most buys dinner on the way home.'

'What if we both lose?'

Ann shook her head. 'We won't.'

'What are you saying? You fancy your chances?'

'I know about horses, Mike.'

'Ah, but I'm lucky – remember?'

'We'll see, shall we? One horse per race, and two fifty each. Agreed?'

'Agreed.'

'Shall we have a nose around then?' There was plenty to see. One of the local hunts had turned up and were milling about in a parade ring with their hounds. In another ring, the young riders in white breeches and racing silks were circling their ponies or saddling them up while the stewards handed out their numbers and the announcer went through the list of runners. Spectators were lined up three deep against the flimsiest of fences, a series of bare wooden posts linked by loops of baling twine. 'By heck,' I said, 'it's a fair old crowd. Every man and his dog is here.' There was certainly no shortage of dogs, or of kids. It was a proper old-fashioned country gathering, with flat hats, tweed jackets, shooting-sticks and red faces everywhere you looked.

'Now then, doing a bit of undercover work, are you?'

I turned round to see who it was. Standing there in a denim shirt and a pair of faded jeans, and grinning at me, was Ronnie Leach.

'Bloody hell,' I said, 'you come for a day out and the first person you bump into is one of your oldest—'

'Customers, Mr Pannett. We're all customers nowadays.' He turned and winked at Ann. 'Isn't that right, Sergeant?'

I looked at her. 'I didn't know you knew each other.'

Ann laughed. 'Ronnie and I have spent a few evenings together. And the odd night – haven't we, Ronnie?'

He smiled sheepishly. 'You mean in the cells at York custody.'

'Small world, isn't it?' I said. 'What are you up to, anyway?'

He held his hands up, as if I'd accused him of something. 'Hey, I'm up to nowt. Just enjoying a day at the races, same as you.'

'I'm glad to hear it.'

'I'm doing as you told me last year. Keeping me nose clean.'

'So I heard. And working too.'

'Aye, bits and pieces, like. Still doing deliveries for my mate out Hovingham way.'

'Well, I hope you've got that old rust-bucket of a car fettled. And what's with all this then?' I was looking at the notebook and pencil he held in his hand.

'It's a serious business, this betting lark.' He tapped his head. 'Lot of information to take in.'

'Go on – you can't kid me. You're working on sommat. You must be.'

'I'm doing t'same as every other bugger here. Trying to make sure them fat-cat bookies don't have too much cash in their satchels when they go home. Can't have 'em stumbling across that field carrying excess weight, can we now?'

'No, that wouldn't do at all.' The crowd was parting to let the pony riders make their way out of the ring and down the hill towards the course. 'So, you got any tips for us?'

Ronnie gave me a sly sort of grin. 'I might have. Need to see the runners first. That's why I'm right here, every race.' He tapped the side of his nose with his finger. 'Paddock-watching.'

'Watching for what?'

'Weighing 'em up. Ann knows, don't you?'

'You look at their size and scope,' she said. 'And you want to see what their coats are like, how fit they look, that sort of thing.'

'Aye,' Ronnie chipped in, wagging his pencil at me. 'Make a note of any that's getting too warm. Or playing up. You can soon sort out them as has a fighting chance.'

'Size and scope, eh?' I replied. 'Sounds a bit scientific for me. I'll go with the old gut instinct – or my lucky pin.'

'Well, if you want a tip,' Ronnie said, 'get on any of Lord Daresbury's horses. I know a lad, backs 'em blind; always makes himself a few bob.'

'Or anything with one of the Greenalls on board,' Ann said. 'They clean up at these events. There's a whole tribe of them.'

'Aye, trouble is, whatever they're on goes off at daft prices. Four to one on and suchlike.' Ronnie tucked his notebook back in his shirt pocket. 'See how you go on, Mike. And if it gets to the last race, have a word. I've had a whisper about a young gelding. He might go off at a decent price.' He winked at Ann again. 'Like that one your old dad rode, eh?'

'You remember that, do you?' I said, but Ronnie had turned and sloped off towards the stewards' tent. I turned to Ann. 'He's a slippery one,' I said. 'So what was that horse he was on about? Did he mean the one your dad was riding when he won the Cup?'

'Yes. Dad knew she'd go well, but he never told anyone – except Mum. He'd already won the farmers' race on her at Easingwold point-to-point a week or two before. It was a similar distance to the Grimthorpe, and she absolutely romped home. Wasn't even out of breath afterwards. He kept on to Mum to put everything she had on it. Go on, he said, it can't be beat.'

'Can't imagine your mum whacking a big bet on.'

'That's the funny part. She only put a pound on it. My dad was totally convinced that he would win, but he couldn't budge her. She wasn't going to lose what she couldn't afford.

I remember when the race started she couldn't bear to watch. Covered her face with her hands and every so often when she had a little peep there was Dad plodding along at the back of the field. Even I could see the horse was cruising. But Mum was giving it "Ooh, look at him, plum last. I knew not to throw my money away!" Then on the final circuit the others started flagging and good old Mary just cut through the field like a knife through butter. Took up the running in the final couple of furlongs and won it going away.'

'Fantastic. Was it a big price?'

'Fifty to one. Mum couldn't believe it. Of course, as soon as it was over she was going "I should've had more on, I should've had faith in your dad." He still teases her about it to this day. There were all these punters who'd backed the favourite, stomping about, ripping up their tickets and cursing their luck, and there was Mum trying to cover my ears. Our bookie was smirking at his mate – till we went to collect. You should've seen his jaw drop.'

'Did she treat you all?'

'She said it was a treat. She bought a brand-new set of top-quality china. Well, the first part of it. Had to wait till Christmas to get the rest. The only good news from our point of view was we weren't allowed to wash it up, it was so expensive. So we were always on at her to use it. You'll know the set I mean: it's that one she wheeled out the first time you came to tea, remember?'

'It's a super story.'

'Yes, but there's a better one, if we could ever get to the bottom of it.'

'Oh aye?'

'Grandad. The rumour was that he had a hundred quid on Dad to win. He never admitted it, but he never denied it either.'

'Well,' I said, 'let's hope we do half as well as they did. Come on, I'll buy you a coffee and we'll study the form.'

A lot of good that did us. Twenty minutes later, after I'd gone through a list of runners as long as my arm, my head was spinning. 'Too much information,' I said. We were sitting on the grass looking out over the course. Away towards the row of bookies' umbrellas I could see Walt chewing the fat with a couple of old codgers in thick knitted sweaters, both of them dabbing at their foreheads with coloured handkerchiefs. It wasn't long before the PA announced that the runners for the first race were on their way to the parade ring.

'Come on,' Ann said, 'I'm going to go and find me a winner.'

I spotted mine from a mile off, a big, powerful horse, almost jet black, striding majestically around the far side of the ring as if it owned the place. 'That'll do for me,' I said. 'What's his number?'

'Can't see. Ah, here he comes now. Five – no, fifteen.'

'Fifteen . . . fifteen.' I ran my finger down the list. 'Look at its name,' I said. 'It's a sign from above. A Fair Cop. How can you not back that?'

'You suit yourself,' Ann said. 'I'm not sure about his attitude. He's still a stallion, and by the look of him his mind's on other things.'

'Like what?'

'Like mares, for example.'

'Oh. Now I see.'

'Whereas that' – she had spotted a plain little bay that to my untrained eye looked half asleep – 'that one I do like.' She handed me a five-pound note. 'Go on. Number eight for me. Two fifty on the nose. You do as you please.'

I got a shock when I went to put the bets on. Ann's was six

to one second favourite, mine was fifty. Not that I was going to let the price put me off. Think of the winnings, I say. But once the race got going in earnest I could see why it was an outsider. It was certainly a sleek and handsome beast, but it was wilful. It just wouldn't do as it was told. After getting the first three fences all wrong it failed to take off at all at the fourth. Ploughed straight through the fence like a Chieftain tank and left the poor old jockey to make his own way over, flying through the air with the greatest of ease before landing in a crumpled heap on the far side. Ann's horse, need I say it, never put a foot wrong and finished eight lengths ahead of the field.

'Don't be fooled,' I said as she went off to collect her winnings, 'it's only beginner's luck. There's plenty more races to come.'

I was repeating the refrain two hours later, except that by now I was betting in the last-chance saloon. Ann had racked up three winners and was showing a profit of £37.50. Walt had come by, full of himself, having backed the same horses. I'd yet to see any of my selections cross the finishing line. Two had pulled up, two had fallen, and one had been left alone on the starting line after refusing to race. I was digging deep to find my next stake while Ann was recycling her winnings at the sloe gin stall.

'You look as though you're fretting, lad.' Walt had his back half turned away from me and was counting out his winnings under his jacket, distributing little bundles of notes into various pockets.

'Why, she's running away with it,' I said. 'She's miles ahead of me.'

'Are you not backing the same hosses then? She knows a thing or two, does your lass.'

'We decided to have a little competition – see who could find the most winners. She's home and dry, three up with one to go. I'm still waiting to get on the bloody score sheet.'

Walt laughed. 'You don't want to get worked up about it, lad. It's only luck at t'end of t'day.'

'Aye, but . . . there's pride at stake, Walt. Pride.'

He shook his head and pursed his lips. 'Take my advice and let the lass win.' Then he nudged me. 'They're a lot sweeter when they think they've got the upper hand.'

'Aye, but I don't like losing, Walt. I never did. Not even when the winner has to pay for our meal on the way home.'

'She's buying you dinner?'

'That's what we agreed: whoever came out on top, it's their treat.'

'Sounds to me like you've played your cards right,' Walt said, buttoning up his coat and patting the little wads of cash. 'Mind, you should be used to it by now – being a kept man . . .'

'Walt . . .' But he'd skipped away to the bookies, to back another winner no doubt, and Ronnie Leach was heading my way with a conspiratorial look on his face.

'Ah,' he said, 'been looking for you.' He cast an anxious look around him and lowered his voice. 'I've had a word for this number ten,' he said, 'a strong word. Comes from the stable.'

'So does that smelly stuff you put on your roses,' I said. I was falling out of love with this game rapidly.

Ronnie took no notice. He was standing on his tiptoes, craning his neck to look over the heads of the crowd. 'Can you see it?'

I took a half-hearted glance at the horses being paraded around the ring. 'That big chestnut, is it?'

'Aye, that's the one. Copper Canyon, they call it. Topical name, eh? They reckon it's got a fair turn of speed so the jockey'll hang back then come with a rush in the last few furlongs.'

'And you reckon it's a good thing, do you?'

'I'm only telling you what I've been told,' he said. 'They're saying it shouldn't get beat. If you wanna back it I'd get on now – before t'bookies get wise and cut the odds any more. I've backed it with four different bookies. Got fourteen to one, then twelves.'

'Ronnie,' I said, and looked him right in the eye, 'I'm counting on you.'

'And I'm counting on that stable lass.' He turned to go, then stopped. 'Pass the word on to Ann, won't you?'

'Course I will.'

By the time I got my money on, the price was down to ten to one. But even as I made my way down the hill towards the course I heard someone saying he'd got eights – and was happy with it.

'And . . . they're off!'

'What you backed?' Ann had joined me. We were standing right by the fence. We had a perfect view as the horses thundered past in a blaze of colour, kicking up lumps of turf as they responded to their jockeys' urgings.

'Oh, some nag with a novice on board.'

'I'm on that number ten. Copper Canyon. Stood out in the ring. Did you ever get that tip off our friend Mr Leach?'

'Ann, you didn't seriously think he was going to come up with one, did you? And if he did, would you trust him?'

'Approaching the second fence, and it's Colonel Ludlow with a five-length lead, Wendy's Choice in second, then a gap to the third, and at the rear of the field Copper Canyon is finding the pace a little hot.'

'Not that it matters anyway,' I said. 'You've won it fair and square.' I swallowed hard and gave her hand a squeeze, and started thinking about dinner. The horses had disappeared from view for now.

'*And as they go out into the country for the final time Colonel Ludlow still has a commanding lead. Wold Rover has moved through into second, and the tail-ender is still Copper Canyon.*'

'Can't say I'm impressed with yours,' I said as they made their way along the side of the hedge that bounded the back straight.

'Just wait.'

'*They're four fences from home and Wendy's Choice has pulled up.*'

We walked back up the hill a few yards to get a better view as they emerged from the trees at the far corner.

'*And now the leader's under pressure and feeling the warmth of the jockey's whip. His lead's down to a length and a half. Wold Rover has moved up alongside – and from the back of the field Copper Canyon is cruising!*'

Ann was on her toes now, watching intently as the field came into view. I tried to keep calm, but my heart was in my mouth. 'Come on,' she said through gritted teeth, 'give him his head.' I kept schtum. With my luck, he'd be throwing his jockey off any time now.

'*We've a new leader now as they approach two out. Wold Rover, with Copper Canyon coming like a train.*'

'Look at that,' Ann said. 'This animal has class.' She was clenching her fists and urging it on. 'Winner number four coming up.'

'*Over the last and the whips are out. They're neck-and-neck with half a furlong to go . . . Wold Rover, by a head, Copper Canyon pressing on the rails – and as they go to the line he gets his head in front for the first time. Copper Canyon the winner by a nose!*'

We decided to eat at the Jolly Farmers. It was near home,

and the odds were we'd catch up with Walt. He was there okay, grinning from ear to ear.

'I hope you've put all them winnings in a safe place,' I said.

He patted his jacket. 'They're about me person, lad. And soon as I get up that hill they'll be in me strong-box.'

'So you've not been home yet?' Ann asked.

Walt shook his head. 'Thought I'd celebrate with a pint,' he said. 'Do you want one, either of you? I can stand a round, I reckon, after a day like I've had.'

'Tell you what, Walt,' I said, 'we're having a bite to eat. Why don't you join us?'

He frowned and looked at Ann. 'You didn't win enough to pay for us all, did you?'

I didn't give Ann a chance to speak. 'Don't worry,' I said, 'his'll be on me.'

'Hold on a minute,' Ann said. 'We had an agreement, remember? Whoever came out on top buys dinner.'

I didn't say a word at first, just took out my wallet and opened it up. 'In terms of finding winners, you won. But in overall cash terms, my dear . . .' I fanned out ten twenty-pound notes in front of her.

'Where'd that come from?'

'I had twenty quid on that last one. So shall we call it a draw?'

Chapter 3

The Ultimate Potting Shed

It's no laughing matter, I told myself as I drove down the steep wooded hillside towards the ruins of Kirkham Priory and bumped my way over the level crossing. No laughing matter at all. But when you're called out to investigate a sixty-year-old male who's been seen on the public highway, on a pushbike, stark naked – well, it's hard to keep a straight face. In this day and age, of course, we're all wary of any suggestion of behaviour that might be construed as sexually threatening – or worse – so this could have been a serious matter. However, I was pretty sure I knew the man in question. It had to be Gerald. Who else could fit the caller's description? He was, according to the lady who'd rung in, 'riding along with his front basket full of old tin cans, smoking a pipe, and not a stitch on him but a straw hat.'

The thing with Gerald is, first and foremost, he's a Yorkshireman. And if you don't quite know what that means, let me say that among his many attributes a real dyed-in-the-wool Yorkshireman is his own man. I always tell people a Yorkshireman is like Popeye. Remember him? 'I am what I am.' And he has a certain cussedness. Like Algy, the time he found out it was illegal to fly a Yorkshire flag within sight of the public highway. What did he do but go straight out, erect a thirty-foot-high pole next to his front gate, then run the white rose ensign up it. Some people say that folk like Algy are just looking for confrontation, that they thrive on it. Others say he's standing up for his rights, and we should all take a leaf from his book. I remember a conversation we had in the Jolly Farmers around this time, when the first rumours were starting up that the government might try to enforce a ban on hunting with dogs. Algy had never mounted a horse in his life, let alone gone hunting, but he stood at the bar that night and told anyone who'd listen that the minute our elected representatives tried to tell him that he couldn't go hunting he'd be straight out to buy a horse and ride with the Middleton hounds. 'And if anyone cares to write that down, by golly I'll sign it in my own blood,' he added for good measure. Fortunately for him, nobody had any blank paper on them at the time. Or if they did they weren't owning up to it.

However, I'm getting off the subject, which is our mate Gerald. I'm not sure what Gerald's background was. He didn't have much of an accent, but he was Yorkshire through and through. He was an educated man. According to Walt, he'd been an accountant in Harrogate years ago, and when you heard him speak you could imagine it. He'd been married and had a family, but for some reason or other he'd dropped out of what we call respectable life and gone off to live in the wilds as an ageing child of nature.

Well, I suppose that's a slight exaggeration: what he'd done was build himself some sort of retreat in the woods, not far from Kirkham, but a long way off the road. It was part way between a caravan and a shed, it was static, and as such I suppose it wasn't exactly legal, but the farmer who owned the woods had never objected, and in any case Gerald only lived there part of the year. April to October, more or less. The rest of the time he stayed at his niece's house over Ripon way. But in the summer months I'd occasionally see him, puffing away on his pipe as he gathered armfuls of firewood, his bike leaning against a convenient hedge or gate; or I'd spot him wheeling it home with a five-gallon container balanced on the handlebars. He had a couple of old army jerry-cans that he used to fill with spring water he collected from the pipe that fed one of the drinking-troughs in a nearby cow-pasture. He rarely had more than a pair of shorts on, but if he'd decided to discard them – well, it was time to put him right about what the law did and didn't allow. These things are best nipped in the bud.

It was a cool, grey day but the rain that had been falling all morning had stopped at last, and the sky was brightening from the northwest. When I came to the green lane that led to his place I saw that it was thoroughly overgrown. There was no way I'd get my Puddle Hopper down there. So I parked on the old forestry track and set off on foot. 'Great,' I muttered to myself as the overhanging branches showered water down my neck and the rank grasses soaked my trouser legs.

I smelled the place before I actually spotted it. It wasn't the sweet smell of burning wood, but rather the pungent aroma of charred plastic. And as I entered the little clearing where the old shed stood, there he was: naked as the day he was born, bent over an old dustbin and pulling out a tangle of electrical cable on the end of a garden fork. I watched as he dumped it into a brazier, then stepped back as black smoke and yellow flames swirled about him.

'Now then,' I said.

'Ah, good afternoon.' Gerald didn't seem at all surprised by my presence. He just stuck his fork into the ground and turned to face me.

'I'm PC Mike Pannett from Malton,' I said. 'I'm your rural beat officer.' It's hard to know where to look when a man's got nothing on, so I nodded at the fire instead. 'At least you've got a nice warm job.'

'Yes, I save them up for days like this.' He reached out with his fork and pulled a strand of copper wire from the blaze. 'Surprising how much this stuff fetches at the scrapyard.'

As he spoke, a gust of wind shook the trees and a shower of fat drops hissed on the glowing sides of the brazier. 'Listen,' I said, 'can I have a word – inside?' I looked across at the door of his little dwelling. It was a wooden-framed thing, painted yellow and glazed with that fluted glass they used to put in back doors thirty or forty years ago. He must have rescued it from a builder's skip somewhere. It still had the original plastic numbers on it: 34.

'Yes, do come in.' Leaning beside the shed was a bike, a plastic bag tied over the fishtail saddle, its large wickerwork basket overflowing with crushed aluminium drinks cans. It certainly fitted the description the complainant had given us – not that I'd doubted for a minute that Gerald was our man.

Inside, he sank into an old leather-upholstered car seat and offered me a wooden rocker. There was barely room for both of us between a folding bed, a black pot-bellied stove and one of those glass-fronted kitchen cabinets, its front folded down to make a worktop. I doubt that Gerald's entire home measured more than about six feet by ten. And was it my imagination, or was the whole place tilted to one side?

I decided to get right down to it. I had little choice. He was sitting there, relaxed, at peace with the world, legs apart, wiping some mud off his foot on a square of old carpet before tamping a fresh wad of tobacco into his pipe.

'Mr Rodgers,' I said, pulling out a notepad and flicking it

open, 'I'm afraid I've received a complaint which I believe may concern you.'

I stared hard at the empty page of my notepad as he crossed his legs and sucked on his pipe. Then I looked up at the ceiling, which seemed to be lined with a patchwork of yellow and blue fertiliser bags. 'Oh yes,' he said, through a fog of blue smoke, 'and what might that be about?'

'It's from a lady,' I said. 'Down in the village. She said she saw someone who answered your description cycling past the other morning dressed in – well, in not very much.'

Gerald took his pipe out of his mouth and balanced it on the edge of the glass-fronted dresser. 'And that's the point, is it? That I wasn't wearing very much?'

'Yes, it is.'

'I think you'll find, Officer, that under British law a man has a perfect right to dress as he pleases. Or has something changed? It's been a while since I read what passes for a newspaper these days.'

'Her exact words were' – I sought refuge in the empty notepad again – 'that you "had all your goods on display". She was quite upset.'

'Look, Constable . . . Pannett, did you say?' Gerald picked his pipe back up, flicked his lighter into life and sucked the flame into the bowl. 'I'm not a paid-up member of the Naturists' Society or whatever they call it, but I believe it is better for my mental and physical health to expose my skin to the sunlight during the summer months. That's the way I believe nature intended us to live.'

'Don't get me wrong,' I said. 'In the woods here, that's fine. But when you're out and about on your bike, would you just think about the public at large – especially the ladies – and try to . . .' I didn't mean to, but I couldn't help it: I gestured towards his nether regions. 'Try to keep things under wraps, eh?'

Cases like this can be difficult. Where does the law draw the line between self-expression and giving offence? We have naturist beaches now, even on the east coast of Yorkshire. And you have to believe that anyone who'll prance about naked on the beach at Fraisthorpe when that wind's coming off the North Sea has to believe in what they're doing. So when you're dealing with a character like Gerald – well, is he just a bit of a character, a determined individualist, or has he some sort of mental health issue? It's a tough call, and as a cop you have to do your best to make that judgement. You think of offences like 'being a public nuisance', 'indecent exposure' or perhaps general public-order offences. But you also have to weigh up what's in the public interest – and the effect on the witness or victim.

Having had my chat with Gerald, I'd decided that a gentle warning and a word of advice would, hopefully, sort things out. We would see if there were any more complaints over the next few weeks. I left him to his scrap-metal reclamation. As I walked back through the dripping woods to my vehicle I thought about the endless variety of cases that come your way as a copper. I certainly couldn't remember dealing with anything quite like this before.

I was debating whether to go back to the station or call in at Walt's for a cup of tea and a chance to dry my trousers when the mobile rang. I bumped to a halt in a gateway and took the call. It was Nick the gamekeeper. 'Now then, Mike, are you up to anything?'

'Not a lot, Nick. Just between calls at the moment. What's on your mind?' I was hoping he'd rung to tell me that his wife was baking. It wouldn't be the first occasion on which I'd timed a visit there to coincide with a fresh batch of rock buns coming out of the stove.

'You remember that feller Jenks I was telling you about the other week? At the Country Watch do?'

'Hmm – sommat about a barn with the windows sealed up?'

'Aye, that's it. Blacked out they were.'

'What's up? Has sommat happened?'

'No, no – just that I ran into him this morning down at Yates's in town, and he was asking me if you'd been and had a look.'

'Tell you the truth, Nick, I haven't had time yet. But I tell you what, it's not far out of my way. I'll maybe pop over there and have a look. Unless you're wanting help with them cakes your missus is baking.'

'Sorry to disappoint you, son. She's in town herself. Market day, isn't it?'

If you wanted directions to the main farm, the one that old Jenks lived in, I have to say I'd be struggling. Not that I was wanting to talk to him at this stage. For now I was just going to have a nose around the rented place. The main farmhouse, where he lived, was only really visible if you were out walking in the hills. I'd seen it a time or two from a track where I some-times took Henry to try to burn off some of his excess energy. It forms part of a long-distance footpath, the Wolds Way, and looks out over one of those beautiful dry valleys the area's known for – dry because as soon as it rains any run-off tends to seep quickly through the chalk base and go underground. As to the rented place I was supposed to be looking for, well, Nick had tried to explain where it was, but as my vehicle bucked and swayed its way along the narrow track, splashing through a succession of milky puddles, I started to wonder whether I'd got it right. However, Nick knew his way around these parts, and there was at least one set of fresh wheel-ruts, so I ploughed on between the overgrown hawthorn hedges that lined my route.

I must have gone the best part of a mile by now, and was starting to wonder whether I'd gone wrong. The hedge had given way to a dark copse, a tangle of ash and elder with ivy smothering the ground in between. Above me, through a gap in the trees, I could see the steep, bare Wolds, dotted with sheep. And then, around a bend, the track suddenly opened out into a large, well-maintained lawn. To one side of it stood a handsome farm cottage and to the other a tall redbrick barn with a pantiled roof, its two rows of windows blacked out with some sort of sheeted material. From this distance it was hard to tell what it was exactly – and I had no intention of going any further. I'd seen all I needed to for now. Just in case I happened to be seen or challenged by the occupants, I had prepared a cover story, but there was no one around. I backed up fifty yards or so to where there was a bit of a clearing, turned around, and headed to town. I needed to have a chat with a man called Des.

Des Carter was our CID man. He came from the West Country and he wore a suit. He was a detective constable. Unlike some DCs I have met, Des didn't assume that he was superior to every uniformed officer he came across. He was odd that way: if it wasn't for the fact that he would dish out gratuitous insults to us plods as a matter of course – always with his tongue planted firmly in his cheek – you could be forgiven for thinking that he saw us as equals, allies in the fight against crime. I liked Des – and not just because his career had taken a similar course to mine. Like me, he'd started out in the Met, then started hankering for the open spaces he'd grown up with – although in his case he made the move to his wife's home territory of North Yorkshire rather than back to his native Devon. We had another thing in common: we both loved fly-fishing. Not that we ever got much chance to talk about it; we didn't see a great deal of each other at work. The CID and the uniformed branch inhabit very different worlds most of the time.

People have funny ideas about the Criminal Investigation Department. They assume that a DC is superior in rank to a PC. Not so. All they are is specialists, like firearms or traffic officers. As their name implies, they investigate crimes, rather than just policing an area. Whereas a PC deals with whatever comes his way, and may well have to break off from working on a burglary to attend to a road traffic accident or a domestic bust-up, a DC does not pound a beat and is therefore free to attend to the long and often laboured enquiries that are a routine part of investigation into a serious crime. They have the time to undertake the detailed interrogation of a suspect that is par for the course in such cases as rape, murder, high-value robberies, and so on. They can also advise the beat bobby in certain specialist areas, although in my case I rarely felt the need for guidance: during my time in London I had dealt with pretty well every type of crime you can think of and was generally pretty well clued up on the procedures. In this case, however, I had no hesitation in going straight to Des. Apart from anything else, he would have a handle on the latest intelligence.

'Now then, you idle bugger!' I found Des hunched over a computer screen with a pile of box files on the desk beside him. 'What you skiving at this time?' Just because I'd marked his cards as one of the good guys, there was no reason why I shouldn't get my insults in first.

Des skidded his swivel chair away from the desk and tapped his finger to his head. 'Listen, you bloody wooden-top, I could explain it to you, but you know what? You'd start complaining that your head hurts – and right now I've run out of aspirins. Just you stick to pounding the pavements, and leave the intellectual stuff to us, eh?'

'Don't you worry about the streets of our fair city,' I said, pulling up a chair. 'They're in good hands. Anyway, I wouldn't dream of sending you out there. Might get that nice new suit all mucky and crumpled. Can't have that, can we now?'

'And on a more serious note?' Des was doing his best not to laugh.

'Young couple, Des. He's working, they have a kid at school, right? They rent a farmhouse way out in the middle of nowhere with a big barn out the back – and they black the windows out. Any ideas?'

'No law against it.'

'No, but it's an odd thing to do, isn't it?'

'Depends what they're into. Not an artist, is he? They like natural light, don't they?'

'I doubt it.'

'He could be a photographer. Or his missus?'

'Des, this ain't a darkroom. The place is bloody huge. Size of a church.'

'Hmm.' Des scooted forward, took hold of the mouse and brought up a file onscreen. 'Tell you what we have had,' he said. 'A bit of info from Crime Stoppers. Came in a few weeks ago. They reckon someone's growing cannabis in industrial quantities out our way.'

'Interesting. I came across something similar to this in the Met one time. It was in Clapham. An industrial unit with blacked-out windows. Turned out to be a huge cultivation site.'

'Yeah, they use hydroponics. Most of the skunk that's out there these days, they grow it in tanks. You know – watering systems, artificial light. And, of course, invisible from the outside.' Des turned away from the screen and leaned back in his chair, stretching, his hands behind his head. 'A big old barn miles from anywhere, you say? If I was looking for a place to grow some weed I'd say it's just the job, mate.'

People tend to assume that most of the drugs consumed in the UK are imported illegally, but research has shown that as much as sixty to seventy per cent of the cannabis supply is actually grown here. And sold at a very nice profit.

'Right,' I said, 'I'll take a closer look.'

'And I'll do some digging around, shall I?'

'You do that, Des. Oh, by the way,' I said as I headed out of the door, 'I hear that North Yorkshire CID have uncovered a new type of drug abuse.'

'Oh yeah?'

'Where the user injects ecstasy directly into the mouth.'

'I haven't heard about that one.'

'Yeah, it's called E by gum.'

'Pannett, get the hell out of here.'

Back on my rounds I thought about what I'd seen, and wondered whether it might indeed tie in with Des's intelligence reports. If it did, I needed no further motivation. People have mixed views on drug use. Or drug abuse: call it what you will. But I've always been dead against it. Having said that, I have to add that, growing up in rural North Yorkshire in the 1970s, I was never really exposed to anything in the illegal-substance line. The nearest we got to it at school was when the big kids, the ones who fancied themselves as hard cases, used to go behind the bike sheds, take teabags apart and smoke the contents. I can't say it ever appealed to me, but they made a big play of it, and staggered around when they came back into the playground, pretending they were high. They impressed one or two first-years, but that was about it. Later on, when I started going into York for a drink on a Friday and Saturday night, my mates and I became aware that there were one or two pubs where you could buy cannabis, if you knew who to talk to. But that was about it: rumours, whispers, a few loudmouths boasting about what they were up to. So going to work in South London, where the cannabis culture really had got hold, was quite a revelation. The stuff was everywhere, along with harder drugs like heroin. And then along came crack cocaine: highly potent, very addictive, and bringing with it all sorts of other issues. For a start, the people who used hard drugs were permanently skint, and soon started funding their habit through street robbery, burglary and suchlike. It was a massive problem, and when I left London I was glad to think I'd seen the last of it. But these days, even in the market towns you see heroin, and more recently cocaine. But up to this point, in Ryedale, we'd only had a few drugs busts, mostly small-scale stuff. And I wanted it to stay that way.

Des and I agreed that I would take a further look at this barn place, but without announcing myself to the occupants. I'd team up with Jayne, go in under cover of darkness, and Des would find out what he could about the people associated with that address: who paid the utility bills and so on, and was there anything untoward about the amount of electricity or water being consumed?

As soon as I told Jayne what I had in mind her face lit up. 'Nothing I like better than a nice night-time operation,' she said. 'Plain clothes, is it? Unmarked cars?'

'Oh yes. We don't want the subjects spotting us, but if they do – hey, we'll be a courting couple looking for a quiet spot for romance.'

'Mike, I've heard some sad come-ons in my time, but that takes the biscuit.'

'All in the line of duty, Jayne.'

'But joking aside, I mean, it's what we joined the force for, isn't it? Proper old-fashioned cops and robbers.'

She was right, in a way. When you decide to go into the police, yes, you're thinking community service, upholding the law, doing a worthwhile job, making the world a safer place; but a part of you is also thinking high-speed car chases, big crime busts, and cloak-and-dagger operations. To be perfectly honest, the amount of routine work you have to do is a bit of a let down when you first start out. At the age we were when we started, we wanted action, not admin. So, by the time Jayne and I had set the thing up we were like two kids on the night before Christmas.

The shift began like any other. We patrolled the town, waiting impatiently for the pubs to close and the streets to empty. Then we checked out the villages before going back to the station for a coffee. It was getting on for two when we changed into plain clothes and set off in an old, nondescript Vauxhall Vectra. For backup we had Ed and Fordy parked a couple of miles away in a marked car. Hopefully we wouldn't need them, the objective of the operation being to gather more information rather than to confront anyone. But all the same, we had to be prepared. The higher the stakes, the greater the dangers. Preliminary checks had confirmed that the residents of the farmhouse were a couple with a small child. Neither were known for violence and no firearms were registered to them.

We drove down the narrow track on sidelights, taking it very slowly and keeping the engine on low revs. We'd gone maybe three-quarters of a mile when we pulled up in a gateway and continued on foot, barely able to make out more than the odd dark shape in front of us. The sky was clear but there was no moon, so it was very, very dark. We'd have been better off if it had been overcast. The amount of light reflected from clouds, even when you're several miles from town, gives you far better visibility than you'll get on a starlit night such as tonight.

I set the pace, creeping slowly towards the end of the track, with Jayne following a few yards behind. When I trod on a stick it seemed to go off like a pistol shot. Otherwise all we could hear was the sound of our own breathing and the rustle of our clothes against the low-hanging branches. I was thinking about Jayne behind me, and what might be going through her mind. I had done stuff like this before, but for her it was a novelty. The first few times you're out of uniform and in plain clothes it's as if your armour is off. You feel exposed, vulnerable.

I whispered back to her, 'You okay?'

'Fine, Mike, yeah. Exciting, innit?'

'Careful!' I whispered. I'd come to a stop and Jayne had bumped into the back of me. I tugged her sleeve and pointed towards the house, its outline clearly visible. We stood for a minute or so, listening. There was no sound save the distant yip of a fox. Somehow that made me even more apprehensive. My biggest fear was that there might be guard dogs on the premises. You only need to be attacked once to be very wary indeed. It happened to me years ago, before I ever joined the force. I was working on a demolition site. Sauntered in one morning and clean forgot about the Alsatian they kept there until he charged across the yard at me. I escaped by jumping into a skip – after he'd taken a lump out of me. I still have the scar to this day, although only a few close friends have seen it.

We crept along the edge of the copse towards the barn, which stood between us and the house. I was feeling more edgy by the minute, and as we approached our target I was overcome with this odd feeling that we were doing something wrong. It was the sort of feeling I might have had years ago on a scrumping expedition. I knew it was daft: we had a perfect right to investigate what we considered suspicious circumstances. Perhaps it was the darkness, the fear of discovery, the fact that we were on someone else's property.

'They got security lights?' Jayne asked.

'Couldn't see any when I recced the place.'

We walked slowly across the yard towards the barn, treading as lightly as we could over the loose stones. At this stage all I was interested in was getting some idea as to what was going on in there. We were within a few yards when I stopped, held my breath and put my hand up to Jayne. I could have sworn I heard a low humming noise. I beckoned Jayne forward again and went right up to the wall. Up above us was a row of windows, all blacked out. There it was again, the humming, like a grain dryer, but not as loud. It was more the sort of noise you'd hear from an old electricity substation. Jayne was right up beside me now, breathing hard. 'What the hell's that?' she whispered. 'Couldn't be radiation, could it?'

'I bloody hope not,' I said. And then, looking up, I saw a ventilator grille. Wafting down from it on a draught of warm, moist air was a familiar smell. 'Hey, recognise that?'

She sniffed. 'Cannabis.'

There was no doubt about it. It's one of those distinctive smells that you never forget. I edged forward a few yards to a ground-floor window that wasn't blacked out. Shining my Maglite through the dusty glass, I saw a room about twelve feet square and more or less entirely taken up with a large blackened container full of water, with copper and plastic pipes running up through the ceiling and back down.

'Right, mate. That'll do me.'

'What's the plan?'

'Get out, quick as we can.'

Back at the car we radioed Ed and Fordy to tell them they were no longer needed, then drove back to the station, where Chris Cocks immediately wanted to know what we'd found. 'Plenty,' I told him. 'The place reeks of cannabis. They've got a sophisticated plumbing system on the go, extractor fans, all sorts. They'll be producing the stuff by the ton, mate.'

'So what you going to do next?'

I looked at the clock on the wall. It was turned half past four. 'Write up a few notes, leave a message for Des, and home to bed.'

I woke up early the next day. I knew I would. Cases like this don't come along very often, and when they do you don't want to miss a thing. Your biggest fear is that some vital development will take place on your day off, or while you're on leave. I already felt proprietorial about this one: it was mine, and I was determined to follow it through. At the end of the day I didn't want this sort of thing happening on my patch, and if it did I wanted to be in on the bust. Still, I reminded myself as I picked up the phone to call Des, there really was no rush on this one. These people would have no idea we were onto them, so there was no reason for them not to just carry on as normal.

Des and I agreed that the first step was to refer the matter to our inspector, Birdie, to bring him up to speed and get his authority to apply for a search warrant. Then the uniformed officers and the CID would sit down and plan a joint operation.

In doing this we had to tread carefully, in case these people were already being watched by the Regional Crime Squad, or the National Criminal Investigation Squad as part of a broader investigation. Back in the 1970s Operation Julie, which netted a massive LSD production ring, brought scores of individuals under surveillance nationwide and resulted in over a hundred arrests. Confidentiality was the key throughout, but at the same time the officers involved needed to make sure that none of the suspects were picked up by a local branch, which would have alerted the others in the ring. So Des and I searched the computer database to see whether anything was flagged up on the farmhouse or its occupants. There was nothing.

A few days after Jayne and I had been down to the farm we met with Des and a couple of his CID colleagues. Inspector Bird was with us, along with Ed, Jayne and Fordy. The young man who lived at the farmhouse, we learned, was known to Humberside Police. He'd been arrested in Hull a couple of years ago for possession of drugs, but that was it. He now worked in a factory in Malton and was, to all intents and purposes, living a normal, law-abiding life. He and his partner had a five-year-old daughter. Des had checked on their electricity bills and reported back that they were no more than an average domestic consumer might run up. That certainly didn't make sense.

After our discussion I went to Pickering to see the magistrate and apply for a warrant. My application was held *in camera*, the only other person present being a clerk. I presented our case and obtained a warrant under Section 23 of the Misuse of Drugs Act, entitling us to search the barn and house or anyone on the premises for drugs or any equipment or paraphernalia used in the manufacture or supply of drugs. We had a month to execute it. If we didn't do so within that time we'd have to apply for a fresh one. With that side of things sorted out, we met again and agreed that we might as well put our plan into operation as soon as possible.

Twenty-four hours later we met with a search team based at Scarborough – a sergeant, four PCs trained in drug searches, a specially trained drugs dog with handler, and a SOCO or scene of crime officer. The following morning we had a briefing at Malton. It felt good to see the team assembled, to know that everything was in place and all the available resources were there for us. I went through the briefing sheet that Jayne and I had prepared. There was nothing dramatic about it. We simply described the location of the premises we were going to search, pinpointed it on the map, then outlined the intelligence we had gathered, mapped out the route we would take, and set out the strategy. Each unit would arrive in its own marked vehicle: the CID, the uniformed officers, and the search team. We nominated Ed as the exhibits officer. He wasn't best pleased, but for such an important job you want an experienced cop. The exhibits officer is detailed to log everything that is seized, the time and date of seizure, the officer finding, a description of the item, where it was found, and the seal and exhibit number of each individual bag. Everyone always tried to avoid that job. It was painstaking and laborious, but it was absolutely vital should the case go to court. It was agreed that if we took any prisoners they would go to Scarborough to be held in custody. Along with all that there were certain other details to iron out: what radio channel we would communicate on, for example. We also made contact with a local vehicle-hire company, and had them on standby to supply a large van to transport any items of evidence should the raid prove successful.

The question of timing was important. For a drugs job, you

either execute the warrant very early in the morning, when people are asleep and less likely to offer resistance or dispose of the goods; or you choose a key time, when they're fully stocked – say for the weekend – and in the process of distribution. That way there's more chance of catching some of the punters too, which provides additional evidence that the people concerned are supplying drugs. On this occasion, with a five-year-old child to consider, we decided to go at nine thirty, when she would hopefully be at school.

After all the preparation it was a relief to be in our cars and heading out along the A64. In fact, it was more than a relief. As we swung off on the country road that would take us towards our quarry, it felt exhilarating. When you look in your rear-view mirror and see that you are part of a convoy of several fully marked police vehicles, and you know you have a sound plan and are fully equipped to implement it, you feel . . . empowered. That's the word.

So for the third time within a week I made my way down the bumpy lane towards the farm. The puddles had dried up now, and when the vehicles fanned out across the yard in the morning sunlight we raised a cloud of white dust.

I went to the front door and gave it a good bang. There was no reply. I knocked a second time while Ed and Des checked around the back. Nothing. The windows were all shut, but there was a car parked in the shade of the house, the driver's side window open and the keys in the ignition. We went across to a stout-looking wooden door set in the wall of the barn. I had the door enforcer in the back of the car, but there was no need for that; as soon as I turned the handle it swung silently open. Inside was a set of wooden stairs with a stout metal handrail. The atmosphere was humid and laden with that same heavy scent we'd smelled a few nights earlier. Above the low humming of what had to be a pump, we could hear water gurgling through pipes, and an irregular ticking as the sun beat down on corrugated panels in the roof. As we stood there I felt my heart beating faster. It's the same feeling I've felt a hundred times before, but it's still exciting. It's precisely what you expect policing to be about when you join up. It doesn't matter how many times you've felt it before or how many different jobs you've been on, it's still there. It's an adrenaline rush, and I think it's what most of us like best about the job.

We walked swiftly up to the first floor. 'Christ!' Ed was at my shoulder, staring. 'Look at that.' In a space the size of a school gymnasium, illuminated by an array of overhead lights, was a sea of dark green: hundreds upon hundreds of cannabis plants, growing in densely packed rows. I jumped as a sudden click was followed by a sharp hissing sound, then felt my shoulders relax as a set of overhead nozzles started spraying water onto the foliage. The only time I've breathed air as warm and wet as that was in the tropical hothouse at Kew Gardens. As to the smell, it was almost nauseating. Even as I stood there I heard a whirring noise as a set of ventilators in the roof were cranked open by an electric motor.

'Bloody place is fully automated,' Ed said. 'They've probably got robots doing the weeding.'

We walked slowly along the rows on duckboards. I could feel the fine spray drifted onto my face. I'd just got to the end of the tanks when I stopped dead in my tracks. In front of me, lying face up, topping up her tan on a sunbed, and wearing a set of headphones and a very skimpy bikini, was a dark-haired young woman, completely oblivious to our presence.

Someone had to say something, and I was first in line. 'Excuse me, madam.' She didn't respond, so I repeated myself, a little louder. At that she turned towards me, pulled an earpiece out, sat bolt upright and said, 'Oh my God!'

'I'm PC Mike Pannett of North Yorkshire Police,' I said. 'I think you know why we're here, judging by all these plants.' She just looked at me, and I went into formal mode. 'We'll be searching these premises under warrant for drugs or material used in the production of drugs. I do need to tell you that you are under arrest on suspicion of cultivation of cannabis.' Then I cautioned her. Given the circumstances, it felt strange giving the official spiel. In situations like these you're tempted to say, 'Look, lady, you're nicked.' But those days have long gone.

She said nothing. But when she took off her sunglasses it was so that she could wipe away a tear.

'Is your husband about the place?' I asked her.

'No. He's at work.' She had stood up now and was putting on a long towelling dressing gown.

'I understand you have a child.'

'She's at school. I just took her in half an hour ago.'

'I see. And what are these plants?'

'I don't know.' She glanced past me at the CID boys, standing there with Fordy. Jayne had stepped past me to stand by the woman's side.

'Well, just so you know what we are doing, we're going to crack on now and search the barn and seize all of the plants and equipment. I'm sorry to say that we are also going to have to search your house.'

'Okay,' she said. 'I understand.'

While Des and the lads set about searching the rest of the place, Jayne led the woman across to the farmhouse to get dressed. By the time Ed and I had followed them across they were both in the kitchen, and the woman's mobile was ringing. I told her to go ahead and answer it; I was hoping it was the husband so that we could get him back and sort everything out. You wouldn't normally let someone answer the phone in such circumstances, but it was a judgement call and I was banking on him not wanting to leave his wife and child to take the rap.

'Yes?' she said, her hand shaking as she held the phone to her ear. She listened to the voice on the other end for a moment, then said, 'Listen, the police are here.'

'Is that your husband?' I asked. She nodded, and I held out my hand. 'Can I have a quick word?'

She passed me the phone. 'Now then, sir,' I said, 'we're at your house and we've found what we suspect to be cannabis plants under cultivation.' He said nothing, just gave out a long, slow sigh. 'Your wife's under arrest,' I said. 'Best thing for you is to come home, I think.'

He seemed very calm. 'That's no problem, Officer. I'll be there in twenty minutes.'

At this point the woman broke down in tears as the reality of what was happening hit home. 'What'll happen?' she sobbed. 'What about my daughter? Will I go to prison?'

'Look,' I said, 'there's no point denying that it's fairly serious, but one step at a time, eh? Have you got anyone who can collect your daughter from school and look after her for a bit?'

'There's my mum.'

'Mike.' It was Des, who'd come across from the barn. 'You realise we have a huge find here?'

'I'd say it could be one for the record books, mate.'

'We're gonna have a problem shifting all those plants,' he said.

'Yeah, I'll get onto Mennel's for the hire van. I saw Fordy arrive at the kitchen door. You need to get yourself to town,' I said. 'The hire van needs collecting.'

A raid such as we were now involved in throws up a number of administrative and logistical problems. Before we shifted anything the SOCO had to photograph the whole place, and Stuart only knew one way of working: thorough and painstaking, which meant that he wasn't one to be rushed. After he was through, every last scrap of relevant material had to be counted, logged and bagged up. It's no good showing up in court with vague estimations of 'lots of plants'. The prosecution want accurate numbers that can't be challenged by the opposition. So – plants, lights, the timers and valves, header tanks, even the wiring system – it was all evidence and it would all have to be dismantled and taken back to the station store. So we now had two members of the search squad going from tank to tank, counting the plants in each row, multiplying them by the number of rows, and Ed complaining of writer's cramp as he logged all the figures. After they'd done that, it was on with the white paper suits and masks to start bagging everything up.

I was glad to leave that job to the search team. I wanted to meet the husband, see what kind of fellow he was. Criminals are rarely what you expect when you meet them face to face. Some of the worst ones look mild-mannered and inoffensive. When this chap drove up in his Astra van it was quite clear he knew what was coming. Some people have a defiant attitude when you tell them they're under arrest. Some will argue, some will fight, some are morose and silent. This guy was simply resigned. I have to say that he and his wife looked a sorry pair. Crestfallen, you might say. And you could understand it.

They must have ploughed a fair bit of capital into setting up the growing system, and here it was being dismantled before their eyes. Funnily enough, a little part of me was troubled to think of a healthy crop being destroyed. Living in the country you learn to respect growing things. We would later establish that from a crop this size they could expect to recoup £100,000, in cash, tax-free. And they would harvest three times a year. It had me wondering why the lad still kept his full-time job in town, but that would be for the investigating officers to find out.

'We're going to have to search your house,' I said, after I'd put the handcuffs on him.

'Yeah, I s'pose you are,' he said, and led us inside.

I don't like searching people's homes. If you do it right it's a tedious business. And the worst part, for me, is bedrooms. It gets embarrassing. You see things you'd rather not know about. It was clear they ran their business from theirs – or he did. There was a computer, which of course we seized; there were notebooks with phone numbers, written orders, bank statements – all of which would be manna from heaven for the Intelligence Unit. There was even a collection of plastic bags for packaging the cannabis, some of them already full, and scales for weighing it out. According to Des what we'd found was Grade A skunk cannabis, twice as valuable on the street as the plain resin. It was clear that this fellow was supplying the stuff wholesale, and leaving it to others to distribute it to local dealers.

By the time we'd got everything dismantled and bagged up it was well past four o'clock and we were all starving hungry. It was at this stage that one of the CID boys called me over to a metal box that was fixed to the creosoted wooden pole that brought the overhead power supply to the house.

'Remember we wondered why their electricity bills were so

low?' He pointed at a black cable that ran out from the box and snaked across the yard towards the barn. 'Looks like they've short-circuited the meter and tapped straight into the mains supply, the crafty buggers.'

'Yeah, right. That'll be a further arrest for abstracting electricity. I'll get onto Control to get the leccy board down to make it safe.'

While Fordy got on with packing all the seized material into the hired van, we took our prisoners to Scarborough where they would be interviewed.

By the time I got back to Malton we were well into overtime. Fordy had just arrived from the farm and was ready to unload the van.

'Birdie's told us to get all this in the property store,' he told me.

'Bloody hell, that's on the third floor!'

'Well, Jayne's been sent to help Des out with the interviews – gain a bit of experience. So it looks like it's you, me and Ed got the short straw.'

Fordy took me round to the back of the van and lifted the sliding door. Two lamps, a tangle of wires and a plastic header tank clattered onto the tarmac, exposing a pile of binbags stuffed to the top with cannabis plants. The entire body of the van was chock-a-block, from floor to ceiling. It took us a full hour to get it all put away, even with the help of a couple of lads off the late turn. Last job was to sweep out the back of the van, which was covered with several hundred pounds' worth of cannabis leaves. And if I thought that was it, job done, I had another thing coming. I had my jacket over my arm and was heading for the door, covered in sweat and looking forward to getting home and showering off, when I bumped into the new chief superintendent.

She stopped and wrinkled up her nose, then looked at me. 'Mike, I've just come down from my office and the whole building stinks of cannabis.' She put her hand into her pocket and produced a small handful of leaves. 'And I found these on the stairs.' She looked at me, and my heart sank. 'There are plenty more as well,' she continued. 'You'll get it sorted before you go home, won't you?'

'Will do, ma'am.'

She paused, then gave a hint of a smile. 'Good job, by the way.'

So, after boxing off the paperwork and sweeping down the stairs, all I had to do was dodge the afternoon desk sergeant. But he collared me as I was opening the door to leave. 'Call from a lady out in the woods near Westow, Mike. Seen a man hanging his washing out on the trees.'

'And?'

'All his washing. Everything.'

'Oh no. You mean he was . . .'

'That's right, mate. Stark naked.'

'First call tomorrow, mate. I promise.'

Back home, after the dog had taken me for a walk, I had a shower and changed into some more comfortable clothes. By the time I sat down to a plate of grub and a bottle of beer, the ten o'clock news was coming on the telly, and Ann was arriving from work. She leaned forward and kissed me, at the same time nicking a pickled onion off my plate. 'What's for supper then?' she asked. 'Supper?' I said. 'This is my lunch – and I'll thank you to keep your fingers out of it.'

Chapter 4

The Fast and the Furious

We were in the Jolly Farmers. Me, Ann, Walt, Algy and Soapy. The team. Everyone was enjoying a beer, except me. I was on orange juice. And mineral water. And cola. And I can't stand any of them. It was a warm, sticky evening, I had the kind of thirst that only a cool pint of bitter was going to satisfy, but I had to be away at half past nine. I was starting a run of nights – and one thing you never do is drink before you go on duty.

There are a lot of things to enjoy about working shifts. Like getting up in a morning and walking the dog around the hills and not seeing another soul; or coming home to our cottage in the woods at half past six in the morning and sitting with a mug of tea listening to the birds as you mull over the events of a night shift. I even relish that precious hour or two of daylight you get after work on an early turn in midwinter, when I can swing the old axe and split a few logs before the sun goes down and the puddles start to freeze, knowing that everyone else is stuck in their offices or shops until it gets dark. But there are times when it works the other way around, and this was one of them. There was Algy at the bar getting the drinks in before the final round of questions, and I was looking at my watch wondering whether I could hang on another five minutes. Just to twist the knife in the wound, I had a headache. But that was no surprise. Quiz night has that effect on me.

It's a funny thing about quiz questions and memory. I mean, I always reckon to know a fair bit about football, cricket and rugby. I'd say that adds up to a good general knowledge, which, as Algy once said to me, is 'a splendid social lubricant'. He meant it's what blokes will talk about when they don't know each other very well. I'm a fair hand at geography, too. That was one of my best subjects at school. Knew all my mountain ranges and rivers, and my capital cities. It helped that my dad was an exceptionally bright man and would impart all sorts of knowledge to us, and always encouraged us to look things up in a big old atlas that lived on the shelf behind the television. But the funny thing is, as soon as you put me under the pressure of a pub quiz, my memory is liable to let me down. It's not that I don't have the answer logged away somewhere; it's just that I can't always call it up. It doesn't help when the rest of the team is looking at you and Algy's tapping his pen on the table and going, 'Come on, Michael old boy, this is your territory.' Of course I usually get it in the end – except that sometimes I get it just after we've handed the answer sheet in. And when that happens your team-mates are inclined to get a bit tetchy. But sometimes you surprise yourself. Sometimes the landlord fires off a question about a song that was a hit before you were even born, or some actor from the age of silent movies, or a baseball team in America, and before you have time to even think about it you hear yourself giving out an answer, and it's right. That always makes me laugh, when everyone's congratulating you, and you're thinking, 'Now where the hell did that come from?'

Ann doesn't have that trouble. Not at all. She's good. She knows about films, books, television, current affairs. Even answers questions on soaps, which she never watches. Reckons she gets it from the newspaper headlines while she's standing in the queue at the supermarket checkout or reading those celebrity gossip mags at the hairdresser. Her mind's just crammed full of random knowledge. More important, she can snap her fingers and summon it up at will. So when she's on a late shift we really miss her. As for Walt, he tends to sit there, fidgeting with his pencil as he waits for his specialist subjects to come up, and tutting. He started tutting when they brought in the smoking ban in pubs, and he's never let the subject drop. 'I need me roll-up,' he'll complain, tapping his head. 'They all play hell about it but I've been reading in t'*Reader's Digest* how tobacco's good for your brain. Stimulates your cortex, whatever that is. Helps you concentrate.' No one ever argues with Walt. It isn't worth it. We just let him have his say. 'Trouble wi' quizzes these days . . .' and he's off. 'It's all them questions aimed at young-sters. And townies. When I were in school we used to have what they called a Brains Trust, last day of term. By heck, we didn't half look forward to that. Old Mister Braithwaite, he'd get his gramophone out of t'cupboard – same as he kept his cane in – then he'd crank her up and play us different bits of birdsong and animal calls he had on an old 78. And we had to identify 'em, d'you see? Then he'd fetch a few sprigs of foliage, or bits of dried-up fur what he had in his drawer – aye, and feathers and suchlike, or maybe a dead insect in a bottle, or a bone, and hand 'em round. We'd all have a look at 'em, then write down what we thought they was. Now that's what I call general know-ledge. Things worth knowing. Not all this here footballers' wives and their going-ons.'

And fair credit to the old fellow, whenever we get a question on the natural world, Walt comes up trumps. Every time.

Quizzes are all about teamwork. And we aren't a bad team. Even when it gets to the music round, which is where Soapy comes in. You play a tune, any time from about 1955 to the present day, and he'll give you artist and title. Sometimes, for good measure, he'll throw the record label in. Phenomenal. The rest of the time he sits there supping his beer and looking at the ceiling. Not even interested. Then when it comes to history, which I know nowt about, we all relax, because that's where Algy shines. Battles, kings and queens, politicians, natural disasters, revolutions, explorers, military leaders: he just reels 'em off one after another with their dates. He's the original case of 'If I don't know it, it ain't worth knowing.' And if you'd seen his collection of books up at his house you'd realise where he gets it from. This particular night, just as I was leaving, we got into a tie-break against a team of students. There were four of them, all lads, and they'd been hiking along the Wolds Way. They'd come all the way from Market Weighton, eighteen miles and more, then legged it six miles from Thixendale with their packs, hoping to win themselves some beer money. When the landlord announced a final round on world history, their faces lit up. 'Magic,' one of them said. 'That's our subject.' Algy just smiled at 'em. 'Well, good luck to you,' he said. 'I just hope you've done your homework, boys.'

I hated to do it, but the clock was ticking. I got out of my chair and took my empty glass to the bar. 'Right,' I said. 'I'm away. See you in the morning.' I kissed Ann goodnight and set off, but not before I'd heard Walt say, 'Never mind, lass. You've got that dog of yours to keep you warm.'

That's one of the few times I feel a bit down on this job,

when I'm leaving Ann and my friends in the pub and driving into town, knowing that while everyone else is having a good time and then going home to bed I have to be out there working. Still, you shrug your shoulders and get on with it. What else can you do?

I was paired up with Jayne that night, which made a change. I didn't work with her that often. If I was with anyone it was generally Ed, sometimes Fordy. More often than not, when I was out and about on my own beat, I was single-crewed.

'Funny how things have gone quiet on that Sunset Gang,' I said as we walked across the yard to the car.

'Yeah, they soon went to ground, didn't they?' said Jayne. 'And I thought they were s'posed to be on a bit of a campaign round here.'

'Tell you what,' I said, 'We better keep our wits about us. Cos with a team like that, you just don't know when they might hit us. We don't want to end up like Pete with a faceful of CS.' I slung my bag into the back and got into the driver's seat. 'You know what I always say.'

'Wass that then?'

'The old saying, Jayne. They'll come again. They always do. Thieves are like gamblers. They know they should quit while they're ahead.'

'But they never do, eh?'

'And that's where they come unstuck. Happens every time. So, what you been up to?' I asked, as we turned into Castlegate and headed down towards the river. 'Haven't seen you in a while.'

'Keeping busy. Been spending my days off cooped up in the house, studying.'

'Studying? What for? I thought you'd already got a degree.'

'Ah well, that's the point, innit?'

'What d'you mean?' We bumped over the level crossing and swung up towards Norton, past the petrol station.

'Well, coming into the force as a graduate. You're expected to move on. The pressure's there to take promotion.'

'That right?'

'Yeah. I've started studying towards my sergeant's exam. Part one anyway.'

'Bloody hell. You've only been here five minutes.' We drove on in silence for a moment. 'Still, I can see where you're coming from.'

'Well, you can't stand still, mate. Not at my age at any rate. 'S all right for you older blokes. Coasting along.'

I checked the traffic at the mini-roundabout, then drove on along Commercial Street. 'Coasting along, you say? Listen, Jayne, it takes time to learn how to be a police officer. It takes experienced cops like me to hold the bloody job together while you graduate types make dodgy decisions from up your ladder.'

I smiled as Jayne raised her eyebrows. 'You crusty old sod,' she said. It was one of the things I liked about working with her: we could wind each other up, and you always knew she'd give as good as she got.

'So you never fancied taking promotion, Mike?'

'Tell you the truth, Jayne, I'm perfectly happy as I am. When I was younger, yeah, I might have considered it, but the thing is, you go for promotion and you immediately close a lot of other doors.'

'Yeah? Such as?'

'Well, take the TSG. I was in that. I got onto murder enquiry teams, and the Area Crime Squad. Didn't half do some interesting work. Exciting too. If I'd gone the way you're heading, well . . .'

'You'd have missed out?'

'I'm not saying there aren't things to get into as a sergeant, but back then, at twenty-five, twenty-eight – no, I was having way too interesting a time.'

'What about now?'

'I dunno . . . Thing is, Jayne, I love me job. Simple as that. I don't want any extra hassle.'

'Oh. You never get frustrated that you have to take orders from plonkers – well, people you don't always respect?'

'Course I do. Sometimes.' We were passing the Costcutter on Commercial Street and I was slowing down. 'We need to keep an eye on places like that,' I said. 'Just the sort of shop our Sunset friends might target.'

The place had only recently been revamped after consultation with a police architectural liaison officer and the crime prevention officer. The windows, the doors, the locks had all been upgraded to improve security, and a set of concrete pillars had been put in the pavement out the front to discourage ram-raiders. It's a process known as 'target hardening'.

'What does Ann think?'

'Think about what?'

'You still being a PC.'

'What is this, a conspiracy? You're the second person to have a dig at me on that topic. No – the third in fact. My mother's on the case now.'

'Well, I don't think I'd fancy it.'

'You mean you'd only want to be married to an inspector or sommat? That what you're saying?'

'I'm just saying I wouldn't fancy staying on the bottom rung all me life, that's all.'

'Well I wouldn't fancy all that bookwork. Last time I did any studying I was at Hendon. And that, my friend, is many moons ago. It's not something that I was ever really interested in.'

'Sure you're not just worried about failing?'

I didn't answer, and we drove on in silence. We checked out a number of warehouses and shops in and around town and then headed for the villages. Fordy and Ed, and Chris the sergeant, would be doing the same in other areas. It wasn't so much that we expected to nab the gang in the act, but there was always a chance. And at least if the Sunset lot were scouting around they'd be aware that we were out and about as well.

All through the shift, as we went from place to place, Jayne took notes which would be fed into the system. Even if a place was okay, we logged our visit, so that if a burglary were committed we could narrow down the time it took place. It was all grist to the intelligence mill.

It must have been about two o'clock when we parked up in a nice quiet spot, tucked inside a gate near Howe Bridge where we could observe traffic along the A169 Pickering road. There was a clump of elder trees in full bloom and I wound down my window to take in the scent of the flowers. I reached out and grabbed a bloom and passed it to Jayne. 'Smell that,' I said. 'My old grandad used to make wine out of this. Gorgeous, it was.'

We gave it half an hour or so, then shifted to another spot on the Helmsley road. Sometimes you get lucky, sometimes you don't, but there comes a time of night in the countryside when anyone on the move is worth taking notice of. But tonight nothing seemed to be happening, so we retraced some of the route we'd taken earlier, and checked the same premises – with the same result.

It was getting on for five when we turned off the bypass and headed back towards Norton, and the first rays of the sun were lighting up the treetops. As we drove along Commercial Street I was just about to suggest we take a final look at Costcutter when a woman in a pinafore stepped out into the street waving a mop.

I stepped on the brake and wound down the window. 'We've been burgled!' she shouted. 'Burgled!' Behind her the shop lights were ablaze, and the door was wide open, but there was no alarm going off.

'Now then, love. What's the problem?' Jayne and I were out of the car and shepherding her back onto the pavement.

'They've come in the back and taken – ooh, all sorts. Spirits, ciggies . . . I haven't checked the till. I'm only the cleaner. But thank heaven I didn't bump into them. What would they have done?'

'It's okay, love, we're here now. Let's just take a look, shall we?'

'Bloody 'ell, look at that.' Jayne was in the shop already, pointing at the metal grille behind the counter. It had been ripped open and the shelves were all but clean; there were just a few packs of cigarettes scattered on the floor, along with a broken bottle of what smelled like brandy.

'Well, how the hell have they got in?' I said. There was no sign of the door having been forced. 'You came in through the front here, did you?'

The cleaner pulled a bunch of keys from her pinafore pocket. 'Always do. I have my own set, see?'

'And was it still locked?'

'Oh aye. I had the same fiddling about I have every morning. Right complicated, them new locks, y'know.'

'Where's the thing for the alarm? The control box?'

'Through here.' She led us past the shelves of foodstuffs into a dimly lit area towards the back. 'You'd think that would've gone off, wouldn't you?'

It was clear that the console had been opened and interfered with. The whole thing had been smothered with some kind of foam.

'What's all this about then?' Jayne was sniffing at it. 'Smells like shaving cream.'

'Search me. Maybe it fouls up the contacts or something.' I leaned closer and shone my light on it. You could see where the wires had been fiddled with. One or two were hanging loose. 'But they'd still have to break into the building first.'

'Yeah, so why didn't it go off?'

We moved through an open door into a side room. There was a desk, a phone, a filing cabinet, a fridge humming away in the corner next to a little sink.

'What's this place?' I asked.

'It's the manager's office. And they use it when they want to make a cup of tea.'

'Here you go.' It was Jayne. She'd gone on past the office, down a narrow corridor to what looked like a storeroom. She was pointing to a rectangular inlet high up on the wall.

'I bet this is where they came in,' she said.

'The cunning little . . .' Standing on tiptoes, I could see right through a ventilation duct and out onto the wall of the property across the alleyway.

'Well, that explains that. They've pulled the outside cover off and wriggled their way through here.'

'Must've been a bloody tight squeeze.'

'Or very thin burglars,' the cleaner said.

I was shaking my head. 'Clever, very clever. Enter through

the one spot that's not wired up, disable the alarm, and help yourself.'

It was getting on for half past five by this time. The morning papers had arrived and the shop would be opening at six.

'Right,' I said, 'This looks like a Sunset job. We need to get the old SOCO on the job.'

'He doesn't come on duty till eight,' Jayne said.

'I know that. We'll call the inspector. He'll authorise Chris to call him out early. Meanwhile' – I looked around at the mess – 'we'd better get this lot protected and secured.' That meant temporarily closing the shop. If the burglars had left any foot-prints, fingerprints, bits of hair or fibre, we needed to make sure they were preserved for the SOCO. We couldn't be having any contamination of the crime scene. And if that was a pain for the shop owners, well, so be it.

We managed to get away about seven, when the SOCO arrived, along with Thommo off the early shift. I was feeling knackered by now, and Jayne wasn't looking exactly chipper. 'Dunno about you,' she said as we drove through town, 'but I feel crap about that.'

I didn't say anything. I knew very well what she was on about.

'I mean, we checked the bloody place three times. For all we know they could've been in there that last time and we wouldn't have known. Cleaning out all them fags and booze and laughing their bleedin' socks off at us.'

'Well, you can only do your best,' I said. 'You know what this lot are like. They're professionals. Chances are they had spotters out watching us check the place.'

Jayne shuddered. 'Gawd, that's creepy, that is.'

'Yeah, but it happens. Stay in touch by mobile, wait till we drive off, then make their move.'

'I'm just thinking about what could have happened if we'd met them face to face.'

'That's why we need to be on our toes. And know where the rest of the team are patrolling – in case we need help.'

I was trying to be positive, but driving home an hour or so later I thought about what Jayne and I had discussed. I wondered just how desperate and violent this gang might be. How far were they willing to go? It led to this other odd feeling skittering across the back of my mind, one that I'd felt a hundred times before in this line of work. It was a sort of shiver of dread tinged with excitement. Part of you is afraid of the challenge you might have to face some cold dark night, on your own – because cops do get seriously hurt, even killed. But a part of you relishes it. You want to know how you measure up, whether you're capable of putting your fears to one side, and concentrating on the job in hand – following the procedure, step by step, constantly asking yourself, what should I be doing here? And here? And what should I do if . . .? I think that's how most of us deal with the fear. Sometimes it's only after the moment has passed that you ask yourself, how the hell did I cope with that?

As I left town behind me and climbed up onto the edge of the Wolds I was also thinking about this gang that was starting to cause us grief. The fact is that in our part of the country it's comparatively rare to have an outfit that keeps on doing the same kind of job, over and over, especially one that's willing to attack police officers. And a part of me was actually quite excited to think that we were pitting our wits against a well-organised team, a bunch of professionals if you like. I have to admit that that same part of me was impressed at their creativity; I even had a grudging respect for the way they operated. If they were the gang we thought they were, these were level two cross-border criminals, coming down from the northeast. So the way I saw it, when we nailed them – when, not if – it would be a real feather in our cap. Ever the optimist, that's me. I think that's what was making my pulse beat a little faster that morning as I drove up through Leavening and headed home.

A moment or two later it was going like the clappers as I turned down the little lane that led through the woods to Keeper's Cottage. There on the lawn, just next to the garage, a group of hooded figures were standing, hands in pockets, the morning sunlight filtering through a haze of cigarette smoke above their heads. I shot into the clearing and slammed the brakes on, scattering stones and raising a cloud of dust.

'Ex-cuse me.' I stepped out of the car, braced for anything, but at the same time completely bewildered. 'Can I help you?' Then as they turned to look at me I saw the familiar faces of the four students we'd met in the pub last night.

'It's all right,' the first one said, his hands spread in front of him as if to ward me off. 'Your wife – she said we could pitch our tent here for the night.'

'Oh, she did, did she?'

'It was after the quiz, and we were looking for a place to camp.'

'Well, there's nowhere in the village.'

'That's what she told us. So she walked us up here.'

'And she said that you might give us a ride to Thixendale in the morning,' the second added, looking nervously at the others.

'Cheers, Ann,' I muttered to myself. 'So what happened in the tie-break last night?'

The first youth looked at the second. 'Er – we won.'

'But we bought your team a round of drinks,' his mate added brightly. 'Out of the winnings, like.'

'In exchange for . . .?'

'In exchange for – you know.' He gestured to the flattened grass where they'd pitched their tents.

'And a lift in the morning,' I said.

'Yeah. She said you wouldn't mind – and you'd get your free pint next week.'

'Come on, in you get.'

It didn't take long to drive the four or five miles to Thix. I dropped them outside the pub and left them to pick up the path that would take them over the hill to Wharram Percy and then away to Wintringham. And as I made my way home I thought to myself, well, that's another lot who'll go home and tell everyone how wonderful North Yorkshire police are. Either that or 'what a soft touch.'

I was back at work early the next night. Couldn't contain myself. An incident such as Jayne and I had encountered does that to you. It puts you on your mettle. You find yourself thinking about the pride you take in your shift – because we all think our own shift is the best, and that's the way it should be. Right or wrong, I knew that the other three shifts would get to hear what had happened and I knew that Jayne and I could expect a bit of banter. We were the plonkers who'd checked a shop three times and not noticed it was being raided. Not quite the whole truth, of course, but that's how they'd see it. And it would hurt, because whatever else you feel, you feel proprietorial about the area you patrol. When people are ripping off businesses on your beat it feels as if they're robbing you too. So I arrived at the station eager to know if there had been any developments.

'Not a lot,' was Chris Cocks's verdict. 'Just this.' He handed me a printout. The CCTV camera down by the level crossing had captured a few images of a Transit van driving into Norton at about four o'clock, and what looked like the same van heading back again at about five. The number-plate wasn't fully legible, but what you could read, and the colour of the van, tallied with the one that Pete had reported from the earlier break-in, when he'd copped a faceful of CS gas.

'It's better than nowt,' I said to Jayne when we met in the parade room. 'Let's just hope they put their heads above the parapet again soon.'

'You wanna be careful what you wish for,' she said. 'We don't want a bleedin' crime wave, do we?'

She was right, but that's another odd thing about this kind of work. We knew that our best chance of nailing this lot was for them to come out and try it again. And for me that meant the sooner the better.

I suppose it was too much to hope that they'd be back at work already, and in any case the events of the coming night were to push the Sunset Gang right out of my mind. That's where I sometimes envy the CID lads; that they can focus on a particular incident and get their teeth into it. Jayne and I were straight back into battle, having to face whatever came our way.

Because it was a Friday night we had the late shift overlapping with us for the first few hours. There were four of them, plus their sergeant, and a couple of specials. And we needed every one of them. It was mayhem from the word go.

Sometimes on a Friday or a Saturday night you can come in, get your bearings, have a cup of coffee and a bit of a natter with the off-going shift, then ease yourself into the job. It helps cement the bonds that make a more effective, close-knit station. Nights like this one, though, you're in action from the word go. There's no chance to take stock. We were straight down town to help the late shift stop an argument in the market square from turning into a full-scale punch-up, then over the bridge to sort out a bunch of lads from one of the villages who thought it would be fun to have a swimming race across the river.

But at least we had plenty of us on duty. Jayne was paired up with Ed, and I was with Fordy. We'd been allocated a brand-new Ford Focus, an 1800cc diesel turbo with barely 1500 miles on the clock. 'Jayne was well pissed off that we got this,' Fordy said. 'It's a bit of a beast, isn't it?'

I had to laugh. 'Compared with that souped-up Vauxhall Nova of yours, I suppose it is, lad.'

'You having a go at my little passion wagon?'

'That what you call it? You don't mean rust-bucket?'

'Hey, the girls all love her.'

'Says a lot about the standard of women you hang out with, Fordy.'

But he wasn't listening. He was winding down the window to shout something at our two specials, who were passing by in what we call the rowdy van. It's a Transit. It not only creates a presence on the street, it's also got a nice cage at the rear for holding and transporting prisoners. If you've got a bit of a roughhouse going on and that shows up, it makes a statement, especially if four or five officers leap out. As Thommo liked to say, 'It makes the buggers think.' In the cities you'll see big vans with plenty of cops on board on a regular basis, but in rural areas it's a rarity. So it was good to see it on the streets on a Friday night. And we would have the added luxury of a dog unit that was due to come across from Scarborough for an hour at closing time before heading back to the coast for when the clubs turned out.

The point about the rowdy van was that we knew we had

the capacity to make several arrests if necessary. Or, as I said to Fordy, 'Enough troops to fight a small war.' Our problem, though, was back at the station, where two of the three cells were already occupied from an earlier job, meaning that if we did make any subsequent arrests we'd have to take them to York or Scarborough. The minute you get involved in a fracas of some sort you have that question hanging over your head: is it worth placing someone under arrest when it could mean depleting your manpower – at a time of night when you need all hands to the pump? But that's rural policing for you. You might say it makes it interesting. Having said that, it's some-times useful, when there's a bit of aggro, to grab a couple of ringleaders and stick them in the back of the van. It makes the others ask themselves, do I really want to be next? It's a judge-ment call. A lot of the time it can work; at other times it can inflame the situation. As Fordy and I chewed all this over I said, 'Anyway, we've a couple of vans from Helmsley and Pickering at the top end on standby, both double-crewed. If it comes to it and we have to make any arrests, at least we have cover while we take 'em to Scarborough.'

The odd thing is that as often as not, when you have plenty of officers on duty, things seem to stay pretty quiet. Then on the days when you're thin on the ground, all hell can break loose. And it often does. Maybe it's true that a show of strength puts people off causing trouble. Or maybe it's just Sod's Law.

As it turned out, we were lucky this particular night. The Pannett charm – plus a very eager dog with large teeth – defused a couple of tense situations, and we were back at base shortly after twelve for a quick cup of tea, looking forward to a quiet night out in the country.

Fordy was pleased to be working with me. As a town copper

he relished the change of scene. 'Yeah, this is a treat for me,' he said when we set off for the country after our break. 'Hardly ever seem to get out of town. Joined the police to see the world and three years later, what have I seen?'

'Malton town centre.'

'Right. I mean, it's okay for action, but sometimes you just wanna – you know – get out and about.'

'Tell you what then,' I said, 'we'll start out by patrolling the A64 in our brand-new car, eh? The old crime corridor. Let's see if we can stir up some action, eh? Cos I tell you what, mate, I don't know what it is but I can feel something happening tonight.'

I had no particular plan in mind as we left town, other than to cruise along the main road keeping our eyes peeled. We made a few routine stops. There were a couple of cars with a light out, another full of youngsters going a bit too quickly, but nothing we couldn't sort with a bit of finger-wagging. We went out as far as the Hopgrove, on the edge of York, then turned around and headed back east. We'd got as far as Scagglethorpe when my mobile rang. I pulled over and fished it out of my pocket.

'Mike, it's Jack.'

'My mate from Staxton,' I said in answer to Fordy's raised eyebrow. 'Now then, lad, what can I do for you?'

'Why, I've been trying to get onto Control but they've had me in a bloody queue.'

'They will, mate. Friday night. You know what it's like.'

'Well, listen. I've just had a gang of lads make off without payment. And a lass.'

'Oh?'

'Aye. The old story: pulled up, filled up and shot off without paying. I should have bloody known. I spotted the lad filling up – kept his back to the CCTV. Hood over his face and all that.'

'Got any vehicle details?'

'Red Astra, four occupants.' He gave me the registration number. 'And they left here heading towards York.'

'Okay, how long ago?'

'Be seven, eight minutes now. I've wasted all this time trying to get hold of someone.'

'Okay, we're on the main road and we're pointing your way. We'll keep our eyes peeled. Just hang on a sec. Fordy mate, put out an all units, will you? Red Astra, Y295 . . .'

While Fordy got on the radio I got a few more details off Jack. 'Right,' I said when he was through, 'we'll catch up with you later.'

'What do you reckon?' Fordy asked.

I put the car in gear and set off towards Rillington. 'Oh, every chance we might spot them.'

'Your mate Jack: he's sure it wasn't an accident then? They didn't just forget to pay?'

'Positive.' You do get people driving off absent-mindedly. It happens quite often. Then you have to trace a registration number, go to someone's house and tackle them about it. And nine times out of ten they're all apologies. But Jack was in no doubt on this one. 'No,' I said to Fordy, 'he's on my Country Watch team. He knows what's what.'

'Country Watch. That how he has your number?'

'Aye. And my roster. They all do. Co-operative policing, buddy. The name of the game. Anyway, we know what we're looking for. So let's see if we can find them, eh?'

The only question in my mind now was, would the suspects

follow the A64 towards York, or would they turn off and take one of the back roads? 'And I tell you what,' I said, as we made our way through West Heslerton, 'if it does come to a pursuit we'll find out what this new car of ours is made of.'

We were doing sixty to seventy on a clear road, watching the oncoming traffic. But even at that speed you don't have much time to read a registration number, so Fordy took responsibility for remembering the first half, while I did the second.

Two, three, four cars went by, none of them remotely resembling what we were after.

'I bet they've gone the back roads after all,' Fordy said.

'You sound disappointed.'

Fordy just grinned, then leaned forward in his seat, squinting at the road ahead. 'Hang about. 295 ... Y295,' he said, and before I could read the last three letters he was banging his hand on the dashboard and shouting, 'That's them!'

'Yep, four occupants. Perfect.' If this had been a film I would've slung the car around, left a nice set of black tyre marks on the road and given chase, lights blazing through a cloud of smoke. And to be honest, that's what your instincts tell you to do. I don't know where adrenaline comes from, but I'm always amazed how quickly it hits your bloodstream, urging you into action. But on this occasion we needed to be just a bit canny. Had we been in the middle of a city, yes, we would have given chase immediately rather than let them get lost in the side streets and traffic. But where we were, with miles of open country all around, you can afford to play out a bit more line – and use a bit of nous. You need to think health and safety, and preservation – of your own life, the suspect's life, and the lives of any other road users. Not to mention your brand-new, turbo-diesel Ford Focus.

As the suspect vehicle receded in my rear-view mirror I eased my foot off the accelerator. 'They might have spotted us,' I said, 'but they've no reason to think we suspect them. The last thing we want is for them to see our brake lights coming on.'

As I spoke I was thinking. So far we were only dealing with a minor crime – making off without payment – but the question in my mind was, why would they do that? They must have known their number would have been taken, so were they stupid, or were they desperate? What else had they done, and what else might they do? Could they be on drugs? On the run? Had they stolen the car? It all goes through your mind when you get caught up in a situation like this.

'Probably just joyriders,' was Fordy's opinion.

'You never know,' I said as the car disappeared from sight and I made a wide U-turn on the empty road. 'Could be a couple of young tearaways out to impress their girlfriends. Could be armed robbers. Could have kidnapped someone. You can't assume anything.'

There was a good couple of miles of open road ahead before the next turn-off, so we had every chance of gaining on them, just so long as the driver hadn't spotted us. This was where teamwork came into play. While I got my foot down Fordy got on the radio, using our vehicle call sign for the night. 'Romeo Mike 23 to Control.'

'*Romeo Mike 23, go ahead.*'

'We've spotted the suspect vehicle. It's westbound on the A64, just west of Heslerton. Four up.'

'*Romeo Mike 23, all received. Any units Ryedale channel to assist?*'

As I accelerated along the empty road I heard Chris Cocks and the lads in the Malton van unit call in. They were both making their way from town.

I was doing ninety by this time, then a hundred, and the car seemed to have energy to spare. You could almost feel it champing at the bit. Up ahead I saw the red lights. 'There they are, Fordy my lad.'

At this stage I still hadn't put the blue lights on, nor the two-tones. With any luck they still wouldn't have figured out who we were. What I wanted was to get close – but not too close. I needed to give other units time to respond.

'Now let's reel 'em in, shall we? Nice and steady.'

'Go for it.' Fordy put the mike to his mouth again. 'Yeah, Control . . . any traffic vehicles nearby?'

'*Romeo Mike 23, all received, just getting onto York and Scarborough now. Keep us updated.*'

'Good move,' I said, as the speedo nudged 105. 'They're gonna take a bit of catching.'

'*Control to Romeo Mike 23. Traffic car on its way from Scarborough, just passing Staxton now . . . Four or five minutes behind you.*'

'Great this, isn't it?' I said.

'What is?' Fordy seemed surprised.

'The car, buddy. Look at it: a hundred and ten and nowt rattling.'

'Just my teeth, mate.'

'*Control to Romeo Mike 23.*'

'Go ahead, over.'

'*The owner of the vehicle has just reported it stolen from a car park near Scarborough railway station, over.*'

'That's all received.'

'Right.' Fordy settled lower in his seat. 'So that's the story, is it?'

The trouble was that we still didn't know why they had nicked the car or what they intended to do. Were they just joyriders, or was something more sinister going on? And would they stop? People imagine that all a copper has to do is catch up with the bad guys and it's hands in the air and they come quietly. Not these days it isn't.

We were through East and West Heslerton now, and within a few hundred yards of the Astra. It was time to ease off. Wait and see how long it was before they twigged who we were, meanwhile buying time for the other units to get nearer. But we didn't have to wait long. The Astra started losing speed rapidly. It crossed my mind that they might be looking for somewhere to bail out. But instead of stopping or turning off the car continued cruising, slowly. It was down to forty, then thirty miles an hour.

'What the hell they playing at, Mike?'

'Not sure, but I think they're having a crafty look at who we are and what we're in. If so, mate, this won't be the first time they've done this. Brace yourself, cos owt could happen now.'

I put the blue lights on. 'I've had enough of this. Get onto Control, Fordy. Tell 'em I'm gonna try and stop them.'

But even as I flashed my headlights to indicate that they should stop, I caught sight of a puff of burning oil as the driver in front dropped down a gear and put his foot to the floor. He had no intention of pulling over.

'Just hope the buggers don't go daft,' I said. You tread a thin line in these pursuits. You want to apprehend them. You want them off the public highway before they kill some poor sod – or themselves – but at the same time you don't want to push them to where they'll take crazy risks. 'Had two lads out at Bulmer a couple of years back. Rolled their car into a hedge. Christ knows how they got away without killing themselves.'

'Tell you what,' Fordy said, 'this lad looks like he can drive.'

'You're right there, buddy. To say he's in a clapped-out old thing like that, he isn't doing badly, is he?'

Trying to stop someone who doesn't want to be stopped isn't as easy as you'd think. You want to get close, and at times you feel you'd like to run them right off the road. But you have to keep a safe distance, leave yourself enough room to respond to whatever they might do – and in a high-speed pursuit with the driver's freedom at stake, there's no knowing how he's going to react. And that assumes he has a clear run. What if a deer runs out in front of him, or an oncoming car? What if he blows a tyre, or simply loses control? This guy was irritating the hell out of me but at least he seemed to be in control of the vehicle. But some of the world's finest drivers have killed themselves driving at speed. All it takes is one error, whether that be yours, or somebody else's.

I was focused on the road now, gobbling up the white line, hands tight on the wheel. There's no getting away from it; there's a real buzz about this kind of scenario. You're exercising all your driving skills, knowing that there's every chance of a result at the end of it. But coupled with the excitement is fear. At over a hundred miles an hour you've not much thinking time. You could duck out if you decided the situation was too dangerous, of course you could. Nobody would blame you for that. But I've never been one to hang back and I wasn't going to this time either. I was calm now, in a groove. I had a superior vehicle, was well trained as a driver, and knew every little kink and gradient of this road, which I doubted that they did. As far as I was concerned this gave me the edge. I wasn't going to let them get away and tell their mates that, hey, don't worry about these North Yorkshire coppers: just get 'em into a race and they'll bottle it. No way. Not on my patch, lad.

We were at Wintringham lane end now: dark woods on our left and that tight narrow bridge approaching fast, with a double bend and an adverse camber. We were still doing eighty, ninety to stay on the other car's tail.

'Bloody idiots, can't be from round here, this lot.'

Fordy was clutching his seat with one hand, pressing against the dashboard with the other. 'He's gotta frigging brake!'

'He will.'

And he did – with the bridge barely a hundred yards away, and smoke coming off his wheels. God help us, I thought, if his tyres blow or his brakes burn up with the weight he's got.

We were through the bridge okay, braking on the approach to the right-hander but still nudging sixty.

'What are they? Stupid, or plain reckless?' Fordy said.

You look for the good in people, but there's some where you have to admit they just don't give a toss about anybody or anything. Not even their own safety, in some cases. They're the really frightening ones.

Fordy continued with the commentary, but I noticed that his voice had gone up an octave and there was a slight tremor in it.

'Romeo Mike 23 to Control, vehicle travelling at high speed, failing to stop, crossing central double white lines. Driving very dangerously.'

'You all right, Fordy?' I asked.

'Yeah, spot on, Mike.' His eyes were narrowed and fixed on the Astra, barely thirty yards ahead of us. I could remember my first pursuit and could imagine how he was feeling. He reminded me of myself when I was younger, when the smells of the hot engines, overheated brakes and burnt rubber were enough to get the adrenaline pumping.

'Bastards!' I was really angry now. You try not to be, but sometimes you can't help it. If anybody had been coming at us on that bridge we'd have had a tragedy on our hands. Despite my years of experience this was getting to me now. Chasing a car in the countryside is a different ball game. I'd done my fair share of hot pursuits in the Met, but they never lasted more than a mile or two. You'd chase them along the Embankment, or down the Old Kent Road, as often as not through heavy traffic, but you rarely got above about fifty miles an hour – and then they'd dive into some estate, abandon ship and starburst: all running in different directions. There was no way we'd ever reach this kind of speed, or pursue them for this long.

'Romeo Mike 23 to Control, suspect vehicle doing seventy in a forty zone at Rillington . . . Now sixty and into the thirty zone, over.'

'Thank God it's dark,' I said. 'At least we'll see the lights of anything oncoming.'

'Romeo Mike 23 approaching red traffic lights at Rillington, speed now forty miles an hour, stand by.'

At this pointed I braked, backed off and held my breath.

'Control, suspect vehicle straight through red light.'

I slowed right down, looked both ways and eased the car forwards as the gap between us opened up again. There was no way we could have gone through at that speed. The fact that the suspects did upped the ante as far as I was concerned. The driver clearly didn't give a monkey's about anybody else.

'*Control to Romeo Mike 23. We've Sergeant Cocks on his way with two specials in a van. He'll be at the roundabout on the Pickering road.*'

But we never got there. Just as we reached the dual carriageway the Astra veered off on the old road, heading for Norton. We were through another red light by the bacon factory and within a minute were haring down Commercial Street at sixty, right across the mini-roundabout and braking hard for the sharp right over the railway line.

'Cameras'll get this,' I shouted to Fordy as we bumped over the rails and the Astra swerved hard left along Blackboards, between the railway and the river. 'You okay? You look nervous.'

'Aren't you?' He was bouncing around in his seat, his brow furrowed.

'Don't worry, bud' – we were into Yorkersgate now and heading up the hill towards the war memorial – 'I'll make sure we don't get ourselves killed. They'll run out of steam before we do – or their car will. Their brakes must be about burnt out. Just make sure you're ready.'

'What for?' Fordy shouted as the engine screamed and I changed down.

'A foot chase. If I were a betting man I'd say they'll bail out and do a runner sooner or later. Most important thing, Fordy lad, is to get the driver. You're the front-seat passenger so he's yours.'

'I say they roll it.'

'I wouldn't bet on it.'

A minute or so later we were racing past the industrial estate. Now that there was no danger of some drunk staggering out into our path, I could feel the tension ease out of my shoulders a little. 'Thank God we got through town in one piece,' I said.

'Yeah.' Fordy shifted in his seat. 'I wonder what happened to Cocksy.'

'Eyes right, old buddy.' We were passing the BMW dealership

and there he was, parked up in his van, giving us the thumbs up before swinging out after us.

We were back on the main road now, swinging past the Huttons Ambo turn-off and up Golden Hill to the blind summit.

'Been to some nasty fatals up here,' I said as I dropped down a gear and saw them swing left round the bend and momentarily out of sight. 'I'll feel a bit better when we're back on the dual carriageway.'

'*Control to Romeo Mike 23.*'

'Yeah, go ahead, over.'

'*Traffic car just coming onto the bypass, should be with you shortly.*'

'Only a couple of minutes behind us, then.'

Past the Kirkham turn-off the road dips steeply onto a long level stretch of dual carriageway. The Astra was now going flat out, touching a hundred, weaving across the lanes to pass a little Nissan. 'Christ!' I pointed at the clock. We were on the steep downhill section at Whitwell-on-the-Hill. The needle was just touching a hundred and ten miles an hour and we were still hardly gaining on them.

'*Control to Romeo Mike 23. We have a traffic car ahead at the Hopgrove roundabout ready to deploy stinger.*'

If I hadn't been gripping the wheel and concentrating so hard I would've rubbed my hands at this point. 'That's the stuff!' I shouted. 'Rats in a trap. These buggers are going nowhere. And I tell you what, Fordy lad, it's a good job too. Cos the last thing we want is a stolen car hurtling through the streets of York. Sod that for a game of soldiers.'

I felt more relaxed now and Fordy was doing a good job with the commentary, which was so important – both in terms of compiling evidence and keeping the other units updated with our location and situation. The next couple of miles was going to be easy enough, and so long as they kept to the main road we'd no need to get too close. If the stinger was rolled out properly it'd rip their tyres to shreds and bring the whole thing to an abrupt end.

We drove on in silence for a minute, which felt strange to me. In my Met days the commentary was nonstop. There's so much going on in an urban chase – names of streets, junctions, other road users – that you struggle to fit it all in.

'*Permission to talk, over.*' It was the traffic car.

'Go ahead.'

'*Just passing the Jinnah restaurant.*'

'Excellent,' I said. 'Puts 'em about a minute behind us.'

'Just our luck if a deer jumps out at us.' Fordy was looking at the dense woods that lined the road. We were now barely a couple of miles from the Hopgrove roundabout, and the lads with the stinger. 'And I tell you what else, mate. It's a good job it ain't raining. Can you just imagine?'

It's a marvellous tool, the stinger, and very simple. They come in different designs, but the one we use is a bit like a section of trelliswork with dozens of sharp hollow metal spikes an inch or two long. The only problem is that some roads are too wide for it to reach fully across. You have to lay it out carefully for maximum coverage.

We were approaching the roundabout, barely fifty yards behind the Astra. The traffic car was in my rear-view mirror, coming up fast, and I was braking hard. The last thing you want is to get your tyres shredded by your own stinger – and trust me, it has happened.

'Right, Fordy mate, we ready to run after these buggers and grab 'em?'

'Oh yes.' He had his hand on his seatbelt ready for a quick release when I suddenly stamped on the accelerator.

'Shit! What ya doing, Mike?' Then he saw what had happened.

On the run-in to the roundabout the road fans out into two broad lanes. The stinger had only reached three parts of the way across, and our runaways had swerved past it, cut across the verge and were now swinging out onto the Leeds road, the driver's hand out the window and his middle finger extended.

'There's times,' I said, 'when you really have to control yourself. Cos if I got hold of them right now . . .'

'Know what you mean, Mike. Know what you mean.'

'Gotta hand it to 'em though. They spotted that stinger coming.'

We continued for a few more moments as lead car until the Scarborough traffic lads came flying past. A few moments later we saw the one from York come up behind us, blue lights flashing. 'All yours, lads.' I eased back a touch on the accelerator. These lads were trained to give chase at high speeds. And they had the high-performance vehicles to enable them to do so safely.

'Wonder where they're heading,' I said. We were already passing the Hull road and a possible route into York, but they kept straight on.

'Leeds?'

'Probably. It's a shame we didn't have a third traffic car available to do the old T-pack.'

'Is that where you box it in?' Fordy said.

'Yeah, cluster round it and gradually bring it to a halt. Causes a few dints in the police cars, but better than letting these idiots kill somebody.'

Right on cue, Control came through to tell us that a third

traffic car was now available at Tadcaster. But we weren't going to need them. We were on the far side of York, and thinking of a possible liaison with the Leeds lads at the A1 intersection, when they threw us a dummy pass, slamming the brakes on and swerving viciously to the right at the roundabout, back towards the city on the old main road.

Passing the Tesco superstore under the orange street lights, we could see – and smell – the haze of smoke as the Astra lurched to the right to pass a slow-moving van, then wove a path around the wrong side of the bollards, forcing an oncoming car to mount the kerb.

The lead traffic car was on the radio now. '*Control, we're on Tadcaster Road, passing the Knavesmire . . . permission to switch to York channel, over.*'

'Good move,' I said as we sped past the Fox and Roman pub with the racecourse on our right. If any of the York units could follow the action and respond, so much the better. 'Any moment now, bud, and they're gonna have to make a decision. Because once they get into town proper they're gonna have some serious problems, especially at this time of night.'

The traffic officer was back on the radio, his voice loud and urgent. '*Control, and any units in the Micklegate area, beware, beware . . . high-speed pursuit approaching the Micklegate area. We need to clear the streets now. Repeat clear the streets now. ETA thirty seconds.*'

'Bloody hell, Fordy. This could be really bad.'

We'd come up over the Mount and were on Blossom Street, passing the old Odeon where a couple of drunks were arguing outside the boarded-up foyer. Ahead was the intersection and Micklegate Bar.

'They surely aren't . . .' but they were: straight across the lights and through the narrow white stone archway set in the ancient city walls.

'Oh, Christ. Look at it.' The clubs along the Micklegate run had turned out and partygoers were all over the street. A young lass in a skimpy little dress tottered out of our way, waving a half-consumed bottle of something blue as her mates grabbed her elbows and dragged her onto the pavement.

Two York PCs on foot were running up the road towards us, screaming at people to 'Move! Move! Move!' and shepherding the revellers back behind the parked cars as the Astra braked once, twice, then accelerated down the street. Some of the onlookers cheered, some of them stared like startled rabbits at the spectacle before them – and then we were past, down the cobbled hill towards the lights.

'Bloody hell, Mike!'

'You won't see much worse than that in your career, Fordy. Thank God for those York PCs on foot.'

'Now where?'

Micklegate slopes quite steeply as you approach the lights at the bottom – and they chose that moment to hurl the Astra round to the left through the heart of clubland, where the streets were still crowded with youngsters in their party gear. Up towards the war memorial it went, with our traffic cars now hard on its tail, over the lights and down past the sorting office into the Leeman Road tunnel.

'They get through here and they could be away out of town again,' Fordy shouted.

'After that performance? I don't think they've got a clue where they're going.' The whole tunnel was illuminated by the flashing blue lights, the sound of the sirens echoing off the tiled roof as I tried to catch up. And then there was a blaze of red as the traffic car in front braked hard, turned sharp left and momentarily disappeared from view. A couple of seconds later, at the exit of the tunnel, I saw it come to an abrupt stop, and the driver's door fly open.

'They're out!' I shouted.

Over the radio came the traffic lad. *'It's a crash, crash, crash! We've got runners!'*

The Astra had swerved off the road into the old station yard, opposite the Railway Museum. It had crashed into a set of bollards, the bonnet was up and steam, or maybe smoke, was rising from the engine. All four doors were open. Shielding my eyes against the pulsing blue lights, I caught sight of three silhouettes disappearing into the car park, heading for the station. A fourth was on the ground, wrestling with one of the traffic lads. It was a girl, eighteen, maybe twenty, swearing and spitting and lashing out with her bare feet.

'Fordy!' I shouted. 'Grab hold and get her in the car.'

I set off like a greyhound with the other traffic officer. I love a foot chase, and as a recreational runner I pride myself on being fit, but I was really up against it here. Not only was it pitch black, but I wasn't quite sure where I was running. They'd disappeared. And to add to that I had a big pair of boots on, my utility belt weighing me down and my radio cord wrapped round my neck. I was also at the age where my body could have benefited from a warm-up-and-stretch session. The suspects, on the other hand, were kitted out in the usual trainers and designer sportswear. And they were young. And they were highly motivated. Their freedom was at stake. I shouted at the top of my voice for them to stop, then threw in a few expletives to vent my frustration.

You wouldn't think it was possible to lose three suspects so quickly. But we had. We were standing in the station, panting, on the footbridge that connects the platforms. The only movement was a guy in dark railway uniform sweeping cigarette ends onto the track outside the little shop where they sell drinks and sandwiches.

The fact is, there were so many different ways for them to have escaped. One moment we really thought we had them; now we faced a major search operation. And we failed. Eight of us spent an hour, maybe an hour and a half, combing the area. We got a dog handler to help, but we still drew a blank. By now, too, there was trouble in Micklegate with a fight outside one of the clubs and Control were calling all cars. It was time to cut our losses.

Fordy and I took the young lass to the police station in Fulford Road. She would be interviewed in the morning. Meanwhile the car was being taken back to the station to be checked for evidence.

It was gone five o'clock when we set off, back along the A64. The road was deserted. Fordy and I didn't say a lot. The adrenaline rush had faded, and we were left feeling like a pair of wet rags. Back at the station I put two sugars in my tea, a thing I rarely do, then sat down with Fordy to write up my notes. When we had finished we went over the events of the night, briefly. We told each other that it would have all been different . . . *if* the stinger had reached right across the road, *if* we had had a third traffic car for a T-pack on the A64; if, if, if . . . But it was all hindsight – and hindsight, as we all know, gives you an unrealistic slant on things.

So I was feeling pretty glum when I got home that morning. First the brush with the Sunset Gang, then this. You never like it when a villain gets away, and it particularly hurts when you know you had them in the palm of your hand. But this time our luck was in, as we found out when we came in for parade the next night. The female prisoner had cracked under questioning. She told the CID that the four of them had taken a train to Scarborough, missed the last train home and decided to steal a car. There was barely any petrol in the tank and none of them had any money, and they'd gone on from there, the whole thing escalating way out of control and putting several lives at risk, including ours. Better than this, she named the other three individuals. All of them were known to the police in Leeds, and had a long string of petty offences against them. They had been arrested that afternoon and now faced a raft of new charges. 'Any luck and the court'll put a brake on their activities,' Fordy said when I told him what had happened.

Before I could answer, Jayne chipped in. 'So,' she said, grinning like a monkey, 'I hear you got a run for your money last night. In the brand-new vehicle. Pity they got away.'

I was about to tell Fordy not to rise to the bait. 'We achieved the desired result,' he said, stirring his tea with unusual vigour.

'Yeah,' I said. 'Four arrests. You wanna get up to speed, girl.'

She only paused momentarily, but it was long enough. Fordy was in like Flynn. 'That's right,' he said, 'and how about this? If you get to drive the new Focus, you'll find we've run it in for you.'

Chapter 5

It's a Bullseye

I'd been fretting about the weather all week. It had been what they call changeable, meaning that it kept raining, then stopping, then, just when you thought it was safe to go out in the garden, it'd start again. Now it was one o'clock Friday, my shift would be over in an hour or so, and Ann and I had a precious free weekend to look forward to. We were off up the Esk valley, near where her folks came from on the northern edge of the Moors. And I'd had the bright idea of camping out. We'll be fine, I'd told her. July? Best time of the year. Short nights and plenty of sunshine. No worries.

I wasn't the only one casting a worried glance at the skies. Everywhere I'd been around my patch that week there was a tension in the air. The crops had just about done their growing and were starting to ripen off. I mean the cereals, of course. Not the spuds: they'd barely come into flower yet. But as I leaned on an old wooden gate on the wold top above Duggleby and looked over towards Sledmere, all around me the cornfields were taking on the pale hue of a rich tea biscuit. One or two were bleached of colour, almost white. By contrast the trees were turning a deep dark green, like those overdone greens you used to get with your school dinners. When you see that you know the season is turning from midsummer to high summer, with autumn not far behind. Along the roadside the first drifts of willow-herb added a splash of bright pink to the drab thorn hedges. Far away to the east I could see the North Sea, a thin line of grey, while above me white clouds billowed up against a great sweep of blue. With a bit of luck we'd be set fair.

There had been a decent amount of rain throughout the growing season: enough to water the crops, but none of those heavy downpours that flatten them, nor any of those cool, drizzly spells you get some years that encourage mildew. Mostly it had been sunshine and showers and a nice breeze, which never hurt anything. And as I stepped through the gateway into a field of barley to look in the other direction, towards the Moors, I could see the bearded seed heads, nicely fattened up. From now on all the farmers would be watching the skies, tuning in to the weather forecasts, and crossing their fingers for a decent dry spell as they made sure their harvesters were fine-tuned and ready to go.

I was out on the Wolds visiting one of my Country Watch people. I made a point of trying to see them all every few months, even if we just had time for a cup of tea and a natter and a glance at my latest newsletter. If ever I mentioned at the station that I was doing the rounds of my contacts, I knew exactly what to expect. Oh aye, they'd say. Slacking again. But in my book it was all about maintaining contact. We might do no more than talk about the prospects for harvest, or the state of the farm economy; or one of them might take me out to the edge of his fields to admire a good crop of wheat and try to explain about the moisture content, but it maintained the relationship, as you might say. And that meant that come midwinter, when I wanted someone to watch a stretch of road till four in the morning on the off-chance that a suspect vehicle might go by, knowing full well that they'd most likely see nothing more exciting than the frost forming on their windscreens, well, I knew I wouldn't feel awkward about asking one of my Country Watch team. The thing is, you can ask a friend to do that, whereas you wouldn't ask a mere acquaintance. And I made it my business to become a friend to these farmers and gamekeepers, and their wives too – even if that meant listening to them as they chuntered about the price of fertiliser, or animal feed or the amount of diesel they were using to run the grain dryers.

Barry and his wife farmed about five hundred acres of wold land between Sledmere and Helperthorpe. The place had been in his family for a long, long time. He didn't seem to know how long. I'd asked him more than once, and all I ever got was a scratch of his head and, 'Aye, it'll be well over a hundred year, Mike.' His parents still lived in the old farmhouse. He and Jackie had built a bungalow about a hundred yards away beyond the various outbuildings, with a beautiful view over the wold tops towards Driffield and the coast.

I found Barry out in the yard with his head under the bonnet of an old Land Rover. 'Now then, what you up to?' I asked him.

'Hey, tek a look at this,' he said, wiping the sweat off his forehead with an oily rag. 'Isn't she a beaut?'

'New, is it?'

'To me it is, aye.' He put his hands in his overall pockets and squinted at me. 'Go on,' he said. 'How much d'you reckon I paid for 'er?'

'Oh, I'm not much good at secondhand motors, Baz.' I looked at the registration plate. 'D reg, eh? That'll make it – hell, must be seventies vintage at least.'

'She's ower forty years old, cock-bod. Dates back to when a Land Rover was a Land Rover, let me tell you, not all bloody show like them Chelsea tractors.' He lowered the bonnet, nice and gently. '1966 this little beauty was registered. And shall I tell you what it cost me?' He stood there grinning at me, a smudge of black across his forehead, and three or four chrome-plated spanners threatening to drop out of his blue overall pocket as he leaned forward and gave the windscreen a wipe. 'You'll never guess,' he said, standing back and touching one of the front tyres with his boot. 'By, look at the tread on them buggers,' he added. 'Hardly worn.'

'Baz,' I said, 'if you don't hurry up and tell me, mate, I shall simply burst.'

'Nowt, matey. Not a brass farthing. T'owd lad had got hissen one of them new four-by-fours and he wanted rid, fast. It had stood in his yard for six months and he couldn't even be bothered to strike it up. D'you know, Mike, I reckon if I'd stood there humming and hah-ing any longer he would've paid me to tek it off his hands. There now.'

'Well, looks like you've got yourself a bargain . . .' I began.

'Aye, and all t'papers in order – before you start asking questions. Mind, I shall only run her around the farm, like. This ain't for putting on t'road, so there'll be no tax to pay, nor insurance.'

Then Baz crooked his finger and winked at me. 'Hey, come over here,' he said, leading the way through the shed, squeezing between his combine harvester and an old grey Fergie tractor. 'Got sommat else to show you.'

Out the back, sheltered under a stand of mature sycamores, was a collection of rickety huts and sheds, each with a wire-mesh run attached to it, and each containing a different variety of bird. He had hens, ducks, guinea-fowl, a couple of turkeys. 'And look here,' he said. 'You ever seen these?'

'Tell you the truth, mate, I haven't.' They were slim birds, standing tall, with great long necks, and they started running this way and that as soon as they set eyes on us. 'You know what they remind me of?' I said. 'Them clothes brushes you used to get – where the handle was a duck's head and it stood on your sideboard in a little stand.'

Baz laughed. 'Aye, they do, don't they? They call 'em Indian runner ducks. Good layers, mind. How you off for eggs, anyway?'

'Oh, I can always do with a few eggs, mate.'

'Over here then.' He slipped inside one of the cages, opened up the shed and lifted a plump hen off a nest of clean straw. 'Go on, help yourself.'

I reached in and scooped up four spotless brown eggs, all warm in the palms of my hands. 'Cheers, we'll have these for breakfast tomorrow before we set off on our trip. Or maybe in our pack-up.'

'Oh aye? Where you off to?'

'Esk valley, mate. A weekend's camping and hiking.' I was looking around. Barry must have had half a dozen separate sheds, each with its own run. 'You ever get a fox sniffing around?' I asked.

'One or two, aye. But if you keep your bods properly fenced in and lock 'em up at night you're okay. Between you and me, Mike, I admire the fox. I ain't saying I wouldn't shoot one if he was getting in here, like, but you've got to admit they're wonderful creatures.'

'I agree with you, Baz. Beautiful.'

'We had a family of 'em this year. Down in the dale yonder. Mum, Dad and a couple of young 'uns. Never bothered me. There's plenty rabbits down there. Way I see it, they're doing me a favour, keeping the buggers down.' He scratched his chin thoughtfully, then said, 'And it's a rum business about rabbits, when you think about it. We shoot 'em, we snare 'em, and I've a lad comes in with his ferrets – and we have to, else they'd devour your crops. I lost five acres of corn one year, little buggers breeding down in the dale there – and that was me profit down t'Swanee river.' He leaned forward and tapped me on the chest, his spanners jingling in his pocket. 'But what gets me about 'em is how people reckon they're furry and cuddly and cute, but no bugger protests about their slaughter, do they now? Whereas your fox – a known predator and a killer – soon as t'old hunt sets off after one of them, folk are all up in arms. Now, are they protesting on behalf of t'fox, or is it sommat about the toffs as ride to hounds?'

'They ain't all toffs, Baz. You know that. There's plenty ordinary folk follow the hunt.'

'Aye, I know that.' He wagged a finger at me. 'And you know it. But what's t'public's view? Eh? Them townies and suchlike?'

'So what d'you reckon to it, then? You pro or anti?'

'The hunt? I've never got involved. But – live and let live, I say. And if the bloody government wants to ban it, they'll have a job on, is all I can say. Cos I don't reckon country folk'll stand for it. I just hope you buggers don't get caught in t'middle, that's all.'

'You mean the police?'

'What else would I mean, Mike? Cos there'll be trouble, as sure I'm stood here. And you'll be called upon to sort it out.'

'Well,' I said, 'let's see if it gets through parliament first, shall we?' I left it at that, thanked Baz for the eggs and drove back to town. I was wanting a quick getaway. Ann would be home from York by about half past two, and we'd got all our gear together the night before. But the first person I bumped into at the station was Chris Cocks, and he wanted a word.

'What is it, mate? I need to get a flyer today.'

He had a note on the desk in front of him. 'I dare say it'll wait,' he sighed, and handed it over to me.

'Oh no. "Naked man spotted in Howsham Woods"?'

'You've dealt with him before, haven't you?'

'Aye, if it's same feller – except he had a pair of shorts on that time.'

'Well, according to these dog-walkers who called in he was stripped right down to his birthday suit and doing stretching exercises.'

'Christ!' I put the note back on his desk. 'All right, mate. Leave it to me. I'll get across there Monday morning. There's nothing that won't wait till then.'

I had a call to make in Norton, so Ann was already home by the time I arrived back at Keeper's Cottage – and she was raring to go. I could see our packs in the back of her car. She had Henry on his lead and was letting him sniff around among the gooseberry bushes at the far end of the clearing. 'Hello, darling. Hard day on the front line?' she asked as I made my way to the back door. 'Or were you delayed at one of your tea stops?'

'You cheeky . . .'

'I've got everything packed and me and Henry are all ready to get going.'

'Give me two minutes. You got the grub?'

'All except supper.'

'Which as I told you is taken care of. Got the wine?'

'Naturally, first thing I packed.'

'Boots?'

'Nearly forget them – but yes.'

'Water?'

'Gallons of it. Look, go and get changed will you? We've got to drop Henry off at your mum's yet.'

We'd been planning this jaunt for a while – or rather, I had. I'd told Ann not to ask any questions. This was going to be a mystery weekend for her. I wanted it to be a proper outdoor trip, just the two of us camping out in the wilds, taking full advantage of the daylight while it was still available. Up in North Yorkshire, given a clear sky, the midsummer light lingers right up to eleven or eleven thirty. In fact, you can often make out a bit of blue on the horizon at midnight, especially if there's no moon. It's like that from late May right through to late July. To me it's as if the earth has stretched the days out as far as they'll go and then takes a breather before the whole process goes into reverse for the long journey back towards winter. I always say you should grab the extra daylight while you can, which is why I always try to get out into the hills once or twice during those magical few weeks.

I got into my hiking gear, found a box for Baz's eggs and locked up. Then I climbed into the driver's seat beside Ann and shoved the dog into the back. 'Right,' I said, 'what we waiting for?'

By the time I'd driven to my mum's I was well glad to get Henry out of the back of the car. He spent most of the journey with his head over my shoulder, drooling and licking my ear. 'You love this, don't you?' I said – and got my ear licked by way of reply. 'Tell you what, though' – I opened my window wide – 'you could do with some breath-fresheners, my lad.' I shoved his face back and asked Ann, 'What the hell's he been eating?'

'You really don't want to know, Mike. It came from under a hedge and – well, let's just say it had been dead for quite a while.'

We dropped Henry off with his bag of food, his water bowl and his basket, and then headed north, to Pickering and onto the narrow road that would take us through Newton-on-Rawcliffe to Stape, then across the moor towards Egton Bridge.

'You going to tell me where we're going?' Ann asked. The road had already become a narrow, pot-holed ribbon of tarmac. The tufts of grass that grew down the middle rustled against the underside of the car.

'No,' I said. She didn't say anything. She was waiting for me to elaborate. 'No, I said it was a mystery tour, didn't I?'

'You did.'

'Well, you wouldn't want me to spoil it, would you?'

'Are you offering your personal guarantee that I'll like it?'

'No guarantees. I can tell you one thing, though. Our first port of call is Egton Bridge.'

'Handy little pub there, if my memory serves me right.'

I looked at my watch. 'There is, and we may have time for a swift pint before we set off.'

'To our mystery destination.'

'Indeed. Our mystery destination. Which, I am fairly sure, you will like.'

'But no guarantees?'

'None.'

By the time we'd parked the car, double-checked our packs and had a leisurely drink in the Postgate Inn, it was getting on for five. As we set off over the bridge that crosses the River Esk I had a look at the sky. The puffy clouds I'd seen earlier at Duggleby had largely melted away, and the wind had dropped.

'Going to be a beautiful evening.'

'Ideal for midges,' Ann said.

I pointed at an outer pocket of my pack. 'What do you think that is?'

She leaned forward to have a look at the plastic bottle. 'Jungle Formula, eh? What you expecting?'

'Nowt we can't deal with.'

'So,' she said, as I locked the car and tucked the keys away in a zipped pocket, 'which way?'

'East and then south. To our first photo opportunity.'

Our way took us along a combination of narrow roads and winding paths, mostly uphill, through cow-pasture and mixed woodland, before dropping steeply down to Beck Hole, where we were sorely tempted to have a swift half of bitter at the Birch Hall Inn. In fact, we were so sorely tempted that we gave in, and by the time we set off up the path that would take us to Mallyan Spout another hour had slipped by.

'Good job we've plenty of daylight left,' I said as I negotiated the jumble of slippery rocks piled along the side of the stream we were following.

'How far have we to go?' Ann asked.

'Good question. If we manage to stay on the right paths it's no more than about three miles. Call it an hour and a half, two at the outside. And then cross your fingers.'

It didn't take long to get to the Spout, where we took turns to stand under the waterfall and take each other's photo.

'I wonder how high it is,' Ann said, looking up through the trees and ferns, the emerald green of the moss-covered rocks, all glistening as the water cascaded over them and sprayed her upturned face.

'Sixty feet,' I said.

'Is that a guess?'

'No – I read it. When I was planning this.'

We were close to Goathland village now. We could see the rooftops not far away past the grassy hillside, and there from the valley came the chuff-chuffing of the steam loco as it made its last journey of the day back to Pickering.

'Be nice to take a ride on that sometime,' Ann said. 'Been years since I went on it.'

'Aye,' I said, pulling the map out of my shirt pocket. To the south of us lay the moor we had to cross before we came to the place I had in mind for our first night's camp. But where was the path?

'Trouble is, there's all these blooming little sheep walks,' Ann said, as she skirted the edge of the hillside, keeping close to the road. 'And then they just give out on you.'

I was fifty yards or so above her, ploughing through waist-deep bracken. 'We want one that goes south,' I shouted. Then I saw her pointing to where two other hikers were striding along towards the village. Heading in the general direction they'd come from, we soon found the path we wanted.

Out on the open moor the going was easier and the path a broad, chalky scar. Now the view opened out and we could see the village behind us, the trees that lined the sides of Newtondale to the east, and ahead of us the dark plantations I was aiming for. Around us it was largely heather and reeds, with drifts of cottongrass making a splash of white here and there. Now and then a curlew wheeled around the sky, giving out its unique and haunting cry. 'This is where you have to be careful you don't suddenly tread on an egg,' I said, 'or a chick. They lay 'em in the unlikeliest spots.'

'Like that?' Ann had seen a bird get up from a patch of coarse grass to circle us, flying close to the ground and squealing its anxiety. I followed her as she walked towards the spot it had got up from. There, on the ground, covered in dark spots, was a large pale brown eggshell, and beside it, lying quite still and perfectly camouflaged, was a fluffy little chick the size of a fat frog.

'Better not linger,' I said, as we moved quickly away. But the parent bird continued to circle us for some time.

'Wants to make quite sure we're off the premises,' Ann said.

All the while, as we walked, I was scanning the dark line of the forestry plantations in the distance. I knew what I was looking for, but couldn't see it. The sun had gone behind a streak of pale cloud over in the west and the light wasn't so good.

'Which way?' We'd come to a fork where another broad track veered off to the right.

'Good question,' I said. 'I reckon we want to stay as near the top of the moor as possible. And head due south.' I pulled my compass off my keyring and squinted through the viewfinder. 'Straight ahead,' I said. 'That other path would take us back to the road, I reckon.'

We'd tramped another mile or so when we started a gentle descent, the ground sloping away on three sides. Ann was about twenty yards behind me. 'Look!' I shouted, pointing ahead to where a group of broad-leaved trees formed a pale green line between the open moor and the plantation. Behind them was what looked like a grass field. 'See that?'

'I can see it, but what does it tell us?'

'It's what I've been looking for. If I've got this right we should find a perfect camping spot down there.'

'I'm about ready for it.'

'Me too. The old stomach's rumbling already.'

I'd been this way many years previously on a TA exercise. I knew the man whose land came down to the moor's edge there, and had paid a call just a week or two previously. When I'd described to him the patch of level ground, the sheep-nibbled grass and the stand of Scots pines, he knew exactly where I meant. And sure, he'd said, you camp there if you like. Been ages since them midges had a good feed.

'This it?' Ann dumped her pack on the grass and looked around.

'Yep. What d'you reckon?'

'Looks fine,' she said, bending to pick up a dead branch and toss it over to where somebody had laid a circle of stones. 'And plenty of firewood lying around.'

An hour later the evening sun was sending shafts of light between the tree trunks, we had a decent little fire going, and Ann had zipped our sleeping bags together on the mats which were spread out nearby.

'Right,' I said, delving into my pack. 'Supper?'

'Thought you'd never ask.' Ann patted her pack. 'So is it time to open the wine then?'

'Aye, why not? But first you've to close your eyes.'

'Oh heck, you're not going down on one knee are you?'

'Just do as you're told.' I pulled out the package I'd picked up after work and unwrapped it. 'Now then, how do these grab you?'

She opened her eyes and laughed. 'Mike, you'll never be the most romantic, but you're certainly the most practical.' She was looking at two beautiful, dark-red rump steaks, dotted with pepper and thyme, each with a little knob of butter pressed into it.

'That's why I was late back from work,' I said. 'Had to pick these up at the butcher's.'

'Hey, I'll forgive a man anything if he brings me presents like that,' she laughed.

We let the fire die down until there was just a bed of hot coals, then set the frying pan over it, waiting for it to get good and hot before whacking the two steaks in. Ann unpacked the rest of our grub, and I poured the wine.

'Cheers.' We clinked together our tin mugs and sat watching the meat sizzle. 'Here's to a good life.'

Five minutes later we sat on an old tree stump, tucking into potato salad, crusty bread rolls and tender, medium-rare steak washed down with a nice, mellow Italian red.

'Doesn't get much better than this, does it?' Ann clanged her tin mug against mine.

'We just want to get rid of those midges,' I said, wafting a hand in front of my face.

'Well, there's three things they don't like: bright sunlight, wind and cold. And if you haven't got any of the above . . .' Ann tugged up a few handfuls of grass and tossed them onto the fire. A cloud of smoke drifted lazily up, and was immediately illuminated by the shafts of sunlight filtering in between the trees. 'There you go. That'll scatter them for a few minutes.'

'Aye, good idea. And with any luck we'll get a bit of a breeze later.'

She looked at the western sky. 'I think we're in for a very still night. I just hope your Jungle Fever does the job, that's all.'

'You mean Formula.'

'Whatever.'

You take a chance when you camp out – especially without a tent, as we were that night. And we got lucky, that's all I can say. A steady breeze blew in from the north, making it a cool but insect-free night. Even better, the sky remained clear. There was no moon either, so we had a spectacular view of the Milky Way – until about three o'clock when the eastern sky turned a pale blue and the stars rapidly faded. Still, if it had rained we had our bivvy bags with us. We wouldn't have drowned, and the car was only a couple of hours' walk away. But getting back to the car wasn't on the agenda next morning. I had plans.

'And what exactly are they?' Ann asked. I was brewing coffee over the rekindled fire. She was still snug in the bags. The sun had been up for two or three hours already, and the day promised to be a fine one.

'You'll see,' I said. 'We've a couple more hours to walk yet, maybe three.'

It was gone seven by the time we'd eaten breakfast, packed our bags and got on our way. It was a fairly easy walk for the first mile or two, on rising ground through still woods and dew-soaked pastures.

'You've surely guessed where we're going, Ann?' We were on a nice wide forestry track, heading east and starting to descend – which was a relief, because we were both hot now. We'd already had to stop and put sunblock on our arms and necks.

'Well, as far as I can tell, without seeing the map, I'd say we're dropping into Newtondale.'

'Correct. And after that?'

She just smiled. 'Listen, you want it to be a surprise, don't you?'

'Yes.'

'So stop asking questions.'

We walked on in silence till we came to a sharp bend in the path. 'We want to be down here,' I said, pointing to a narrow track that dropped steeply through the rank undergrowth and into a stand of beech trees.

Twenty minutes later we emerged from the woods onto a rough road that ran along beside the railway line and the beck. 'They call this the Murk Esk,' I said. 'Great name, isn't it?'

'Which way?'

'Good question.' I pointed to the steep, wooded hillside, almost a cliff, that faced us across the gorge. 'We want to be up there. There's a path that gets us across, but I'm not sure whether we've come out above it or below it.'

'Let's have a look at the map.'

We soon found the right way, crossed the water and started the steep zigzag climb up the other side of the gorge, through bracken and birch trees, finally emerging onto a flat expanse of rough grass and heather with a narrow path snaking through it. We must have walked a couple of miles when we heard the familiar sound of the steam loco, whistling as it approached a crossing, then puffing its way towards us from the north. At first there was nothing but the dense woodland, the fluttering of a startled wood pigeon, and the huffing of the engine. Then we saw the first plume of steam blasting through the foliage, and finally the kingfisher blue of the streamlined locomotive, the *Sir Nigel Gresley*.

'Here she comes,' I said, looking at my watch. 'One of the fastest steam locos in the world. A legend. Just about on time too. Should be in Pickering in about half an hour. And if my calculations are right we'll be riding her back up in about an hour and a half.' I took off my pack and sat down to watch it steam along the valley.

'Ah, so I was right.' Ann sat down beside me on the bracken.

'Right about what?'

'The surprise.'

'That's a part of it,' I said. The loco was into the trees again already, the string of eight or nine maroon coaches rattling after it. 'Used to do this ride with Mum and Dad when we were nippers,' I said. 'They used to take all four of us for a treat. A Spam sandwich and a bottle of Tizer . . . Ee, lass, you can't whack it. Specially when you're sat on a train and there's all smoke and smuts drifting past the window. Great days.'

'Aw, can you still buy Tizer?'

'Course you can. Goes down great with one of each, y'know.'

Ann pulled a face. 'No,' she said, 'not with fish and chips. You want dandelion and burdock.'

'Dandelion and burdock? Now you're really showing your age.'

'Less of that, Pannett.' She sat there, her hands clasped around her knees, watching the last wisp of smoke fade into the trees. 'So you reckon we'll pick it up on the way back, do you?'

'Aye, at Levisham. Should get there in an hour from here.' I stood up and put my pack back on. 'Providing we get a shift on.'

We made it with about ten minutes to spare. The platform was lined with people, but most of them were there to watch the train's arrival and take photographs rather than to ride. We had four seats to ourselves when we got on board.

'How far we going?' Ann asked.

'Up to Grosmont.'

We were both standing squeezed together with our heads out of the window, watching the engine as it pulled us slowly out of the station and across the level crossing.

'You know what, Mike, being on the steam train always reminds me of those old war movies.'

'I know what you mean. *Brief Encounter* and so on.'

'I was thinking *Von Ryan's Express*. Anyway, what next, lad?'

I sat down, and wiped a smut from my eye. 'We'll be hungry, won't we?'

'You bet we will. That was a fair hike along the top there.'

'Right then.'

It's a spectacular ride on the North York Moors Railway. For the first few miles it's all mixed woodland. Sunlight flickered between the branches, and the cool, damp air was spiced by an occasional tarry whiff of burning coal.

'Amazing to think people used to ride this way to go to work,' I said.

Ann had her eyes closed and her head resting on my shoulder. 'Pity they closed them all down,' she murmured, her head nodding to the rhythm of the wheels clickety-clacking over the rails.

We stopped at Newtondale, a little wayside halt, not much more than a wooden platform and what looked like a bus shelter. A party of hikers climbed aboard, swaying through the carriage in search of vacant seats as we trundled steadily on towards Goathland. The crowds were out in force there, with several buses parked outside the station. Ann was fast asleep now, and ten minutes later when we pulled into Grosmont I had to give her a gentle nudge. 'All change for Whitby and Middlesbrough,' I said.

On the platform we shouldered our packs. 'Right,' I said, 'are you up for it? A short walk, then a drive?'

'And is lunch involved?'

'Ann, what do you take me for? You're in the hands of a master planner. It is all sorted. Okay?'

'Okay. But does this involve stopping every five minutes because you've spotted a sea trout in a river?'

'Would I?'

'Yes you would, but let's crack on. I'm starving.'

It only took forty minutes or so to walk to Egton Bridge. And it was pleasant enough, along the river, the air scented by the meadowsweet that grew in great clumps along the hedgerows. This time we resisted temptation, walked straight past the pub, got into the car and drove on up the Esk valley to Lealholm, arriving just before one.

'Ah yes.' Ann smiled when she realised where we were going. 'Nice one.'

Her great-grandparents came from around that way, and while

I'd taken her to Staintondale the previous year to show her some of my old childhood haunts, we'd yet to visit the village where her ancestors had lived and worked. Even now, though, she was going to have to wait a little while before she showed me around.

'Have you booked?' We were standing under an enormous linden tree outside the Board Inn, a splendid eighteenth-century stone-built pub that overlooks the river and its graceful stone bridge. 'Because I've tried to eat here before, and—' She ducked. The tree was still in flower and the bees were working it for all they were worth.

'I know: you need to book. Listen, I've got it all organised.'

Three-quarters of an hour later we'd demolished a magnificent roast-beef lunch, washed down with a pint of hand-pulled ale. Then, while we deliberated about pudding, I made a big mistake. I challenged Ann to a game of darts.

'Okay,' she said. 'Bit out of practice, mind.' She winced as she stood up. 'And a bit stiff. What I wouldn't give for a long hot bath. One night in the wilds is okay, but you can't beat full en suite facilities.'

'Don't be a wuss. You can get all that at home.' I'd got the darts from behind the bar and was wiping the scoreboard with a cloth. 'Right,' I said, 'you want me to give you a start? A hundred, maybe?'

I wish I could describe the look she gave me as she stepped up to the oche and took aim. It was somewhere between contempt and pity. Thud, thud, thud. In they went. Two double twenties and a single.

She pulled them out of the board and chalked up her score. 'A hundred start, did you say? There you go, Mike.'

I didn't answer her. I was casting an anxious look around the bar. There were a couple of lads standing there, but if they were watching they had the good grace to pretend they weren't.

'Right,' I said, taking careful aim and letting the first one go. 'There's twenty . . . and another . . . and . . . bugger!'

'Forty-one.'

'I can add up, Ann. Hey, once I get my eye in . . .'

She held onto that lead. I kept threatening to overhaul her and she kept getting away from me, but finally, when she was down to sixteen with one dart left, she faltered. And I was in.

'Right on your tail,' I said, as I pulled my darts out one by one and totted up my score. 'That's treble nineteen, double top and twenty. Double ten required. Nervous?' I handed her the arrows.

She said nowt, just lined up her first dart and sent it, straight and true, thwacking into the double eight.

I wiped the scoreboard clean and grabbed the darts off her. 'Best of three,' I said. 'Different story this time. I'm first away.'

'Fair enough.' Ann was grinning at me as she raised her glass to her lips. 'I like to give a fellow a chance.'

'Well, pick the bones out of those,' I said. I was in the zone now, no doubt about it. 'Forty, twenty . . . And the treble.'

For some reason, as I heard myself say the words, I was reminded of my old teacher in primary school. Whenever I started getting full of myself he'd puncture my mood with his favourite saying, 'Yes, Pannett, and as the Good Book says, pride goeth before a fall.'

I looked at Ann, totally focused on her game, but perfectly relaxed and poised. In they went. Forty . . . forty . . . and sixty. And then I heard one of the lads at the bar, laughing as he shouted, 'One hun-dred and for-ty!'

It was a tense old business, requiring more lubrication from the bar, and once again I managed to claw my way back to level par, but once again it came down to a double. Ones for me, threes for Ann.

'Here we go again,' I said, 'except it's my first go this time.' The first dart whacked into the wooden surround and bounced back within a few inches of me. I was on the balls of my feet, certain that the second had found its target, but it pinged against the wire and fell to the floor. The third one, though, that went in straight and true. And boy, did it feel good.

'Get in,' I shouted. 'One all!'

'Looks like we've got a contest on our hands.' Ann narrowed her eyes and seemed to take longer over her aim this time. We were both in the groove now, firing off twenties and treble twenties, but this time luck was on my side and I got away from her, banging in 140 to leave myself wanting a double four. I handed Ann the darts. She was on 144. It was all over, surely – much to the disappointment of the lads at the bar, watching intently. 'Go for it, sweetheart,' one of them said. But even he was doubting her now. I kept schtum, just sat back in my chair and picked up the dessert menu. Not that I had any intention of reading it just yet.

Ann ran her fingers through her hair, turned her face to the ceiling and closed her eyes as she did a little calculation, then stepped up to the oche.

Thud. 'Double top! Nice.'

'Thank you, lads.' She took aim again, balanced herself, leaned forward and – thud! Planted it right in the treble eighteen.

'Oh yes! Now the bull. Go on, lass. There's money riding on this.'

I really was reading the menu now. I couldn't bear to look. The thud was greeted by a mighty roar from the bar.

'Where the bloody hell did you learn to play like that?' I asked her as I tucked into my sticky toffee pudding.

'Misspent youth,' she said. Then she shook her head. 'No, seriously, it was in my cricketing days. Whenever it rained half of them would get the cards out; but we had a dartboard in the clubhouse, and . . .'

'You never told me you played cricket.'

'Ah well, I did say, many moons ago, that I'm a woman with a past. We used to play on a night down on the farm. And in winter-time all sorts of friends would come down. We'd hang around in the farmhouse kitchen by the Aga and play darts for a laugh.' She looked at her watch. 'Anyway, shall we crack on? It'd be nice to look around the village; it's been a while since I was last here.'

As she spoke she picked up a leaflet that was tucked in behind the menus. 'Hey, this looks all right. They have a room here with a four-poster bed. And you can get complimentary chocolates, a bottle of bubbly, and a view of the river.'

'Aye, but look at them prices,' I said, taking the leaflet from her and putting it back where it belonged. 'Why would you want that when you've got me, a sleeping bag and the stars, eh? Better drink up, if we want to look around the village.'

We crossed the river and walked up towards the church, through the iron gateway and up the path that led between two venerable yew trees to the graveyard. 'Here's a Barker,' I said. 'Man and wife.'

'No, they're nothing to do with me. Mine are Shepherds. Or was it Laceys? Never remember which one my great-grandfather was. He was the blacksmith in the village.' She walked on between the slabs. 'But my great-gran's buried here somewhere. I'm sure she is.'

'Let's have a look.' Most of the older gravestones were illegible, the lettering almost entirely eroded away by the weather.

'You won't find them,' Ann said. 'My gran knew where her mum was buried, but I'm not even sure it's properly marked.'

As we left the graveyard we stopped at the war memorial.

'Well, there are Laceys and Shepherds on here,' I said.

'They must have been relatives,' Ann said. 'It's such a small community. I wonder where they served, what happened to them? I must get round to doing my family tree.'

'Can you imagine, setting off from a place like this and ending up in some foreign battlefield? The Flanders trenches? The mud?' I looked down towards the river where a bunch of children were throwing sticks and splashing about. 'It's a beautiful place.'

'It is. It's in the Domesday Book, you know.'

We moved on to explore the rest of the village, pausing at the cosy little coffee shop across the river. It had started to cloud over by now. Half an hour later as we walked over the stepping stones that cross the beck, we felt the first few drops of rain. The children had already gone home, and a chill breeze was blowing.

'Not promising,' Ann said, looking up at a leaden sky. 'We could be in for a wet night.'

'That roof's been there since 1742, my girl. I don't think it'll start leaking tonight.'

'What roof?'

'The Board, Ann, The Board. Four-poster, free chocs, bubbly, en-suite facilities. Booked it months ago. C'mon, let's get our bags out of the car before we get soaked.'

Chapter 6

Naked Truth

After a glorious weekend such as we'd had, you know you should feel revitalised. You expect to feel that your batteries have been recharged, that you're ready for anything. Even work. But at twenty past five on Monday morning as I kissed Ann goodbye she said exactly what I was thinking.

'Let's hope for a nice quiet start to the week.' She looked at Henry, who seemed unable to decide whether to keep straining at his lead or have another go at jumping up to lick my chin. 'Unlike some members of the family, I'm not exactly raring to go.'

'That's the trouble with a relaxing couple of days, isn't it?'

She got into the car, stifling a yawn. 'Yep. You relax.'

'Okay then, see you sometime this afternoon.'

I followed her down the drive, with Henry doing his damnedest to pull my arm out of my socket and then drooling over my freshly cleaned uniform trousers. 'Steady on, lad,' I said. 'You've got twenty minutes, max. Then I'm off to work too.'

It was, after all, too much to hope that I'd be able to ease myself gently into a new working week – although the station was unusually quiet when I got there. Ed had yet to arrive, and I'd passed Jayne's car in Castlegate, parked outside the newsagent. But Chris Cocks was at the desk – nice and early as usual.

'Owt doing?' I asked.

'Not a lot. Oh – just one message for you. Fellow called Easton. One of your farmer mates, isn't he?'

'Aye, Country Watch. What's he want?'

'Was on the phone when I got here. Twenty to six. Says he wants you to pop in, soon as you can. Sounded a bit agitated.'

'Will do.' I didn't like the sound of this, and I said as much to Chris, bringing him up to speed with the fact that Bob, who was generally a decent bloke, could be a bit of a hothead.

'Oh, and before you get too involved . . .'

'Go on, Chris,' I sighed.

'The little matter of the exhibitionist. The fresh-air fiend, remember?'

'Oh, hell. Him up at Howsham Woods, you mean?'

'Him. Yes. It's a couple of days since those dog-walkers rang in to complain, and I told them you'd be onto it. Didn't know you'd be sloping off for the weekend.'

'Leave it with me, Chris. I had it on my to-do list anyway.'

'And one more thing . . .'

'I thought there would be.'

'Malton Show coming up. Inspector Finch is on about having a bit of a briefing later in the week.'

'Right. I've booked the Police And Wildlife Show vehicle. Should be really good. We've never had it up here before. Only trouble is . . .'

'Go on.' He knew what was coming.

'We'll need some time to get down to Warwickshire to collect it. It's a two-man job – and I was thinking of taking Fordy.'

'I'll have a word with Birdie.'

I decided to visit Bob Easton first thing. He was a bit of a handful, one way or another, and the fact that he'd called in that early didn't augur well. Don't get me wrong: he was a sterling member of the Country Watch team, keen, resourceful, self-reliant. But it was that last aspect of his character, admirable as it was, that occasionally bothered me. Like most country people, he reckoned he ought to be able to sort out his own problems – even when he should, by rights, fetch the law in. He called it standing on his own two feet. I called it wading in with his size-twelve wellies on.

It was a cool morning and we'd had the first proper dew of the season overnight. You could see the rank grass on the road-side glinting in the sunlight. As I left town and drove up past the gallops a string of racehorses was being led out from a gateway, their legs wet and their breath coming in clouds. It always makes me shiver when I see that. Still only July, but a reminder that autumn isn't so very far away. The harvest had already started. In the fields they'd been cutting the winter barley, and great round bales of yellow straw were scattered across the stubble.

Bob had a small mixed farm. He grew the usual cereal crops, the odd field of rape, and he kept a small dairy herd. He had plenty on his hands with his sons grown up and moved away, and, like a lot of small farmers, he relied heavily on his wife to help him run the place. It was well out of the way, down a long track cut deep into the limestone. It was a rough ride in the old Puddle Hopper, although you could see where he'd made an effort to improve it. Here and there he'd filled in a hollow with builder's rubble, and there were a couple of stretches where he'd managed to get a bit of tarmac down. You often get contractors knocking at your door in these country places asking if you'll take a part-load that's left over after they've finished a job. The last thing they want is to take it to a tip, where they have to pay for the privilege of dumping it, but the longer they carry it around the more likelihood there is it'll set hard in the back of the lorry. Then they've got serious problems.

I found Bob in the yard. He'd got his combine out and had the engine running, which is why he hadn't heard me drive up. Plus the fact that he was standing with his back to me, watching the sky.

'Now then, lad. Is it going to hold?'

'Oh hello, Mike.' He reached into the cab and switched the machine off. 'Aye, she doesn't look bad. Another hour, it should've dried up nicely.'

'Let's keep our fingers crossed, eh?'

'You going to come inside?'

We walked across to the back door and into the kitchen where his wife was unloading the dishwasher. 'Morning, Mike. I expect you'll be thirsty, will you?'

'You know me, Jean. Always thirsty.'

She put the kettle on and I sat down at the table with Bob. 'Well?' I said. 'You wanted me to come by.'

'The truth is . . .' He took his cap off and ruffled what was left of his hair. 'Truth is I've done sommat a bit daft.'

'Not like you, mate, but fire away.'

He forced a grin. 'Why, it's the same old story. The minute you start harvesting the buggers are in like a rat up a drainpipe.'

'You're talking about poachers, I take it.'

'Aye. You get sick of it. It was a couple of nights ago. Saturday. Must've been two-ish, cos it was still dark. I woke up and heard the dog barking downstairs.'

'No, you didn't,' Jean interrupted. 'I woke up and had to nudge you in the ribs.'

'Aye well, fact is I opened t'curtains and there they was, right there in t'yard with their dogs. Two of them.'

'Two what? Men or dogs?'

'There was two fellows and two dogs, but there could've been more for all I knew. Anyway, I opened the window like and shouted at 'em. "Oi," I goes, "bugger off!"'

'What did they do?'

'You know what they're like. "Sorry, pal, we're just exercising our dogs."'

'As if they had a perfect right to walk onto private property at dead of night.' Jean put a mug of tea in front of me, and a plate of biscuits. 'The nerve of some people.'

'So I told 'em to bloody well clear off and exercise 'em somewhere else.'

'And did they?'

'They said one of the dogs had got loose and they were chasing after it. As if they expected me to swallow that.' Bob took a biscuit and dunked it in his tea. 'Anyway, they moved off right enough. But not far. I could see they had their vehicle parked up, about a hundred yards along the lane there.'

'I told him to phone through to Malton,' Jean said, 'but he wouldn't have it. You know what he's like.'

Bob looked at me. 'What, that time of night?' he said. 'You'd have enough on your plate.'

'We might've done,' I said, 'but you still should've called. It's what we're there for.'

'Well, I thought I'd seen 'em off by this time. I was all set to go back to bed. Then of course . . .'

'What?'

He dunked another biscuit and shoved the plate my way. 'Go on, help yourself, Mike, before I polish 'em off.'

'Ta.'

'Well, I watch 'em go, and then blow me they're barely another hundred yards down the lane, on go the brake lights and they're out again. Bugger this, I says, I'm going to have a word, so I get dressed and set off after 'em.'

'I told him not to, I mean, they could've been . . . well, who knows?'

'Could've been armed. Easy. Some of these poachers are not nice people. I've had a few run-ins myself – and some of them are violent. They'll have a pop at a police officer without batting an eyelid.'

'Well, the fact is I went,' Bob said. 'Took the mobile, like, and me stick. But by the time I got to their vehicle they were away across the stubble. I could see their lamps. I knew what they were up to. So . . . sod this, I thought, I'll teach you.'

'Go on,' I said. 'Tell us the worst.'

He leaned back in his chair. 'Why, I let their bloody tyres down.' Before I could say anything he was holding his hand up. 'I know. I shouldn't have. But I did.'

'And then he woke up next morning fretting, didn't you?' Jean was by his side, shaking her head and looking at me. 'Spent all Sunday chittering on about it, then got up this morning and decided to call in.'

'Well, you got that bit right, Bob. Bit late in the day, mind. And of course, technically speaking you've committed an offence. Y'know that, don't you?' He nodded, and looked into his empty mug. Jean took it from him, gathered mine up and refilled them both. 'I could be round here now, Bob, having to arrest you for criminal damage.'

'Oh, bloody hell, Mike.'

'Listen, we need to think about what you might have got yourself into. These lads can be a right handful and if they haven't come to us with a complaint, it may mean they intend dealing with it themselves. I had an incident not so long ago when a couple of gamekeepers decided to make a stand against this type. They ended up with damage to their vehicles and bricks through their windows.' I looked at him, his face lined and weary. 'I really wish you'd called us, Bob. Even if it meant ringing me on my day off.'

'Sorry, Mike.' He ran his fingers through his hair. 'I wish I had now.'

'Anyway, fortunately for you – and me,' I said, 'aye, and Country Watch too, there's been no complaint made. But for God's sake, Bob, don't be taking the law into your own hands. As wrong as they may have been – well, number one, you've no evidence of what they were up to, and number two you've put yourself firmly in the wrong.'

'I did get one thing right, though.'

'Aye?'

'Got the number of their vehicle.'

'Right, that's more like it. I'll make a note of that and see if they're known to us. I've set a new system up. Anything like this and I send them out a letter, telling them they've been seen in the area and pointing out the offence of poaching with dogs. What I'm hoping is, it'll deter them from coming back. But if it happens, you know what to do. Call me. Make sure he does, Jean. These poachers can be really nasty.'

I left Bob and his missus to it, and headed back towards Kirkham. Like it or not, it was time I dealt with my mate Gerald, the naturist or whatever he called himself. To tell the truth I'd almost forgotten about him over the last few days.

It can be an embarrassment, dealing with a fellow like that, and as I drove up towards his place in the woods I realised I was on edge. Seeing him naked the one time was plenty for me; I didn't fancy a repeat showing. Still, I told myself, as I parked the car and set off down the pathway that led to his little glade, it's all in a day's work.

Once again, I didn't spot the caravan until I was almost upon it, the way it was tucked away among the trees. It looked as though he was in. The door was propped open with a length of two-by-four and there on the grass outside was a little folding table with a teapot and a mug, a half-empty milk bottle, a loaf of bread and one of those old-fashioned, wedge-shaped china cheese dishes. His pile of copper cable was still there, but just about smothered in bindweed by now. I got the impression that Gerald wasn't a man to rush at a job.

'Mr Rodgers!' I called out. 'Are you home?'

'Who is it?' came a muffled voice from inside.

'PC Pannett, Malton police. I'd like a word.'

'Just one moment,' he said. Then I heard him mutter something to himself before he called out, 'Better make myself decent – as you call it.'

He came out with a towel wrapped around his middle. Well, I'm saying it was a towel. A dishcloth would be more like it.

'Am I disturbing your lunch?' I asked.

'No, no – I've finished. But I dare say there's another cup of tea in the pot if you'd like one.'

'Ah, that's very generous of you,' I said before I could stop myself. It's force of habit, I suppose, but sometimes you realise when it's too late that you really ought to decline.

'Have a seat.' He reached behind the door and pulled out one of those folding canvas deckchairs, the type old people sink into and can't get out of again. 'One moment, while I get you a cup.'

He popped back into the van and emerged a moment later with a china mug in his hand. He paused at the bottom of the steps, looked inside it, gave it a quick wipe with his loincloth and set it on the table. I did my best not to think about it. They say you have to eat a peck of dirt before you die, don't they?

I tried to keep it brief. There was no point beating about the bush. 'Mr Rodgers,' I said, 'I'm afraid I've had another complaint.'

'Oh yes? And what is it this time?'

'Have you been walking in Howsham Woods over the past week or two?'

'I've been going there for years,' he said. 'I find it's an excellent place to do my stretching exercises. And to engage with the *genius loci*.'

'I beg your pardon?'

'Latin. It means "the spirit of the place".'

'Ah, I see. And what sort of – I mean, what do you wear when you go there?'

'At this time of year? As little as possible.'

'Does that mean you sometimes wear nothing?'

'I dress appropriately to the conditions.'

'So if it's a fine day, warm sun?'

'Look, Constable, we're all born naked. Clothes are an invention of man and not always entirely necessary, nor even desirable.'

The trouble with a fellow like Gerald is that you can't really find a fault in his logic. In a perfect world I'd be with him all the way. Let it all hang out, I say. I mean, why not?

'Look,' I said, 'if the world was populated by people who thought as you did, well, absolutely, why not go around naked in the warm weather? But as you well know, there are rules and there are conventions, and the vast majority of the population don't want to see naked men in public places.'

'I have a perfect right to live my life according to my own principles. I don't bother other people, and I don't expect them to bother me.'

'Yes, Mr Rodgers, I appreciate what you're saying, but we have had members of the public make a complaint, and I'm duty-bound to investigate.' I had to think carefully about this – and fast. It was no good invoking the law on indecent exposure, because that requires you to demonstrate that the offender, if male, intended to insult a female – and I was pretty sure this wasn't the case here. The law on public order, however, is a bit more flexible. Causing harassment, alarm or distress can constitute an offence. Maybe that was the way in. 'Listen,' I said, 'you say you're living as nature intended, but if a member of the public makes a complaint, I could end up arresting you for being a public nuisance, or under the Public Order Act, and then you could end up in court and your name would be in the papers.' I looked around the glade, the sun filtering through the canopy of green, insects droning about the wild honeysuckle, a few clumps of wild cherries ripening off on the tree behind the caravan. It was like his own private Garden of Eden. 'Look,' I said, 'you've got a good life out here. Nobody bothers you, so let's leave it that way, shall we? So long as you're out of sight, you do as you please; but once you venture into public spaces, you're simply going to have to take account of other people's feelings and the law of this land, whether you like it or not.'

He didn't have much to say to that, but the way he looked at me, then at the ground, I suspected that the message had sunk in.

'So,' I said, 'can we leave it at that, d'you think?'

'Yes, well, if that's the best we can do I suppose I shall have to, as you say, be a little more circumspect.'

I stood up, nodded and strode away. I wouldn't normally do that, but I was trying to reinforce in Mr Rodgers's mind the seriousness of the matter. At the same time, my abrupt departure got me out of a quandary. It's not often I leave a cup of tea undrunk, but this was threatening to turn into one of those bush-tucker trials you see on the telly – and it was time I got myself out of there.

I felt good about the way it had gone with Gerald. Or should I say relieved? I'd been worried that he might turn out to be a really awkward customer. Maybe I had a knack for dealing with people like him, I thought as I drove back to town. Maybe I'd found just the right way to approach him and put my case. Maybe I'd found a skill I didn't realise I had. Yes, PC Mike Pannett, Rural Community Beat Officer and Skilled Negotiator. As it turned out, I was going to need all my peacemaking skills before too long.

It was a few days later, Thursday, and we were all waiting for the inspector to talk about the upcoming show. Normally, when you come to work on an early, there's the commotion of the outgoing night shift packing up to leave, and then us getting ready for our briefing with them. But this time they were nowhere to be seen.

'Is something going off?' I asked Chris as we trooped into the parade room.

'Yeah, bloody big fire out at that bloke Easton's. Apparently the barn's gone up and it's all hands to the pump.'

'Shit, I'd better get up there.'

'No problem, Mike. But it's all in hand at the moment. We just need to have a quick get together about Malton Show with Inspector Finch.' We sat ourselves down and waited for Birdie to come in. As he did so, Chris nudged my elbow. 'The good news is, he's agreed to let you and Fordy go and collect the roadshow tomorrow.'

The briefing lasted about half an hour. Birdie covered such things as which officers were assigned to what duty, and showed us where the temporary traffic lights would be set up to ease the traffic flow. Then he got into the Police And Wildlife Show thing, and gave it a bit of a build-up. 'As well as Mike's PAWS wagon,' he said, 'we'll have the community bus there. My over-riding aim is to put on a good police presence and mix with the public. This is one of the biggest community events of the year. It brings the rural community together . . .' Normally I would have been all ears, and full of suggestions. But this morning my mind was elsewhere. I wanted to find out what had happened with Bob Easton.

When the night crew finally showed up, looking tired, dishevelled and muddy, they filled me in. 'Been up to your mate's place. Easton, is it? Up above Kirby Grindalythe?'

'Aye,' I said. 'What the hell's been going on?'

'Oh, bloody Trumpton out in force . . . All sorts.'

'What happened? Are they all right?'

'They're okay, but their barn's a right mess. Looks like arson. Must be thousands of pounds' worth of damage. Tons of straw ruined, and the roof's a goner.'

I drove up there as soon as I could get away. I could see

where the fire tenders had been. All along the lane there were branches that had been ripped off the trees, and the pot-holes were worse than ever. It was a still morning, and as I approached the farm a drift of dirty grey smoke seemed to be clinging to the roof of the barn – or what was left of it. Blackened scallops of melted, corrugated plastic were hanging down from the metal trusses. The yard itself was awash with water, with a huge puddle between me and the back of the house. As I stepped out of the car, Jean came to meet me.

'He's in the shed there, calving. As if we haven't enough on. Go on in – he said you'd be coming by.'

'Are you all right?' I asked her.

She sighed. 'We're still standing. But we could've done without that.' She nodded towards the burned barn.

'You are insured, aren't you?'

'Oh, of course – but you know what'll happen. They'll bump the premium right up. They don't like paying out, do they?'

I went across to the shed. In one stall a cow stood licking a newborn calf that teetered unsteadily on its spindly legs. In the neighbouring one Bob was on his knees, next to a second cow who was lying on her side. 'Here,' he said, 'give us a hand with this one, will you?'

As soon as I got inside the stall with him I could see he had a problem. The cow was only showing the calf's nose and a foot. She looked exhausted. Bob took his watch off and knelt down by the cow. 'It'll be that bloody fire's set 'em off,' Bob said. 'Weren't due while next week, neither of 'em. Started bawling as soon as the flames took hold. Now this 'un's got its leg twisted back.'

'Do you think it might be a vet job, Bob?'

He had his arm inside, elbow-deep, feeling for the calf's foot.

'Don't want to be paying out for that,' he said. 'Ah, there you are,' he grunted as he tried to get a grip. 'Just need to ease her round. You just concentrate on holding the hoof, make sure it doesn't damage the cow as you bring the leg round.' He slid his other hand in, grimacing. 'Gotcha,' he said.

I knelt down next to Bob and the cow, itching to help, but not quite sure what to do. I remembered as a young lad, watching Billy and Jack using soap and ropes to deliver calves at the farm at Staintondale.

'Shall I fetch some rope, Bob?'

He didn't answer. The top of the youngster's head appeared, and Bob got hold of it with both hands, easing it into position. The mother seemed to shudder, then snorted – and out came the entire head, followed soon after by the rest of the calf in one smooth sliding movement, landing on the straw, its black and white hair all matted, wet and steaming, its pink little nose glistening as the sunlight angled in through the barn door. It was a beautiful sight, quite moving really, but what stuck in my mind was the way the mother just sat there, and started to chew gently as if nothing had happened.

While I knelt there staring at the newborn calf, Bob popped his fingers into its mouth, making sure the airways were open, then grabbed a handful of straw and told me to rub its chest and get it breathing. Then he nudged the cow. 'C'mon, Henrietta lass, get to work.'

Reluctantly, the mother turned and nudged her baby, then started to lick it. Bob got up off his knees. 'Aye, she'll be okay now,' he said. 'Touch and go for a moment though, with both of them calving together.' He went to a tap in the corner and washed his hands, handed me a cloth to wipe the muck off my trousers, then led the way back to the house.

'So tell me about that lot,' I said. We were sitting in the kitchen, with the door open, looking out at the charred pile of sodden straw still steaming in the yard.

'Why, I heard t'dogs barking. This would be . . .' He glanced at Jean.

'Three o'clock,' she said. 'And we thought we heard a vehicle drive off. He went back to sleep. I was lying there, wondering who it could've been, and about ten minutes later I saw the flames – well, the reflection of them, on the bedroom ceiling.'

'There was nowt we could do,' Bob said. 'The fire had hold. Mind, them fire brigade lads got out here right fast, to say we're so far from town. God knows it's done enough damage, but it could've been a lot worse.' He sighed, and took a handkerchief from his pocket. 'But I tell you what,' he said, wiping the sweat off his face, 'there's times when you really do wonder what's going to hit you next. I was out in my bottom field last night and guess who I found on the roadside?' I knew what he was going to say, but I didn't answer. He clearly needed to get it off his chest, and he'd probably feel better when he had done. 'Travellers,' he said.

'You would,' I said. 'Seamer Horse Fair coming up, isn't it? There'll be a fair few coming through.'

'I wouldn't mind, Mike; I've had plenty of gypsies stop over the years, proper travellers I mean, and never caused me any real problem. But I had this lot a few years ago and they were always trying it on. Petty stuff most of it, but I fell out with them in the end. I thought I'd seen the back of 'em. I just hope they don't decide to start nicking my fence-posts again, that's all. Cos I shall have to have 'em if they do.'

'Bob,' I said, 'just you be careful, mate. If you have any complaints, you know where to bring 'em. Right?'

Bob nodded agreement, but he wasn't happy. And to be honest, who could blame him? Here he was trying to get a harvest in and it was all happening at once. I knew the travelling family he referred to, and yes, they did sail close to the wind. I'd had dealings with them a bit back when a couple of lambs went missing from another farm, not that anything was ever proved. It was another 'watching' brief, as far as I was concerned, and I made a note to go and see what they were up to.

I didn't linger up at the farm. Not even for the cup of coffee Jean was offering me. I wanted to get back to the station to see what Des Carter had found out about that vehicle they'd seen earlier in the week.

The CID man was ready for me. 'Barnsley,' he said, picking up a printout. 'Owner well known to the local police, and well into poaching – except that he lives in a three-bed semi in town and keeps his dogs in the back yard. Known associates – also well recorded. History of violence and burglary. Not nice people. Your mate was lucky he didn't come face to face with them, if you're asking me.'

'Well,' I said, 'I reckon they want pulling in. Suspicion of arson.'

'Maybe so,' he said. 'I've already spoken to my counterpart at Barnsley CID. We're just waiting for the fire report and if that confirms it's arson, they'll fetch them in.'

We didn't have long to wait. The report arrived the following day, and more or less confirmed our suspicions. Now it was a matter of waiting for the Barnsley officers to round them up.

It was turning out to be a busy old week, and before we knew it it was Friday, and I was teaming up with Fordy for our drive to Warwickshire to collect the PAWS wagon.

'We've played a blinder,' I said to him as we set off.

'Too right,' he said. 'Got me out of a late shift, this has.'

The whole idea had been kick-started when I was on my wildlife course and we were shown around the specially kitted-out vehicle. It was crammed with all sorts of exhibits connected to wildlife crime. There was everything, from crocodile-skin shoes and handbags, ivory and walrus tusks to a whole array of eggs, stuffed birds of prey, foxes and badgers, prohibited traps and even medicines and poisons. I knew it would go down a storm with the visitors at the Malton Show.

It was about a three-hour run down to Warwickshire and it was good to have a bit of company. I'd grown to like Fordy. He reminded me of myself when I started out. He was mad keen on countryside matters. In fact, he told me, he envied me my job.

'Yeah, you've got it good, Mike,' he said. 'When you move on I reckon I'll take over from you.'

'Move on? Where to, mate?'

'Oh, I dunno . . . when you retire, get promoted.'

'I'm a long way off retiring, buddy. And as for promotion, nah, I like things the way they are.'

After a bite to eat and a chat with the Warwickshire officers, comparing rural war stories, I headed back up north. Fordy followed in the car, and we arrived in the yard just in time to meet Ed and Jayne arriving for their late shift. I reversed the wagon into the corner, making sure the CCTV cameras had a good view of it.

Ed couldn't resist having a go. 'Bloody hell, Pannett, there you go again. Swanning off and leaving us to deal with Friday night at the sharp end.'

'Look on the bright side, Ed, you've got Thommo covering for me.'

'Don't remind me,' he said. 'Anyway, how did you manage to swing it – getting this beast?'

'Never mind that, come and have a look,' I said.

He and Jayne climbed on board. 'Hell,' he whistled, 'Must have cost a right packet to pull this together.'

'You'd be surprised, matey. Everything on board – all those exhibits – have been seized by customs over the years. Tell you what, though; it's worth a bloody fortune, so you lot better keep an eye on it tonight.'

Fordy had parked his car and joined us at the wagon. 'Well, Mike,' he said, 'I don't know about you, but I've got a cold pint and a hot date waiting for me in town.'

'Right,' I said, 'and I'm meeting Ann down the Jolly Farmers. A perfect way to spend a Friday night.' I glanced at Jayne.

'All right, all right,' she said. 'No need to rub it in. Anyway, we've been shifted back for the show, so we're free after work on Sunday. How about we all get together for a drink?'

'You're on,' I said.

After two days of thundery showers the weather didn't look promising, but on Saturday evening the skies cleared and Sunday got off to a dry start with bright sunshine. Malton Show has been going on for donkey's years. It always used to be held in the week, and all the local kids would take a day off school to attend. Now they'd decided to change it to the weekend, to try to attract more people. And the venue's changed too. Instead of having it in town – and giving us one giant traffic headache – it's held at the Scampston estate, on parkland laid out by Capability Brown in the 1770s. It's a beautiful, level, spacious site, all lush grass with a scattering of mature trees, perfect for an event like this.

Normally we take as many officers as we can round up, which usually means half a dozen or so going down in a carrier van. We also had to man the mobile police station, which is kitted out with lots of literature and bumf all about the police and crime prevention. If we're lucky the youth liaison PC will come up with some goodie bags or balloons to give out to the kids. We arrived in a proper little convoy with the carrier van, the mobile police station and the PAWS wagon.

At the showground we found the space they'd designated for us, and Fordy helped me set up the exhibits, posters and information leaflets. As the place started to fill up we attracted quite a queue of visitors. The snakeskins and tiger-skins, the stuffed badgers and foxes, the rhino horn, the elephants' tusks – while the kids inspected them, I explained to the parents about the massive trade in illegal wildlife and wildlife artefacts. Not many people realise that it's second only to the illegal drugs market in terms of its monetary value.

We'd been at it for an hour or two when I decided to leave Fordy to it and take a walk around, to be seen and say hello to everybody. 'I'll have half an hour, then we'll swap over,' I told him. 'Do you good to take charge.'

I wandered around between the various exhibits, ranging from tractors and farm machinery to birds of prey and framed pictures of country scenes, and stalls selling everything from homemade cakes to hats, boots and candy-floss. There were the usual amusements too, and over the far side the beautifully groomed show animals – sheep, pigs, cattle and poultry – all awaiting the judge. I was over at the equestrian ring, where riders young and old were taking their turn to go over the fences, when I heard someone calling my name.

'Mike, you got a minute?'

Turning round I saw the familiar lank hair and bow-legged stance of Ronnie Leach.

'Now then,' I said. 'Backed any winners lately?'

He had his hands thrust deep into his jeans pockets, his shoulders hunched, and he was casting furtive glances to either side. As I approached him he edged away from me and slipped behind a large oak tree.

'What we playing? Bloody hide-and-seek?' I said.

'No. Thing is, Mike, I've got sommat for you.'

'Oh aye, where's it running? Thirsk? Ripon?'

'It's not a horse, Mike.' He leaned forward and peered around the tree as a young lass led a pony past us and tethered it to a fence-post. 'I'm talking about – you know, information – like we talked about.'

'Ri-ight,' I said. 'You mean intelligence?'

'Aye, that's it. Intelligence.'

'Well, go on then, spit it out.'

'It's about the takings.'

'I'm all ears.'

'Y'know over yonder where you pay your fiver to get in?' Ronnie began.

'Yes.'

'And how they gather it all up in them Tupperware boxes and suchlike?'

'Go on.'

'And then the head lad comes round and collects it in a satchel?'

'Get to the point, will you?'

'Well, they take it all to that little tent, don't they? And they count it up, like. I mean, there's bloody thousands, isn't there? And no security.'

'Ronnie, you seem to know a hell of a lot about the money situation here. You're making me nervous.'

'I told you last time I saw you, Mike. I'm on the straight and narrow.'

'Come on, Ronnie, let's have it. What do you know?'

'Right, I don't know their names, but I heard three lads talking about how they were going to have it.'

'What, here? Today?'

'Ten minutes since.'

'Who were they? Local lads?'

'They sounded local, but I haven't seen 'em before. Youngsters. Sixteen, seventeen, about that.'

'Can you describe them?'

'Right, one of them you couldn't miss. Had his head shaved, tattoo round the top of his arm a barbed-wire type job. Right little punk.'

'Any more?'

'Aye and one of them was' – Ronnie patted his stomach – 'carrying plenty.'

'Plenty of what?'

'Weight. He was – you know . . .'

'Fat?'

'Stoutish. And a carrot-top.'

'And the third?' I had my notebook out now and was jotting this all down.

Ronnie sighed, and rubbed the back of his head. 'I dunno. Average. Jeans, T-shirt, normal size – nah, nowt to remember about him. Just the stout kid with the ginger hair and the tattooed lad.'

'Okay, Ronnie. That's good. If you catch sight of them let me know, won't you?'

'Where'll you be?'

'Either in that wildlife wagon over by Yates's stand, or there's a community safety bus next to the show ring. There's a fellow selling coffee from a van right by us.'

As soon as Ronnie had gone I got onto Control and relayed the information he'd given me. Then I tried to contact the rest of the guys: Ed, Chris and Jayne and our two specials. But I was fighting a losing battle, what with the loudspeakers announcing the entrants in the dog show and the screams of the kids on the merry-go-round. I hurried back to the PAWS lorry where Fordy was sitting drinking tea.

'Where's all your punters?' I asked. 'There was a queue a mile long when I left you.'

'They found better things to do. Like snapping up bargains in the cake tent.'

'Well listen, buddy, we're on the lookout for three youths who think they're gonna get away with the bloody takings. I need to alert the secretary and his crew.' I gave Fordy the descriptions and hurried over to the tent where the various officials were stationed. The secretary was there, his desk awash with cash. He had the treasurer and a couple of volunteers with him, bagging up coins. 'What should we do?' he asked when I told him what I'd heard.

'Forget about counting, for a start. The first thing is to get it all into a vehicle where it can be locked up and watched over. Then you want to get it away from the showground as fast as possible.'

While they got on with scooping the money off the table-top and back into their plastic tubs, I stood guard outside. What we could have done with at this point was a couple of officers in plain clothes to keep an eye out. Preventing the crime from taking place was one thing, but ideally I wanted to find these youths and have words. As ever, the problem was manpower. With only seven of us on site, and a crowd of between ten and fifteen thousand, we were spread pretty thin.

'*1015, receiving.*'

It was Chris Cocks, on my radio. '1015, go ahead, over,' I said.

'*I reckon I've spotted your lads. Three of 'em, right? One with a tattoo round his arm, and a big fat lad with red hair.*'

'Sounds right. Whereabouts are you?'

'*I'm over by the – the guy who has the birds of prey. You know where I mean?*'

'Yeah. Be with you in two minutes.'

The lads were still there, huddled together beside one of the portable toilets, and deep in conversation, with Chris watching from a safe distance.

'Tell you what,' I said to him, 'it's tempting . . .'

'What, to let 'em try and nab the cash and catch them in the act?'

'Aye.'

Of course, realistically we knew that was far too risky. With a crowd that size there were just too many dangers. What if they got aggressive? We couldn't have innocent bystanders getting caught up in a running fight. And what if, by some fluke, they actually got their hands on some of the money and did a runner – and got lucky again?

'No, we've no choice but to tackle them now,' Chris said. 'And anyway, look – they've spotted us. Come on.' The lads tried to make a dash for it, but they got themselves hemmed in by a queue for the burger stand heading in one direction and a girls' marching band coming the other way.

Chris grabbed the tattooed youth, I got hold of the stout lad and the third one simply froze.

'Need a word with you three,' Chris said.

'We haven't done nowt.'

'Care to show us your entry ticket?' I said.

The lad with the tattoo spoke up. 'I lost it.'

'What about you, then? Where's yours?'

'Ah, you found 'em.' Fordy had come running up, panting and sweating.

Good, I thought, that makes three of us and three of them. Perfect. 'You know what,' I murmured in his ear, 'I reckon we can give them a hard turnover.' The way I saw it, Malton Show is a nice, old-fashioned community event, a perfect day out for families – and the last thing I wanted was to see three undesirables like this ruining it. What I meant by a turnover was that we would separate them and search them for any weapons or anything that could have helped them or be used in a possible theft. We would detain them while we ran all the usual checks on their details via Control – if only to ensure that we'd identified them correctly. This involved seeing whether they were known to the police or wanted for any crimes, or whether any warrants had been issued against them. At the same time we would check the intelligence system to see if they had previously come to notice – as well as checking their names against the voters' register to verify that the addresses they had given were genuine.

They were a pushover. Once we'd established that none of them had tickets they admitted they'd come in the back way, over the fence. The fact that the lads on the gate didn't issue tickets, just took your fiver and let you in, was neither here nor there. If they had paid, they would've known that. But, as we like to say, that was for us to know and them to find out. And as if to vindicate my decision – bingo! Their names popped up on the intelligence system. They'd never been in any real bother, just been stopped and searched in the past in suspicious circumstances, and been seen associating with known offenders. 'So what was on your mind? I asked them. 'What were you planning?'

'We wasn't planning anything. Just wanted a day out,' was all the answer we got. And we didn't push it any further. As far as we were concerned it was job done. Would they really have tried to take the money? Who knows? Maybe what Ronnie had overheard was just a bit of bravado on their part, geeing each other up, trying to sound hard. The fact was we'd prevented the situation developing beyond the planning stage. More importantly, we'd exposed a dangerously insecure and amateurish system of cash handling which would, we were assured by the show secretary, be reviewed immediately. All that was left to do was to give the three youths the hard word and get them off the site. Chris left this job to me; he knew I would drive the message home.

I lined all three of them up and explained that I had had information that suggested they intended to steal the takings. I spelled out in no uncertain terms that this was my patch and I didn't take kindly to people who wanted to come and rip off the community and ruin the show. I had their cards well and truly marked, and if I ever caught them up to no good in the future, I'd come down on them like a ton of bricks.

This seemed to take the wind out of their sails. To be honest, they didn't exactly look like hardened criminals when I escorted them off the site. They looked young, and pretty sheepish. I hoped it was a lesson for them. And if they had indeed intended to steal the cash, they would spend a long time trying to puzzle out how we got onto them, and perhaps it would make them think twice in the future.

As for Ronnie, my own personal 'supergrass', I caught up with him when I popped into the tent where they'd been auctioning off the cakes. He was there with Soapy, polishing off a plate of fruit tarts.

'Didn't know you knew each other,' I said.

Soapy wiped the crumbs off his lips. 'Oh, we go back a long way, cock-bod. His old man and my old man ran a couple of wagons – used to tek us to do the potato harvest.' He laughed, and nudged Ronnie in the ribs. 'Aye, remember that time he got his lorry weighed, went for a pint, then come back and got it weighed all over again.' He laughed, spluttering crumbs all down his T-shirt. 'Crafty sod got paid twice for t'same load.'

'It's no wonder you turned out to be such a fly couple of lads,' I said, casting an eye over the empty plates that were scattered around the tables. 'And thanks for saving a few cakes for me and the lads. Really appreciate that.'

'Oh sorry, Mike.' Give Ronnie his due, he did at least try to look guilty. Soapy just laughed.

'Mind,' he said, 'we have got sommat for you, Mike. Haven't we, Ron?'

Ronnie looked around him. The tent was more or less empty now, just a couple of women gathering up the mess and rolling the white paper covers off the trestle tables. 'Aye, I've had a word for one in t'Ebor meeting.'

'Oh yes?'

'Be a decent price an' all.'

'Go on, then.'

'They call her – oh, some Arab name. I can never get me tongue around them.'

'Whatever it is,' Soapy said, 'you wanna get on her, Mike. Antepost. I'll let you know the name.'

'We'll see,' I said. 'I remember somebody once telling me a tale about a bloke who owned a whole string of shops, but got into the old gambling lark in a big way, ended up losing everything. He made the national headlines. "Fast women and slow horses", they said. I was always taught to leave well alone.'

The rest of the day passed without any more dramas. After Fordy had had his break the two of us took it in turns to patrol – well, walk around really, because it was a good-humoured affair and everyone seemed to be enjoying themselves. And of course, you can't wander about an event like that without bumping into people you know. Walt was there, with his lady friend, crowing about how his sister had won first prize for her pies. I spotted Algy too, casting an eye over an antiques stall, and a couple of lads from the Jolly Farmers.

It was getting on for seven when Fordy and I arrived back at the station with the PAWS wagon. Just as I was leaving I learned that we'd had word from South Yorkshire. The CID had rounded up the owner of the vehicle whose tyres Bob Easton had let down, and one of his mates. They'd arrested both on suspicion of arson, seized some items of clothing and gone over the car looking for anything that would link him to the fire. It was unresolved as yet. The hope was that they'd find some sort of evidence linking them to the scene – straw, ash, maybe animal droppings. Meanwhile, after questioning them, they'd released the suspects on bail.

It had been a hectic few days, but if I thought my troubles were behind me I had another think coming. I'd made a note in my diary to call by the next day and check on the travellers that were camped beside Bob's field. To my great surprise they'd beaten me to it. Chris stopped me at the desk as I arrived at work. 'Now there's a first,' he said. 'Travelling folk using state-of-the-art technology.'

'Why not?' I said. 'They've always moved with the times if it suited them. Motorised transport, TVs, washing machines.'

'Aye, I know, but I never thought I'd see the day when they were ringing us on a mobile. And this one concerns you, Mike. Family out Kirby Grindalythe way. What do they call them? Riley?'

'Yep, that'll be them. And why do I have a bad feeling about this?'

'They reckon some farmer's been down threatening to turn their caravans over.'

'Oh they do, eh? Right, leave it with me, mate.'

I can't say I looked forward to sorting this one out. If, as I suspected, it involved Bob, then this could be trouble. Which, to tell the truth, would be a bit of an embarrassment, seeing that he was supposed to be on our side. But maybe I was getting ahead of myself. The first job was to go and talk to the main man, old Mr Riley.

It was a familiar scene: the caravan parked up against a tall hedge on which an assortment of clothes had been hung out to dry, a white Sherpa van under an ash tree, a couple of horses grazing by the gate, and a smudgy sort of fire sending a drift of smoke across the road. A couple of young men were sitting on the step of the caravan as I got out of the car, but they didn't even look up, just edged aside as the door opened and out stepped Riley Senior, the head of the family. In truth he was only sixty or so, but his family had been passing through here around the time of the Seamer Fair for generations.

'Now then, Mr Riley. Cracking morning.'

''Tis that,' he muttered.

'I understand you called the station.'

He walked across the rough grass towards me, adjusting his trilby hat and tightening his belt. 'I did that, Mr Pannett sir.

And I got to tell you, it's the first time I ever had to call a copper out in my life.' He looked back at the two younger men sitting on the steps, pulled his hat down lower and said, 'I don't like to say this, but I'm telling you now I'm not having it. There now.' He shook his head. 'We put up with a lot, us travellers, but we ain't having that, no sir.'

'What aren't you having, Mr Riley?'

'Threats.' He waved his arm towards the field. 'That daft bugger.' It was obvious who he meant. If we'd gone to the gate Bob and Jean's farmhouse would have been visible, about a quarter of a mile away across the field. 'Come down here accusing us of all sorts. In his tractor he was, and he had that bloody great fork on the front. Threatened to tipple the caravan over. Frightened me missus half to death – and the little ones too. He should be locked up, he should.'

'Now, try to calm down, Mr Riley, and tell me what's been going on, will you.'

'It's him you want to be asking, Constable. Coming down here accusing us of stealing his gas cylinders. What do we want wid his gas, eh? We cook on the fire here.'

'I don't know about that,' I said, 'but don't worry. I'll check with him.'

'We have a good understanding with farmers, us Rileys. We don't go stealing things what don't belong to us. You should've seen him, Officer. Raving he was. I feared for me life, I'm telling you.'

I took out my notebook. 'D'you want to step into the car a minute, sir, and I'll take a statement from you. Won't take long.'

'Statement?' he repeated. 'What d'you want a statement for?'

'It's standard procedure if you're wanting to make a formal complaint.'

'Ho no,' he said, backing away from me. 'I'm not having anyone arrested on my account. I just want you to put a stop to it, that's all.' He stepped back again, holding his hands up. 'No, no paperwork. We don't want any of that. I don't deal wid the police. Fight me own battles, I do.'

It occurred to me to tell him that Bob Easton felt the same way, but I thought better of it. 'Well, look,' I said, 'I tell you what I'll do. Let me have a look around here – just in case some of his gas cylinders have got mislaid, you understand – and then I'll go and speak to him. If he has been threatening you, you have my word he won't do it again.'

'He won't get the chance,' he said. 'Don't you worry. We shan't be stopping here. Soon as the missus fetches the youngsters back from town we're off. We don't want any more to do with him – nor your statements and complaints neither.'

'Well, the choice is yours, but I can't prosecute anyone without you making a statement.' Before I left I had a good look at the site, checked out the back side of the hedge and poked around under the van. There was nothing to incriminate them, and I was soon on my way.

Up at the farm Bob was looking sheepish, to put it mildly. 'I've been expecting you,' he said.

'Bob, what you been up to this time?'

'Oh hell, Mike. It's just been one thing after another, and then I went t'check me crowscarers and the bloody gas cylinders had gone. Three of 'em. They cost me twenty-five quid a throw, and I've to drive to Westow to collect 'em.'

'Well, there was no sign of any cylinders down at Riley's place. I mean, what would he want with them anyway?'

'Sell 'em on?'

'Maybe. But where's the evidence?'

'And what about me fence-posts? There must be a dozen gone missing this last week or two.'

'Bob,' I said, 'let's not talk about your fence-posts. They may have had them, and they may not. What you should be doing right now is thanking your lucky stars for a traveller's suspicion of authority. If he'd given me a statement about what you threatened down there, I'd be arresting you, not supping tea at your kitchen table. You're putting me in a right old spot here, Bob. So what've you got to say about that?'

I laid it on the line to Bob, and I made sure that Jean was in attendance. Then I trailed back to the lane and had another word with Mr Riley. 'Right,' I said, 'I've had a talk with the farmer up yonder. He's had a lot of problems lately with someone burning his barn down. He regrets what he did and promises me it won't happen again.'

'Too right it won't,' said Mr Riley. 'I told you, we're moving on.'

'Now he tells me his gas cylinders and a whole load of fence-posts have gone missing. The man's had enough.' I walked over to the blackened circle where the fire was still smouldering. 'You wouldn't have been burning them on your fire here, would you?'

Mr Riley pulled his hat down over his eyes. 'No, that wasn't us, Officer. We just collect and burn . . .' He pointed to a pile of brushwood at the side of the caravan. 'Aye, fallen branches and that.'

I gave him the hard stare. 'So,' I said, 'you're moving on are you?'

'In the morning, aye.'

'Well, let's not be having any rubbish left lying about, eh? Where you going, by the way?'

'Weaverthorpe.'

'Ah, still on my patch. I'll be seeing you later then. And when

I do I don't want to hear of any fence-posts going missing over there.'

'I can promise you you won't. Not us, Officer. Not the Rileys.'

'I'm glad to hear that.'

It had been a funny old week, with all that had been going on at Bob's, the three lads at the show, and now this business with the travellers. Sometimes things just aren't as clear cut as we'd like them to be. Sometimes there is no black and white, only a grey area. Some people think you can just go arresting everybody on suspicion and sort it that way, but I prefer to apply a bit of common sense. But it's always a fine line. If you don't step in things can escalate out of all control; but step in too soon and people will look on you as petty-minded, out of tune with the community. And for me, the trust of the community is paramount. Treat people squarely, and it ought to come right, that's what I say. But then I always was the optimist. When push comes to shove, I always go back to what I was told as a young copper: What would that average commuter on the Clapham omnibus make of it?

I left old man Riley to it, and made my way back down the lane, then headed over the tops towards Rillington. I thought I might have a word with Nick the gamekeeper. But before that I was going back to Scampston. Ever since I'd watched Ronnie and Soapy polish off those cakes I'd had sweet things on my mind. It was time to pay another visit to the little baker's shop in the village there and grab a treat for me and Ann to enjoy later.

Chapter 7

The Sun Goes Down

'Dog days,' I said, yawning. 'That's what we're in, I reckon.' It was Sunday evening. Ann and I had been attacking the undergrowth that was encroaching on the gooseberries, but we'd soon come to the conclusion that we needed mechanised help. She was slumped in a folding canvas chair nursing a nasty scratch on her wrist, and I was perched on my log – we still hadn't got round to carving a second seat in – trying not to rub at my nettle rash. As the sun went down behind the trees, one or two mosquitoes had come up out of the beck side and were starting to whine about our ears. I hardly had the energy to wave them away.

'Dog days. I've heard the expression,' Ann said, 'but I've never worked out exactly what it means.'

'Nor me. Maybe we should ask Henry.' Henry was unusually quiet, lying in the grass and half-heartedly snapping at the odd wasp droning past him.

'Always meant to look it up in the dictionary.' Ann turned and looked at me. 'Go on, pop inside and fetch it, will you? You never know. Could be a quiz question.'

I groaned and eased myself upright. 'The things I do for you. Mind, it's time I stirred myself anyway.' I looked at my watch. 'Due at work in forty minutes.'

I brought the big book out and left Ann to thumb her way through it while I went back in, grabbed a quick shower and got changed. When I came out with my bait tin and flask she gave me a big smile. 'You were right,' she said, pointing at the entry with her forefinger. 'Dog days: sultry part of summer supposed to occur when Sirius, the Dog Star, rises at the same time as the sun, often reckoned to be early July to mid-August.'

'Y'see, Ann? You're living with a compendium of useless knowledge, and you didn't realise it. I knew there was a reason why we felt so lethargic. Let's just hope it has the same effect on the villains, eh?'

The weather had been hot and sticky for a week now – although the last day or two we'd been having more of the sticky and less of the hot. An outbreak of thundery showers had cranked up the tension among my farmer friends as they tried to get their harvest in. They weren't at their chirpiest, and I was having to look to old stalwarts like Algy and Walt when I needed a quiet five minutes and a refreshing brew. Not that I had much time for that. Ever since the weekend off with Ann I felt I'd been chasing my tail. Okay, I'd put the naturist fellow to bed, so to speak, and saved the takings down at the show from that gang of young tearaways, but now we were getting all the petty problems that come with the peak holiday season: antisocial behaviour, shoplifting, opportunist burglaries as windows and patio doors were carelessly left open, people complaining about noisy neighbours, kids playing ball where they weren't supposed to play ball, and so on and so on. It's not the kind of stuff you see in police dramas on TV, but it's part of our daily diet in the summertime – along with the occasional flare-up on the streets at the end of a long evening. On top of all this somebody reckoned they'd seen a big cat out at Hovingham Woods. Twice they'd rung in, wanting to know what we were going to do about it. They'd even found out that we had a trained wildlife officer at Malton – meaning me – but as I said to Ed when I got to work that night, call me a hard-boiled old sceptic, but I'll start taking the Ryedale Panther seriously when I see it with my own eyes, in broad daylight, with witnesses present . . . and after I've taken a breath test.

At the same time as dealing with our own community, we'd now got to that time of year when we had to keep half an eye on the influx of visitors to places like Castle Howard, Eden Camp and especially Flamingo land. The vast majority of people you get at these places are ordinary, decent holidaymakers with nothing more on their minds than having a good time. But when you get several thousand gathered in one place the statistics suggest that sooner or later someone's going to fall out with someone else, most likely at night when they've got a couple of drinks inside them. I've said it before: August isn't my favourite month. And this year, I had another worry on my mind.

'Y'know, this is really starting to get to me,' I said. 'It's winding me up.' I banged the table. 'I am not happy about it.'

Ed wiped up a splash of tea with a crumpled paper towel. 'Steady on, Mike, we're only two weeks into the season, y'know. A lot of games to be played between now and next May.'

It was just approaching one o'clock. We'd tidied up in town and were sitting having a quiet drink before we went out on our country rounds.

'I'm not talking about York City,' I said. 'It's this bloody Sunset Gang. You seen the reports?'

'They do seem to be pretty active.'

'Active? I should bloody say so. Off-licence in Yarm, mini-market at Guisborough, warehouse at – where was it?'

'Pocklington, somewhere like that. Or was it Market Weighton?'

'They're taking the proverbial, Ed. They need sorting out.'

'From what I've heard, we're pulling out all the stops. As far as the budget allows at any rate. These jobs aren't cheap.'

'Aye,' I said, 'a bit of surveillance here and there . . . From what I've heard, this team is very surveillance-aware. Makes it difficult.'

Ed shrugged his shoulders. 'It all costs money, my friend.'

Money. Funding. As a policeman you know what you'd like to do to rein in gangs such as we were dealing with, and you always have this feeling that if you could get one more piece of equipment, one more car backing you up, one more officer watching your rear . . . but the fact is there's always some high-profile crime going off that scoops up what limited resources are available. One time it'll be a murder investigation, another time a manhunt, or a serial sex offender – and don't get me wrong, nobody would begrudge the effort that's put into those cases, but there are times when you just wish you had that little bit extra. We'd like to have used a tracking device on the gang's vehicle – except that this lot kept changing vehicles, parking them up in various lock-ups and the like. We'd like to have brought in helicopters as part of the surveillance but that was a non-starter, what with them operating at night in rural locations. And then again, as I'd found out some time back when I got a helicopter in to control the crowd leaving that rave in the woods, you'd better be damned sure you can justify it when the bill comes in.

'Well,' I said, as Ed and I rinsed out our cups and headed for the door, 'I'm backing this.' I patted my stomach.

He looked at me and pulled a face. 'Meaning?'

'Gut instinct, buddy. I've just got this feeling in here that we're going to have them.'

'You mean tonight?'

'Soon.'

'Mike, I didn't want to tell you this, but . . .'

'What?'

'You had a gut instinct about York City this time last year, and look what happened to them.'

For some weeks now we'd run to a pattern on the night shift. All of us – Jayne, Fordy, me and Ed, Chris if he was out on patrol – would make a point of checking what we thought were likely targets for this Sunset outfit. Everywhere from little out-of-town places to the big supermarkets in Malton town centre. We'd check the doors and windows, make sure all was safely locked up and the security lights working, look around for suspect vehicles parked nearby, and generally put on a bit of a show for anyone who might be watching. Flying the flag, as we call it. Then we'd try and get back to as many premises as possible later in the night, just in case. But in an area the size of Ryedale, you soon started thinking needles and haystacks. What we needed was for Lady Luck to pay us a call. Because this was the sort of gang who would lie in wait for you, watching, taking notes, ready to pounce when your guard was down. Any little thing we noticed we'd feed into the intelligence network. Piece by piece a picture would emerge of the people we were looking for. That was the idea, anyway – but my goodness it was slow progress.

'Y'know what? I reckon something's in the air,' I said. We were driving out along the Castle Howard road. We'd just had a second look at the supermarkets in Castlegate and then Jackson's in Newbiggin, and were on our way towards Terrington. One of my Country Watch members had called in to say he thought he'd spotted a couple of lampers – men with dogs and torches – probably looking for hares in the stubble-fields. 'Did you see that latest intelligence report?'

Ed yawned. 'Which one was that, Mike?' He was losing interest. I could tell. But when a case like this comes up I'm like a dog with a bone. I won't rest – can't rest – until it's sorted.

'Officer over at Hambleton. Stopped a fellow on a pushbike, middle of nowhere.'

'No, must've missed that one.'

'Did a stop and search,' I said. 'Wanted to know what he was up to. Turns out he's from Middlesbrough, and there he is cycling through the woods yon side of Easingwold.'

'No law against that, is there?'

'Yeah, right. At four in the morning? With a walkie-talkie in his pocket?'

'Oh.'

'Aye, reckons he's trying to get fit for the Great North Run. I mean, the crap they come out with. Anyway, they got a name off him, and when they fed it into the computer it threw up a link to the Sunset lot.'

'What sort of link?'

'Known associate of.'

'Not much, is it?'

'All part of the jigsaw, mate. You mark my words, Ed, the net is closing.'

'That's what I like about you, Mike. The irrepressible optimist. Glass always half full.'

We were through Coneysthorpe now, slowing down before crossing the long, straight, tree-lined avenue that divides the Castle Howard estate.

'You've got to hand it to them,' Ed said. 'They're a very professional outfit we're dealing with.'

'Oh, don't get me wrong. There's a part of me has a sneaking admiration for them. I mean, it's all clever stuff, isn't it? Reconnaissance mission, a look-out on a bike – more or less silent, more or less invisible. You hear someone coming and you sling it over a hedge; and you've got your radio link to feed your oppos all sorts of information – like our bloody movements, for a start. Aye, they're a smart bunch of lads okay. But sooner or later they'll get over-confident. Tell me a gang that hasn't, in the end.'

Our ride out to Terrington didn't bear much fruit. We spent the better part of an hour cruising around the lanes, concentrating on the stubble-fields and the edges of the woods, before we finally caught up with a couple of suspects from Cleveland just as they were putting their dogs in the back of a Jeep. But apart from the fact that they were carrying lamps there was nothing to incriminate them – a fact they were quick to point out to us. They knew where they stood and were cocky enough with it. Even so, I couldn't resist having my say. 'Yeah,' I said, 'maybe you are just exercising the dogs this time, but I know what you'll be up to first chance you get. And don't you worry – Pannett's the name, and I'll be watching out for you. We don't want your type in North Yorkshire.'

Ed was a bit taken aback by the way I spoke to them. 'You in the habit of talking to people that way?' he asked, after we'd watched them drive off.

'Not at all,' I said. 'I'm Mr Nice Guy, I am. I try to get people onside. I'm all for – what's that new word? Inclusion?'

'Inclusivity, mate.'

'Aye well, that's my middle name. But when it comes to outsiders, thinking they can ride roughshod? No, I'm sorry, bud. They need the hard word. I don't want 'em on my patch and I'm not afraid to tell them so.'

'Sort of – exclusivity, like?'

'You could say that, Ed, aye . . .'

We drove slowly back towards town, going the long way through Ganthorpe and Welburn. It was a clear night and a bright half-moon was illuminating the fields, some of them stripped bare and awaiting the plough, others heavy with ripe corn. We'd just turned onto the main road and I was starting to think about home – and bed – when the call came in.

'*Control to all units. We have a call from a security guard at Jackson's supermarket in Newbiggin. Suspected burglars on premises.*'

'I don't believe it!' I shouted, as I put my foot down and accelerated towards Golden Hill. 'We checked the bloody place twice already. C'mon, it isn't far from here. Let's have the bastards.'

'What's the betting the buggers were watching us?' Ed said, as he took out his gas and gave it a shake.

Within four or five minutes we were turning into Wheelgate, just behind Fordy and Jayne.

Ed got on the radio. 'We'll take the back and you do the front.' There was a blaze of light out the front of the shop, and the interior was all lit up. 'That'll be the security guard,' Ed said as we swung left off the road and made our way round to the rear. I had the headlight on full beam, lighting up the small car park and the shop's rear entrance.

'Ch-rist.'

You hear people say 'my jaw dropped' and you think it's just a figure of speech. But as I turned to Ed there he was, his mouth open, his chin hanging slack, staring past me at the rear wall of the building. There was a neat hole, about four feet square, with alternate bricks jutting out. For a moment I thought maybe they'd got the builders in, but then a light flashed and out came the security man, on all fours and clutching a torch.

'Oh, there you are, lads.' He straightened up and came towards us, brushing the dust out of his hair.

'What the bloody hell's happened here then?' I asked him. We were out of the car and walking towards the hole. Sometimes you can hardly believe what you're seeing.

'Guess they tried the door and couldn't get in.' The security man looked at the hole and shrugged, then shook his head. 'Sorry, mate – but you have to laugh.'

'They still in there?'

'No. At least, I haven't seen owt. Unless they're hiding. I just came in ten minutes ago. Walked through the shop and never realised what had happened till I wandered into the manager's office.'

Ed pointed towards the hole. 'That where this leads then?'

'Aye.'

'What they done with the bricks? They haven't half-inched them too, have they?'

The security man jerked his head towards the hole. 'Inside.'

Just then we heard a vehicle turn off Castlegate and come towards where we were standing. It was the dog handler, from Scarborough.

'We'll let the canine corps go in first,' Ed said. 'Just in case. Wouldn't be the first time we've had an intruder tuck himself away out of sight.'

I was looking around the car park. 'There's no getaway car,' I said. 'Unless they're being really canny and have one parked out of the way.' Then I saw lights behind me. It was Chris Cocks.

As he wound his window down I heard him say, 'Bloody hell. They don't mess around, do they?' He got out of the car and walked towards us. 'This the Sunset lot, d'you reckon?'

The lad from Scarborough had the dog out of the van and straining at the lead. 'If it is,' he said, 'and they're inside, you're just in time to see my mate here round them up.'

'Who whistled you up?' I said.

'I was just on my way back from York when I heard the call.'

'Brilliant to have you here, mate. Let's hope they're still in there, but I doubt it somehow.'

Before we sent the dog in we surrounded the building, covering every possible exit. Then we waited, ears cocked, hoping to hear the bark of the dog indicating a find – or a stream of expletives from the cornered suspects. But not this time. We stood there for a full five minutes, then the dog reappeared at the hole, snuffling at the ground. 'There's nobody in there,' the handler said as he ducked down to climb back through the hole and lead the animal out of the building.

'Right,' I said. 'Let's go in.' We needed to double-check that the dog hadn't missed anyone, secure the scene for the SOCO, then find out what was missing from inside.

The security man opened up the back door and we followed him in. I looked around, expecting to see the usual empty booze shelf, the cigarettes scattered across the floor, but at a quick glance there was nothing to suggest that anybody had been in the place. It wasn't until we entered the manager's office that the picture started to emerge. There on the desk, neatly piled up, were the missing bricks, with the breeze blocks from the inner wall stacked on the floor beside them. The tiles around the hole were covered with orange dust marked with footprints and deep gouges. 'Don't be treading in that,' I said, as the security man stepped forward. 'Scene of crime. We need to get that taped off, Ed. Already got dog prints all over.'

But they weren't listening. The security man was standing pointing to an empty square of floor on the other side of the desk, under a set of shelves. You could see by the colour of the tiles that something that should have been there no longer was.

'The safe,' he said. 'They've taken the bloody safe.'

'That explains why they came in round the back then,' Jayne said.

'Shit,' I said. 'I wonder how much was in it.'

'Probably the entire weekend's cash takings,' the security man said. 'Doesn't usually get collected till Monday morning.'

'What d'you reckon?' Ed asked me a few moments later as we went back outside to take a look around. 'Our friends from up north again?'

I looked up at the CCTV camera that covered the front of the shop. Like the others, its lens was smothered in white foam. 'It's got all the hallmarks of the Sunset crew,' I said. 'There's no doubt about it. The thieving . . . You got to hand it to them, though. Clever as a cartload of monkeys.'

'And cheeky with it. I mean, all that chipping away. You'd think someone would have heard.'

'I dunno.' We walked back to the hole in the wall and looked around the empty car park. The nearest dwellings weren't that far away. 'Assuming they had the van here, all they had to do was gun the engine for a minute or two. I mean, once you've got the first brick out the rest come pretty easy.' We went back to the car and got the blue and white police tape out. 'But trust me, Ed, they will come unstuck. They always do in the end.'

As I tied the tape off on a wheelie bin, I heard Chris on the radio, ensuring that Control were circulating the details to crews in neighbouring areas. They would be watching routes in and out of Ryedale for any likely vehicles.

But that was little consolation to me at that stage. What a bloody nerve this gang had! To think that I'd been in the same car park earlier on in the evening. They must have been keeping obs on me. It must have taken at least an hour for them to chip away and remove the bricks, and then they must have had a right job on moving the safe. And that wasn't a one-man job. Far from it. That's what was frightening: that they could be so cocksure. It was blatantly obvious to me that they had considered the chances of being apprehended and decided that they could deal with a couple of country bobbies if they needed to.

It must have been four thirty when we showed up at the supermarket. We were still there at just after seven, when the SOCO arrived with Des the CID man. We briefed them and left them to it. We were all ready for our beds.

I was off the next two days and would then be going onto a day shift, so I grabbed a couple of hours in bed and was up by half eleven. Walt was supposed to be coming round with an industrial-strength strimmer and we were going to tackle the undergrowth together. I was just tucking into my cornflakes when he showed up with his best brown suit on, and a rather fetching trilby hat to match.

'Now then, Walter! You finally decided to go for it, did you?'

'What d'you mean, lad?'

'You're gonna make an honest woman of her, then? I was

just saying to Ann last night, it's time old Walt and that Muriel tied the knot.'

'Nay be buggered,' he said. 'Getting hitched? At my age? I've too much bloody sense. I'm off to t'races at York.' He stood in the doorway, watching me butter my toast. 'Aye, and eat up, lad, cos you're coming wi' me.'

'Walt, there's a jungle to clear out there. I'm under orders.'

He pulled a shiny pocket-watch on a silver chain from his waistcoat and flipped it open. 'Aye,' he said, 'and so'll them hosses be if we don't crack on. It's midday already and first race is two o'clock.'

'But what about me undergrowth?'

'You back what I back, young fellow-me-lad, and you'll be able to pay somebody else to fettle this lot while you sit on your log there watching them, with a glass of beer in your hand. Now, eat up and get your car out of t'garage.'

'Oh, it's my petrol we're using, is it?'

'Listen, lad, it ain't many fellows get to go to the races with their own personal tipster.' He tapped the side of his nose. 'I've had word for one today. It come straight from t'stable.'

'Aye, like that pig that's just flown past,' I said under my breath. 'All right, you win. Is it a best bib and tucker job then? We in the county stand with all the nobs?'

'No, it's t'course side, on the grass. Can't have you paying them fancy prices – not on a constable's wage, lad. Maybe when you catch up wi' that lass of yours . . . Besides, we've to pick up another party yet – and you won't catch 'im in a suit.'

'Who's that then?'

'Soapy. I told him we'd call round for him, so come on, let's get moving shall we?'

By the time we'd battled our way down the A64 and reached

town it was getting on for one o'clock. Soapy was in the back seat with bits of newspaper scattered around him, concentrating hard, with his pencil working overtime. Every so often he'd punctuate the silence with some amazing form statistic or a speed rating – none of which meant anything to me – or he'd give us the name of some horse who'd been shipped all the way from Ireland and had to be kept an eye on. Walt was sitting beside me, getting more and more fidgety as we edged our way down Knavesmire Road a couple of car lengths at a time with the sun beating down. 'We're going to be late,' he said. 'Them fellers in t'yellow jackets there – can't you pull rank on 'em? Flash yer warrant or sommat?'

'Come on, Walt. That's not how it works, and you know it isn't.'

'Well, squeeze up a bit, lad. Get under t'shade of that tree there before we all start melting.'

I edged the car forward to within six inches of the one in front. 'Better?'

'And what about your lass? She's in York now, isn't she? Couldn't she fettle it so's you go to t'head of t'queue? There has to be some sort of perks, else the job ain't worth having.'

'You sprang this on me, Walt, remember? So don't be complaining. I was going to put in a day's gardening, and I seem to remember some grumpy old bugger from up the hill was going to help me.'

But Walt was too busy reading the signs on the roadside. 'You'd think they'd have a special one for pensioners. They put us in that field wi' all them other folk, we'll have too far to walk. We'll miss t'first race at this rate.'

By the time we bumped our way across the grass and into the parking area, I was ready to concede that Walt might have had a point. 'I mean, what's Ann been up to all this time working in York and she can't even get us into the owners and trainers section? I shall have to have words, mate. What do you say, Soapy?'

'No worries,' he said as he followed me and Walt towards the turnstiles. 'We've twenty minutes to go yet. Job's a good 'un.'

'Picked your winners, have you?' I asked.

He grinned and held up his *Racing Post*. 'They're all in here, cock-bod.'

'Oh aye?'

'Aye. All you have to do is find 'em.'

Ten minutes later we were through the turnstiles and making our way across the broad expanse of grass where the bookies were lined up, thirty or forty of them in a double row. Behind them two giant TV screens showed the horses circling the parade ring, and further back we could see the beer, tea and fast-food stands, along with the tents they put up for corporate hospitality. All around us people had spread out their picnic rugs, folding tables, chairs and windbreaks and were cracking open food hampers, beer and chilled bottles of wine. Across the track the grandstands rose, tier upon tier, into a bright blue sky and down below the crowds milled around in the sunshine.

'Right,' said Soapy, 'I'm away yonder to do a spot of price comparison.' He glanced around as a party of women in short dresses and wide hats teetered by on high heels. 'Aye, and maybe just check out the form,' he added, running his hand through his hair.

'Meet us over by t'old Tote board then,' Walt said. Then he turned and grabbed my arm. 'C'mon,' he said. 'You and me want to be over here first off.' He led me down to the rail, right opposite the parade ring where the horses were being led round by their stable lads and lasses. 'We'll weigh the buggers up and pick us a nice winner, eh?' he said.

'What we after, mate? I'm no judge of horseflesh.'

'You want a calm sort, and you want a good shape. Aye, and you want good proportions too. Then there's your coat. That can give you a pointer.'

'Walt, I'll leave it in your capable hands. Can't see 'em properly from this distance anyway.'

'Don't worry, they'll be out in a minute and cantering down to the start. Here they come now, look. First couple. Now, that's a beauty, isn't it? Don't like that one . . . too much condition on him. That's a nervy type, looks a bit green . . .'

'Tell you what,' I said, as a big grey went past, tossing its head. 'I fancy that beast. The number three, look.'

Walt wrinkled his nose and checked his racecard. 'Female jockey?' He shook his head. 'Never trust 'em.'

'Aye, but don't forget I'm living with a lady rider now, you know. Maybe I should be sticking up for 'em.'

'You do as you please, lad. But the pair of 'em look temperamental to me.' He ran his finger down the list of runners again. 'No form neither. Won a seller at Catterick last July and hasn't made t'frame since.' He looked up as another horse cantered past. 'Now, this here's more like it. Good hind quarters, nice action – and see how he holds his head high? What's the number, mate, I missed it.'

'Twelve, Walt. Number twelve.'

'That'll do me.' He slipped me a five-pound note. 'See what price he is, and if it's short, a fiver to win. Double figures, two fifty each way. And I'll see you over by t'Tote board yonder.'

I hurried over to the bookies. Walt's choice was favourite.

Even as the fellow in front of me placed fifty quid on the nose, the bookie was altering the price from 5-2 to 2-1. I looked for my number three horse. 33-1, and now out to 40s. That did it. With the racecourse commentator calling out, '*Going behind the stalls and starting to load,*' I handed him the money. 'Five to win, number twelve,' I said. 'And the same again.' There was no way I was going to throw away a hard-earned fiver on a complete no-hoper. I'd stick with Walt. If he couldn't pick them, nobody could.

I slipped the tickets in my shirt pocket and made my way across to where Walt stood watching the big screen as the last of the field of thirteen was put into the starting stalls.

'*Last one in, and . . . they're off, over ten furlongs in this opening handicap worth eight thousand pounds to the winner . . .*' From where we stood at the top of the bank we could just see the horses, making their way down the far side of the course, then passing the woods before they negotiated the long sweeping left-hand bend that would bring them towards the top of the home run.

Five furlongs out our horse went wide, picked up nicely and stole a length on the field. 'Aye, he's maybe found a bit of better ground out there,' said Walt. 'C'mon, lad, we can watch the finish down here.' I followed him as he picked his way nimbly between the groups seated on the grass, hopping across picnic blankets and arriving at the rail, about a furlong from the finishing line, just as the horses came into view.

'He's got it!' I shouted as they thundered past in a blaze of colour. Ours was two lengths to the good and going flat out. Walt turned to watch the final stages on the big screen, grinning from ear to ear, and I'd already got our tickets out to see what we were going to collect. But in the final half-furlong the whole field started to close rapidly. Suddenly they were spread out across the track, five wide and all seeming to cross the line together.

'*Photograph, photograph.*'

'How long have we to wait for that?' I groaned, as Walt stood there on tiptoes, watching the replay on the big screen.

He pursed his lips, and shook his head. 'Looks close,' he said. 'Ours is in there okay . . . Might have got there, but by golly it's close, lad. Could even be a dead heat.'

'Can't see the numbers, can you?'

But before he could answer the announcer was on again. '*And the result of the photograph . . .*'

'C'mon,' I said, come *on* . . .' All around us people were on their toes, clutching their tickets. A lass in a pink dress had her eyes shut and was holding onto her mate's arm.

'*First number three, second number twelve, third number one and the fourth horse was . . .*' Among the curses and groans there was a single shriek as the lady in pink jumped up and threw her arms around her mate; otherwise there was silence.

'Number bloody three?' I gasped. 'Walt, that's the one you told me was no good. The one you said not to back.'

'I said you mek your own mind up, lad.'

I was ripping the tickets into as many pieces as I could when I felt a whack on my back that made me scatter the shreds of paper all over the grass. 'Now then, cock-bod. Forty to one, eh? Were you on it?'

'Was I hell,' I said. 'I was all set to back it and this bugger put me off. We were on the second, both of us. What about you?'

He stood there grinning, and flashed a wad of ten-pound notes.

'You jammy . . .'

He looked at me, sort of puzzled. 'What's up, don't you remember? That was the hoss old Ronnie gave us at the show.'

'You what?'

'Aye, he said it'd be a big price and you weren't to be put off. I had twenty quid each way. Off to a flyer, cock-bod. That's nine hundred and odd I've collected. Hey, and I tell you what, mate, them bookies weren't happy. Get in!' He stopped laughing. 'Cheer up, Mike. Early days yet. Plenty chances to get your money back.' He looked at Walt, who was already sliding away to check on the runners in the next.

'No good blaming him, Mike. You know what they say: always back your own judgement.'

I took Soapy's advice – and by the end of the day I was wishing I hadn't. Walt stuck to his principles as a paddock-watcher and found three winners. I stuck to my gut instincts and ended up . . . well, gutted.

But it had been a nice little interlude – if an expensive one. We wound up the day at the Jolly Farmers, where Soapy spread his winnings all across the counter and treated us to a plate of game pie and chips, plus a pint of bitter. By the time Ann joined us I'd put the disappointments of the day behind me. And next morning Walt showed up bright and early with his strimmer to help me clear away the brambles and nettles. He didn't mention the forty-to-one shot, for which I was grateful; just put on his goggles and gloves, got on with the job and left me a nice pile of debris to burn when I felt in the mood.

When it came time to go back to work after my two days off, I was fully refreshed and ready to renew hostilities with the Sunset Gang. At least, that's what I told Des the CID man when I went to ask what he'd got from the scene of crime.

'Not a great deal,' he said. 'A few footprints, which could be useful when we finally collar them. And there's these.' He brought up some grainy images on his screen. 'Got them before they sprayed the camera lenses.'

Three separate figures could be seen approaching the supermarket entrance. You couldn't see their faces, but you could make out their general build. One in particular stood out: a tall fellow with a domed head, his hair tied in a kind of top-knot. 'Thinks he's a bloody pirate,' Des muttered as he tried to enhance the image, 'but at least it gives us something.' Indeed it did. It was all grist to the mill: if you can tell a suspect that you have footage of him at a particular job he's more likely to cough to it or add it to his TICs – that is, the list of crimes he asks to be Taken Into Consideration. The other useful piece of filmed evidence – and the one that seemed to identify this lot as the gang we were after – was of a familiar old van that had been used in one of their previous jobs.

'Progress,' I said, as Ed and I prepared to go out on patrol. 'Slow but sure.'

'And have you heard the news?' he said.

'What news? What they been up to this time?'

'Ah,' he grinned. 'So you haven't. Remember what we were saying last week about resources – funding and that?'

'You mean the lack of.'

'Yeah, well, pin back your ears, old lad. It turns out that Des has been taking the lead and is working with a dedicated girl from the crime analysis team.'

'Is that right? They've kept that a bit quiet.'

'Yep, they've been linking up with Cleveland, Teesside and Northumbria. And they're hopeful they'll soon have enough for a conspiracy to burgle charge.'

'That's brilliant . . .'

'Yeah, they reckon it's taken a fair few weeks to piece it all together.'

I felt buoyed up by the news. Maybe we'd get somewhere now. But of course, that's when Sod's Law kicked in. After a spate of two or three burglaries within a matter of days, everything had gone quiet. We found ourselves in that familiar but odd position of hoping the villains would break cover and pull another job. But a full week went by and there was no movement. Nothing at all.

I was on nights again. It was a Tuesday. I remember it well because on the way into town I'd seen a huge full moon rising – what you'd call a harvest moon, I suppose. Real ghostly, and a sort of ruddy pink colour. And then when I got to the station everyone was sat around cutting slices from a homemade chocolate cake. I don't know what goes through people's minds, but it's quite surprising the amount of goodies we get brought in for us. Sometimes it's the cleaners, sometimes it's the wife or mother of some member of the public we've helped out. In this case it was Ed's missus – and she can cook. By the time Chris Cocks came in to do the briefing you'd have needed the combined forces of the CID, the SOCO and the forensic science boys to find a trace of her latest creation.

After some routine notices, Chris had news that made us sit up and pay attention. 'It looks like our friends have emerged from their lair again,' he said. 'The Sunset Gang. Pulled another burglary up in the Cleveland area. Retail premises. And they're getting very smart now. This was another one with no forced entry.' He looked around to see that we were all listening.

'How'd they pull that off then?' Jayne asked.

'You'll like this. An informant tells us that they installed a miniature camera. Must've just done it in ordinary shop hours. Aimed it at the keypad where the staff turn on the alarm, and filmed them putting the code in. Came back at their leisure and Bob's your uncle. They got off with about eight grand worth of electrical goods. Turned the entire system off.'

'Very smart,' I said to Ed as we made our way to the car. 'You got to hand it to them. They're a very professional outfit.'

'Yeah well, let's not get carried away, buddy. They may be clever, but they're thieving scum all the same. Let's hope we can get them put away, eh?'

Town was very quiet that night, and a little after eleven we were called out to Helmsley to investigate a burglar alarm that had gone off. We had a look around, but we didn't find anything untoward – although of course these last few weeks we'd been getting jumpy. One of the things we suspected the Sunset Gang of doing was setting off alarms, lying in wait to see what the response was, then setting them off again an hour or two later. They knew that if the alarm sounded a third time people would shrug it off as faulty and not even call us out, unless it was to get us to contact the key holder. At the same time, they would be making a note of how long it was before anyone showed up. So, after we'd investigated this one we parked up a few hundred yards away and waited for half an hour or so. Then we poured some coffee from our flasks and waited some more.

'Funny how it shrinks as the night goes on,' I said.

'I beg your pardon.' Ed coughed and spat out a mouthful of brew back into his mug.

'Look at it.' I pointed at the moon, high in the sky now with a halo around it.

'Oh, that.' He dabbed at the front of his uniform with a tissue. 'Wondered what the bloody hell you were on about.'

'It was a proper harvest moon when I was driving in this evening. Big fat thing.'

'Oh aye . . .' Ed put his mug on the dashboard, picked up a paper and started flicking through the sports pages.

'Must be the earth's atmosphere magnifying it. And now it looks quite small. D'you ever wonder how it stays there? I mean, why it doesn't fall to earth, or fly off into space?'

'I lie awake many a night, Mike, worrying myself to death about it.' He folded up the paper and threw it into the back seat. 'No, course I don't. Look, it's been going round planet earth since the dawn of time. If it is shrinking it's shrinking very slowly. It'll see us out.'

'Ed, you're missing my point. What I meant was—' But Ed was leaning forward, turning up the volume on the radio and shushing me. The lads at Easingwold were reporting an incident that had taken place right under their noses.

'*Yeah, he was on his way home from work. Saw three men loading boxes into a van outside the Co-op.*'

'*Okay – and let me get this right. He called you but you couldn't pursue because . . .*'

'*Because they'd let our tyres down.*'

There was a moment's silence. I stifled an expletive. Ed held his hand up, frowning.

'*You mean all of them?*'

'*Correct. All three police vehicles in the yard, over.*'

'*Are you needing assistance?*'

'*Proceeding to scene in own vehicles, over.*'

Ed couldn't wait to cut in. 'Romeo Mike 23 to Control, over.'

'*Go ahead, over.*'

'We're on our way from Helmsley on the A170, over.'

'It's like a bloody Carry On film!' I said as I buckled up and turned out on the Kirkbymoorside road.

'Keystone bloody Cops, more like it. Wonder which way they'll go.'

Control were asking themselves the same question, and organising as many units as possible to cover potential routes out of the area.

'This is where you and I have to think like criminals, Ed. Assuming they'll head north . . . you wouldn't go the A19 way, surely?'

Ed had half an ear on what I was saying, half an ear on the radio. 'They've put a vehicle at Stillington in case they go that way and there's a York traffic car on the A19 at Shipton. Thirsk lot are holding the A19 up near Sessay.'

'It's a bloody guessing game,' I said. 'They've still got plenty of options. Could go cross-country to Whitby, or maybe out this way, through Helmsley, then across the Moors to Stokesley.'

'In which case maybe we should stay put.'

'Yeah, and then they decide to go through Hutton-le-Hole and Castleton.' I banged the wheel in frustration. 'Manpower, mate. It always comes down to that. We need a car up at Chop Gate, somewhere like that. And the bugger of it is, every minute we head in one direction they could be two miles the other way.'

'*Zulu Papa 42 to Control, over.*'

'That's the armed response lads, from Thirsk.'

'*Go ahead, over.*'

'*We've just been passed by an Audi 80 travelling at speed, east up Sutton Bank on the A170. We're going to turn round and try and get behind it. Any other units to back up?*'

'Right,' said Ed, 'Romeo Mike 23 to Control, show us making our way from Helmsley, over.'

We left town at speed and headed west on the A170. The adrenaline was in full flow. This had got to be them. Over the radio we heard that a traffic unit from Thirsk wasn't far behind.

'Keep your foot down, Mike. Quicker we get there . . .'

'I tell you what, Ed, it's times like this I wish we could still carry a stinger.'

'Aye, and deploy it.'

'What the hell were they thinking of?'

It was only recently that our top brass had decided to restrict their use to traffic officers.

'All that training I did, and here we are ahead of the game and every chance we'll end up watching them fly past us.'

'I reckon we'll have 'em, Mike.'

Ed was listening intently to the radio. The ARV and the traffic cars were now behind the Audi and were going to attempt to stop it.

It's a decent stretch of road out there, with excellent visibility at night, and we were soon doing ninety or a hundred. Within a few minutes the horizon was lit up by twinkling blue and white lights.

'Re-sult!' The suspects had pulled over. There was the Audi, its nose angled into the roadside verge, its lights illuminating a field of ripe wheat.

The ARV boys were just getting out of their car. As I opened my driver's side door they were shining their lamps in through the driver's window. 'Right, out of the car. You two – not him!' As well as the driver and front-seat companion, there was a third man in the rear. The first thing you try to do when you've stopped a group is to separate them, and keep them separated.

If they're novices it'll rattle them, and whoever they are it'll stop them concocting a story – or hatching a plan.

The driver was the first to stumble out, shielding his eyes from the Dragon Light as one of the ARV officers shouted, 'Put your hands out in front of you.'

'We haven't done f*** all, so you can piss off.'

I recognised the speaker immediately from the little knot of hair tied up on top of his domed head. He looked larger in the flesh – and more frightening. He was taller than the ARV lad and was eyeballing him. But it didn't cut any ice.

'Well, that's to be established, isn't it?' said the ARV man. 'Meanwhile you are going to be detained while we search you and the vehicle.'

He was met with a torrent of obscenity from all three at once. My experience from the Met told me that this was a sign that we were not dealing with ordinary criminals. Certain villains – especially the hardened cases – will turn aggressive as a deliberate tactic, trying to intimidate you and put you on the back foot. But these three were in for a bit of a shock. They had several seasoned police officers to deal with, and we weren't at all fazed by a few verbal threats. We decided right away to get all three in handcuffs, with Ed and me taking hold of the male in the back seat. Once they realised that we meant business, they quietened down. But our search revealed nothing of note, other than their mobile phones.

We put Mr Top-Knot in our car, his mate in the ARV vehicle, and the driver in the traffic car. Each one was left with an officer watching him while the remaining officers began to search the Audi.

'Bastards!' Ed had swung the boot open, expecting to find the night's haul – or at least a few tools of the trade. But it was empty. Clean as a whistle.

It was a blow, but on the basis of all the evidence, and the circumstances, we had grounds for arresting all three on suspicion of burglary. All we could do now was hope that the forensic team would come up with something to link them with the Easingwold job.

'Looks like we're in for a long night, Ed,' I said as we watched the ARV boys head off towards town.

'Aye, but if we get a result, who cares? This might be the breakthrough we've been hoping for.'

We took all three suspects, and their car, to Northallerton. While they were booked into custody the car was searched more thoroughly. In fact 'search' doesn't really tell the whole tale. It was taken apart piece by piece. The seats were removed, the door panels, the floor and the dashboard. And in the end we struck gold. We found an assortment of incriminating items ranging from latex surgical gloves to walkie-talkies, all hidden away inside the door panels.

That was great, but there remained the matter of loot. Where was it? It took a while to get to the bottom of that mystery, but it came out in the end that the gang were using a second vehicle, one of the vans that the CCTV had picked up previously. They'd parked it in a residential street not far away, and we were led to it by an observant resident who'd called in to say it looked out of place. The gang had planned to leave it there overnight, then drive it off the next day when there was plenty of traffic about and it wouldn't arouse any interest. It turned out that they'd used this simple but clever tactic on a regular basis.

When you make an arrest – especially after the drama and excitement of such a significant stop as we'd had up above Sutton Bank – you'd like to feel you could close the book. In a film, that would be it. The bad guys would be led away in cuffs to serve their time, the cops would go home to their wives and sweethearts as the credits roll. But in reality the capture and arrest is only the start of the lengthy and tedious business of securing a conviction and hopefully, in this case a lengthy custodial sentence. First thing, the CID had to interview our suspects. And because we only had suspicion, rather than actual evidence linking them to any particular crime, they were released on bail. That can be maddeningly frustrating for everyone involved, but on this occasion we only had to wait a few days for good news to come through. Enough evidence had been gathered from the various crime scenes – matching footprints, CCTV images and so on – to convince the Crown Prosecution Service that we had enough to press charges. All three captives, plus a couple of associates who were picked up later, were charged with conspiracy to burgle and remanded in custody. Faced with the evidence, they all asked for a number of other offences to be taken into consideration.

It had been a long drawn-out business, but in the end we'd got a result, although we would still have to wait – weeks, perhaps months – to see how things worked out when the case came to court, and what sentence might be handed down. It had been a genuine team effort for Ryedale and the region, with a great debt owed to Des and the crime analyst, who had pieced it all together and kept plugging away until we brought it to a successful conclusion. It all went to prove what I like to say: If you don't catch 'em one night, or even the next, don't panic: they will come again.

Chapter 8

A Dark Night

There's a lot of satisfaction to be had in seeing a gang of serial burglars rounded up and, hopefully, put away for a spell. Some people think I'm a bit old-fashioned, but I get a real buzz out of helping to piece the evidence together and actually track a bunch of villains down – especially when we've more or less caught them in the act. Call it the thrill of the chase. It's part of the dream many of us had when we joined the police as raw youngsters. You see something wrong being done, and you want to do something about it. You work out who's responsible, decide how best to deal with them, then put your plan into action. And when you have to take offenders like that out of circulation, then good riddance. One way or another, you've left your community a little bit safer and a little bit better off. Once in a while you do the criminal some good as well, and manage to put him back on the straight and narrow.

But there are some cases you work on which bring you no joy and little satisfaction. Domestic assaults are high up the list of cases I'd rather not deal with. By the time we get called in it's usually too late to salvage the relationship – or the family unit.

Yes, you're glad to have the job done, but there's never the same satisfaction as you get when you bring a burglar to justice, for instance. You can't dust yourself down and tell yourself everything's sorted. There's still the victim to think about, and the aftermath. It's not always the end of the story when the offender is prosecuted. Family ties will have been severed. It can be messy, rather than clean cut. I'm not saying that people who've had their houses broken into or their property stolen aren't traumatised – plenty of them are, in their different ways, and it can take them a long time to get over it. Some never quite do. I've dealt with some victims of violent crime, who just can't function normally for years afterwards. In a few cases, thankfully quite rare, they never really get over it, and have to live with emotional as well as physical scars, often in dread of their assailant being released, scared to go out of the house. In some, extreme, cases they lose their jobs. As a policeman dealing with people who've committed violent assaults, you have to rein in your personal feelings. You've seen the victim, and here you are face to face with the perpetrator. All sorts of things go through your mind, human, instinctive feelings, but of course you're an officer of the law, and you have to behave as such. It's not always easy, but, to do a professional job and ensure the best case is put before the court, it has to be done.

And then there are the sexual assaults. These can be very difficult and testing to deal with, but some officers do volunteer to undergo specialist training in the area. Some even volunteer to work on specialist units dealing with child abuse. Brave souls, I'd say. It is not an area of work I would choose to do day in, day out. What you have, as often as not, is a traumatised victim who's going to be suffering long after the case is closed – if it is – and an offender who, let's face it, is mentally unwell and in need of psychiatric help.

We were getting towards the end of August. The summer holidays were still in full swing, but the shops were full of 'back to school' offers, the new football season was well under way, and the previous few days the weather had been cool and windy with heavy showers. It was definitely back-endish, as we say in Yorkshire. But on the Friday it had calmed down, the sun had come out and everyone was looking forward to a settled weekend. Except me. I was working the late turn, four in the afternoon to two in the morning, or until such time as we got on top of things. You could never tell when you'd get home from that shift, and Ann knew not to wait up for me.

I was paired up with Jayne. She was quieter than usual as we did the rounds in town, and when we got back to the station at about midnight she left me to mash the tea while she went and struggled with her in-tray. Everyone at the station had at least one of those. They're a bit bigger than A4 size and about three inches deep. They're made of plastic and they slide into a large wooden frame. There were about fifty in total, each with the name and number of the owner on the front, together with various added stickers and graffiti reflecting the character of the owner – or maybe the football team he or she supported. We were all allotted one tray, but those who claimed to be the busiest – or who, like me, had additional duties, such as wildlife crime – managed to obtain a second. There was no way that the trays could contain all the paperwork generated by modern-day policing methods, so they were always stuffed full, if not overflowing, much to the annoyance of the shift sergeant. What we all dreaded was him coming round and 'spinning' the trays. It was a normal part of supervision, designed to ensure that you were on top of your work, but there was always a risk, if you'd had a busy run, that you might have missed something.

Mind you, I had devised my own strategy to keep prying hands off my tray, as Chris Cocks learned when I mentioned to him that I'd put a mousetrap in it. 'Well,' I said, 'there's a lot of vermin about, Chris. And our job is to catch 'em, isn't it?' He took it all in good part. And as to whether there really was a mousetrap in there – well, it was that old saying again: for me to know, for him to find out.

When I came into work that afternoon I saw that some joker had moved Jayne's tray from the bottom of the rack to the top, some seven feet above ground and almost out of reach. As Jayne stood on tiptoes to reach for it I could hear her chuntering and fully expected a volley of expletives, but somehow she managed to get it down without spilling the pile of papers, which was topped by a fat brown envelope.

'What you grinning about?' she said. 'Did you put this up there?'

'Not me, Jayne. But I'd keep my eye on Fordy if I were you. Anyway' – I sat down and shoved her mug across the table – 'what's that lot?'

She was sifting through a pile of documents, looking as glum as I'd ever seen her. 'Sergeant's exam, part one. Managed to get hold of some old papers.' She sighed, put them to one side, and wrapped her hands round her tea.

'You're still going for it then?'

'Oh yeah, course I am. Set meself a deadline, didn't I?'

'And when's that? This year?'

'It was going to be. Might be next year now, though.' She flicked the pile of papers. 'You start going through this lot and you realise what you're up against.'

I couldn't help taking an interest in what Jayne was doing. All those years as a copper and I'd never really thought about promotion, but here she was – been with us about five minutes and all set to take the sergeant's exam. I reached across, picked up a sample of the part one, multiple-choice paper and scanned it.

'Hm – well, I could answer the first one,' I said. 'And the next. Not sure about question six though . . .'

'What's that then? Let's have a look.' I passed it across to her and she read it aloud. '"A female is pushing a pushchair containing her two-year-old child when she is approached by a male. He holds a knife towards the child and demands her purse. Has the male committed A – Theft, B – Robbery, C – blackmail or D – all of the above?"'

'Isn't it the CPS's job to decide, Jayne?' I said. She frowned and curled the edge of the paper with her thumb and forefinger. 'Anyway,' I continued, 'he sounds like a nasty sod and needs locking up.'

'Thanks, Mike, that's really helpful.'

'Sorry, mate. End of a long day and all that.' I looked at my watch. 'Should be off home soon,' I said. At which point Chris Cocks came in.

'Got a job for you, I'm afraid.'

'You would have,' I said. Then I looked up. I didn't like the expression on his face. Chris tends to go through life wearing a permanent grin, but right now he was looking very sombre indeed.

'Go on. Let's have it.'

'We've got a very distressed female up at the theme park.' He glanced at Jayne, who still had her head in her exam papers. 'Allegation of rape. She's staying with friends. Sounds serious. If you go up with Jayne and see what's what, I'll make contact with the duty inspector, find out who our CID cover is tonight and give them the heads-up.'

Chris gave me the name of the party concerned and the person I had to contact up at the theme park. Jayne took a deep breath and puffed her cheeks out. 'Christ,' she said, then slid the papers back into the envelope. 'Guess we'd better get going then, eh?'

We went to the car in silence. There was nothing to say, and in any case my mouth was dry. This sort of thing is a rarity in Ryedale, thank God. I'd only ever been called out to one or two since I left the Met. But as soon as Chris told us what we were dealing with the memories came flooding back. Some of the incidents you handle are ingrained on your memory forever because of the level of violence used, or the circumstances in which they take place. The one that keeps coming back to me is a woman who'd been attacked by a man with a knife. She'd put up a fight, and in the process her hands had been horribly sliced up.

'I don't suppose you've dealt with a rape before,' I said as we drove along Old Maltongate, heading towards the bypass.

I couldn't hear Jayne's answer at first, and she had to clear her throat and repeat it. 'Yeah. I mean no. We covered it in training. That's about it.'

I was driving fast and my heart was thumping. I was wishing we'd had more details. What I'd learned from those cases in the Met was that rapes are frequently committed by people known to the victim. Sometimes it's date rape. Alcohol is often involved, of course, and sometimes you find that a drink has been spiked. Sometimes it'll be a current or former spouse or partner, which throws up a whole raft of issues. I found in the Met that you also got quite a few allegations from prostitutes, which again throws up complexities. They're all bad, but what you really dread are the ones committed by total strangers, where a woman has been grabbed, perhaps abducted, then viciously assaulted, or even murdered.

'Well, they can be really testing to deal with,' I said. 'It'll be good experience for you.' Jayne said nothing, just stared at the road ahead. Glancing to one side I caught her face in profile. I realised I'd forgotten how young she was. Probably no more than twenty-three or -four. 'You realise it'll most likely be down to you to do the talking?' I said.

'You mean with – like with the victim?'

'Yeah.' I eased the car onto the roundabout and over the bypass, past Eden Camp where the wings of the old Hurricane glinted in the moonlight. 'One of the joys of being a WPC, I'm afraid. Let's just hope it's not some bloody psycho we're looking for.'

It's only a six- or seven-minute run, along the main road and then a mile or so down the lane that runs through the village. Just time for me to run through things with Jayne, covering the procedure and the things she needed to think about. As well as trying to boost her confidence, it served to refresh my own memory of the procedures.

At the site entrance we were met by the security guard coming out of his cabin to raise the barriers. He told us that the girl was back in her caravan.

'Not alone, is she?' I said.

'No, no – she was down with a mate, they reckon. And family of some sort.'

'Any details of the offender yet?'

'Afraid not. She's in a right state.'

'Okay, where do we go?'

'You'll need someone to guide you in. It's a bit of a maze out there. I'll call the boss. He can take you down.' He went back into the cabin to use the radio.

The boss, when he arrived, was a big tall fellow. Six foot four, at a guess. He said his name was Graham. He gave us the number of the caravan, what row it was in and the name of the particular part of the estate where it was parked. 'What do you want?' he said. 'Shall I drive down in the van and you follow me?'

'You'll have to,' I said. 'I haven't a clue where we want to be.'

We followed him down the main drive, past the deserted carousels and the huge rollercoaster, silhouetted against a full moon. It was well gone midnight but there were still people in shorts and T-shirts strolling about the place looking happy and relaxed. It was a typical summer-holiday scene, except that someone, not far away, had been sexually assaulted.

We drove on into the caravan park. TVs flickered behind half-closed windows. Here and there people were sitting on the decking enjoying a late drink. One group, gathered around a barbecue, raised their beer bottles and waved at us as we cruised slowly past.

'Jayne,' I said, 'you need to get onto Chris, keep him up to speed.' I was thinking it would be good to keep her occupied. I could almost feel the tension coming off her. She was gnawing at her lip. 'And maybe call Control. Find out who else is coming up here. We may need extra hands, depending on what the score is.'

But she was already thinking ahead. 'So . . . am I going to go in on my own? To talk to this girl?'

'Yeah. I can't come with you. It's like I was saying when we drove up, you can't risk cross-contamination of evidence. You do that and the whole prosecution case goes down the toilet.'

I was making an assumption here. Sometimes you find that a female victim prefers to talk to a male officer. Not often, but I've known it happen. As to the issue of cross-contamination of evidence, there's a risk – however slight – that a hair or a fibre could be transmitted from a victim to an officer, and from there to a suspect. Or sometimes the defence will try to wreck a case by suggesting that that scenario could have happened. So the golden rule is that no officer should come into contact with both suspect and victim, nor visit the scene of the assault after having any contact with either of the parties. And if you put the victim in your vehicle, that's it: you can't transport the suspect. Jayne would deal with the victim on her own, which would leave me free and uncontaminated to deal with any offender who might still be nearby. So with a victim, a potentially violent offender and also a scene to deal with, we knew we'd need further officers and vehicles.

I saw Graham's brake lights glow red as he pulled up outside a caravan. The curtains were drawn but all the windows were illuminated. I could see two shadows moving about inside.

'Right, Jayne, you clear what you're after?'

'Yeah, think so.' She was counting out the points on her hand. 'What exactly is she alleging? Is the offender known to her? Who is he? And where can we find him?' She opened the door.

'Good luck,' I said. 'Got your mobile with you?'

She patted her hip pocket.

'Right. If you need to call me, use that. We don't really want to be discussing this over the open radio.'

As I watched her walk up the steps I saw a curtain twitch. As soon as she knocked on the door it opened, and I caught a glimpse of a middle-aged couple ushering her inside.

'*Control to 1015.*'

'Yeah, go ahead.'

'*Mike, you've got PC Ford and PC Cowans on their way. Should be with you in seven or eight minutes.*'

Fordy and Ed. Good, I thought. In a case like this I'd prefer to be dealing with our own lads. I got out of the car. Graham was lighting a cigarette and offered me one. 'Yeah, cheers,' I said. Pure habit. 'This your full-time job,' I asked him, 'or are you just here for the summer?'

'Year-round,' he said. 'Came as a casual about fifteen years ago and never left.'

'So do you know anything about what's happened?'

'Afraid not, we just got alerted by the family she's staying with.'

We chatted for a few minutes, but I was only half paying attention and eventually Graham got back in his car. I was wondering how Jayne was getting on, whether the girl was coherent or not, whether an ambulance would be needed. She'd surely let me know if she was struggling. But so far, I'd heard nothing from her.

A young couple walked by, arm in arm. The lad looked at me curiously. As the girl climbed the steps of a neighbouring caravan and fumbled in her bag for the key, she was caught in the glare of approaching headlights. I heard a car coming up behind me.

'What's the score?' It was Ed, pulling up alongside me.

I nodded towards the caravan. 'Jayne's in with the girl.'

'Any word on who the offender is?' Fordy asked, leaning across from the passenger side.

Before I could answer my mobile rang. 'Yeah, Jayne?'

She told me the girl was eighteen. She was called Debbie. 'She's very upset. I mean really, really distressed. To be fair Mike, she's also had a few to drink. She's down from Sunderland with her mate. And her mate's mum and dad. You can imagine the state they're in.'

'Christ yeah. Probably told her folks she'd be safe with them. So have you got the details from – Debbie, did you say?'

'Yeah, they come down yesterday, meet a couple of lads from the northeast, spend the afternoon with them and arrange to meet up tonight. They get along well, have a few drinks. Then Debbie decides to go back to the lads' tent.'

'On her own?'

'Yeah. Well, with this one lad. Anyway, they have a couple more drinks in the tent and next thing – well, it gets out of hand.'

'Is she injured? Any signs of assault?'

'She says not – and nothing visible at this stage.'

'Have you ascertained exactly what we're dealing with?'

'She's alleging rape. And we have a first disclosure to the best friend. She rang her as soon as she got out of the tent.'

'And have you spoken to her mate?'

'Yeah, she confirms that that's what Debbie told her. Although like Debbie she's – well, she's had way too much to drink. I've got the boy's name though.'

'Boy? Or man? What we talking about here?'

'She says he's about nineteen, twenty. I've got the name and a description.'

'Right, I've got my pen. Fire away.' I jotted down the details. 'And where did it take place, do you say?'

'At this lad's tent.'

'Right. Well, security should be able to help us identify which one it is. You stay with the girl and her parents. I'll get onto Control and get the ball rolling for the examination suite, yeah?'

'Will do.'

There was a lot to think about now. First off I got onto Control and confirmed that the girl was definitely alleging rape. That would trigger certain procedures and give everybody involved the chance to prepare themselves. Then I spoke to the night duty inspector and the on-call CID man, a detective sergeant from York, who needed to be brought up to speed. The CID man confirmed that we were to try to locate and arrest the offender as soon as possible. While all this was going on another unit was sent out – Thommo and two specials. We would need them. As soon as Jayne was ready with Debbie, she'd have to take her to what we call a victim examination suite, the nearest being at York or Scarborough. Control would whistle up an unmarked car so that Jayne could escort her there.

As I mapped out the plan, I reflected on how it would have been just a few years ago. Unsophisticated would be the kindest way to put it. The victim could be made to feel like a criminal, being taken to a police station and questioned by officers in an ordinary interview room. It's easy to imagine why so few women were willing to come forward back then. Thank God that's all changed now, and the training and therefore the attitude of the average police officer has changed too. The new examination suites are designed to offer a less intimidating and more comfortable atmosphere. They're like a small flat, with a kitchenette and a bathroom, comfortably furnished with sofas and coffee tables, and attended by specially trained doctors.

But that was all Jayne's side of things. Right now I had to go and find the offender, with the help of Graham, the park manager. 'According to the victim they're in a tent over by the wash-house,' I said. Graham had a plan of the camping and caravan areas, and was flicking through a register of names. 'Here we go,' he said. 'Two lads, Middlesbrough address. Site number . . .' He circled it on the map and handed it to me.

'Right,' I said. 'We'll go and see if we can find them. Can you make sure nobody leaves the site?'

'Easy,' he said. 'There's only one road in and one road out, and that's the entrance you came in through. I've already told our man there. Nobody leaves.'

I was about to make my way across to the camping area when the mobile went off. It was the night duty superintendent, wanting to know what had happened and what we were doing. 'If this guy's on site I want him arrested right away,' he said.

Throughout the incident so far I had been fully aware of the need to act with great deliberation. Rape is a serious crime, and an accusation of rape has to be taken very seriously indeed. As I drove slowly towards the tented area with Fordy and Ed behind me, I thought about how, whatever we did, we needed to consider our actions carefully. Every move had to be properly thought out. If we ended up in court, the slightest flaw in our case and the defence lawyer would have a field day. In other words, one mistake on our part and we could end up with a rapist walking free. We didn't want that on our hands.

As I drove slowly past the lines of caravans, Control came on. They'd traced the two lads whose names I'd given them. '*Yeah*,' he said. '*They've got recent form. Minor public order in the Middlesbrough area, nothing more.*'

The next moment I heard Thommo's familiar voice. '*Aye, where you wanting us, Mike?*'

'I'm just entering the caravan site at Point . . .' I had to stop to look at the sign. 'Tell you what,' I said, 'we'll wait for you to catch us up. In case there's any bother.'

A minute or two later he drew up behind Fordy and Ed and we drove in convoy towards the camping area. There were only a dozen or so tents scattered about this particular part of the site, and each pitch was clearly numbered. We soon found the one we wanted.

Thommo, Fordy and I approached it together. The rest of the lads remained by their vehicles. It was one of those little lightweight tents that backpackers use, long and low with very short guy lines. It was all zipped up and there was no light from inside.

'Maybe they're no' in,' Thommo muttered.

I nudged him and pointed to a pair of shoes that were poking out from under the hem of the awning, before reaching out a foot to give the tent a good shake and shining my Dragon Light onto it. 'Police,' I said. 'Anybody in?'

I heard something stir and a muffled 'Eh?' as the side of the tent bulged.

'Police,' I repeated. 'Come out now.'

Two of them emerged, shielding their eyes with their hands. One was broad and muscular, the other shorter and skinny; weedy, I suppose you'd say. They both wore jeans and T-shirts. Neither had shoes or socks on. Even from several feet away you could smell the booze on them.

'Is that all of you? Nobody else inside?' I asked.

The thin one shook his head and half turned away from the beam of my lamp.

'We're looking for . . .' I read the names from my notebook.

'Aye,' one of them said. 'That's us. What's the problem mate?'

'Which one of you is . . .?'

They looked at each other, and the weedy lad stepped forward. 'What's up?' he said. 'I ain't done nothing.'

Thommo led the other youth away to one side while I addressed his mate.

'Now,' I said, 'what have you been doing this evening?'

'Had a few drinks, like.'

'Were you with a girl at any time?'

He looked at the ground, shivered, and wrapped his arms around himself. 'For a bit, aye.'

'Debbie, was it?'

'Aye, is there a problem?'

'I have to inform you that an allegation has been made that you have committed a serious sexual assault. I'm placing you under arrest . . .'

'What d'youse mean, sexual assault?'

I took hold of his arms and put the cuffs on. He was shaking now, and not just with the cold.

'Listen,' he said, 'she was up for it. I never raped her. She was well keen. Ask me mate. It were her idea to come back here.'

'I must caution you and remind you that anything you say . . .'

'No, she bloody wanted it, mate. I never raped her. She's trying to stitch me up, the f***ing bitch!'

I had hold of him by the arm and was leading him back to the van. He started to struggle. Fordy had to step forward to help me restrain him.

'F***ing lemme go. I told yer, I ain't done nothing.'

'All right, mate, calm down,' I said. 'Look, this is a serious allegation and we need to get it sorted out. Kicking off is not going to help your cause.'

'That's f***ing easy for you to say.'

'I know, but this is a serious business and we can't sort it out here. Now, stand still while we search you. Once we've done that we're taking you to the station.'

The lad continued to struggle. Fordy held him against the side of the van while I searched him, then opened the back of the van and prepared to hold the lad's head down as I helped him inside.

'F***ing bitch!' He spat the words out, then called across to his mate. 'Hey you, tell him, will yer?' But before the other lad could reply we had our suspect inside and were closing the door. He seemed to calm down then, quickly. I suspected he'd gone into shock. Fordy sat in the van and kept observation on him. To tell the absolute truth I was feeling strange myself. In all my years I'd only ever arrested someone for this crime a handful of times. And it's always felt very serious indeed. People can get the heaviest sentences – years and years in prison, not to mention the impact on your life when you are known to be a rapist. If this young man were to be found guilty, how would he ever get a job in the future? Or, for that matter, find a wife and have a family?

Just as we were about to leave, Chris Cocks arrived. He would make arrangements to secure the crime scene and deal with witnesses, the first of whom would be the lad's friend. He would need to be interviewed and found alternative accommodation for the night, because the tent was now out of commission.

Forty minutes later I had the suspect in front of the custody sergeant at Northway, Scarborough. He'd gone very quiet by this time. In fact, all the way there he hadn't said a word. Apart from anything else, I think he was sobering up fast. He certainly never stopped shivering. And he seemed to be snivelling most of the way. All he said as he got out of the van was that he needed the toilet.

'It'll have to wait until you're booked in,' I told him.

After the formal booking procedure, where his details and the circumstances of his arrest were logged, he was given his rights. The custody sergeant then told him that his clothing would be seized as evidence.

In a rape case, forensic evidence is absolutely crucial, and has to be gathered in a methodical and prescribed manner. Fordy went to the storeroom and brought back several large sheets of brown paper, the kind of stuff you'd wrap a parcel in, some brown paper evidence bags, sellotape and exhibit labels. Then he helped me take the youth down to the cells.

'Right.' We were standing in front of the prisoner. He was seated on the wooden bed in the cell, staring at the floor. 'I want you to step forward onto this paper and take your clothes off,' I said.

'We really have to do this?' he said. 'I haven't done anything wrong.' He looked at me, then at Fordy. Under the encased fluorescent lights, which shimmered off the dull cream walls, he looked pallid and unhealthy. His face was blotchy. His eyes were moist, as though he'd been crying. He'd given us his age as twenty but he didn't look it. You couldn't see him getting served in a pub. 'What you gonna do to us?' he said. He was hesitant, uncertain, maybe even fearful.

'Like the sergeant said, we need to take your clothing as potential forensic evidence. That's all. Nobody's going to touch you. Just do as you're told. We've got a zip-up suit for you to put on afterwards. Soon as we've finished you can use the toilet in the corner there.'

It seemed that the seriousness of the situation was sinking in now. I explained to him how it was going to work. He would remove each item of clothing, I would place it in a property bag and Fordy would seal it up, then label it as an exhibit. He pulled off his T-shirt and handed it over, then stepped out of his shoes.

'I can't believe this is f***ing happening,' he said. 'I haven't done anything wrong. Honest I haven't. I'd never do that to anybody.'

'Listen, it's early days yet. There'll be time to give your side of the story.'

'Yeah, but I want you two to know it's not true. I never raped her. We had a few drinks and that.' He shrugged his shoulders. 'Y'know how it goes. One thing led to another and next thing she's away home. Then you guys turn up. I can't f***ing believe this.'

'Save it for your interview,' I said. 'Your solicitor'll be here soon. Let's just crack on, shall we.'

He fumbled at the top of his jeans as he tried to unbutton them. The object of this exercise was to preserve any hair or fibre or DNA – from him or the victim – as evidence. Later, all of the bags of clothing would be taken to the forensic laboratory at Wetherby.'

'Socks next,' I said. 'Sorry, mate, boxers too.'

He was shaking like a leaf as he did what we told him. When he was completely naked Fordy handed him a paper one-piece suit and a pair of black plimsolls, just like the ones you used to wear for PE at primary school. 'Now step aside and put those on,' he said. I carefully folded the brown paper groundsheets and placed them in another exhibit bag. If the least bit of forensic evidence had fallen from the offender or his clothing, it was now preserved.

You try not to get emotionally involved, and you certainly try not to judge anyone before a case is proven, but as we carried the evidence out I remember thinking, this is going to be a difficult case. How do you establish the truth? And a part of me was thinking, 'Well, did he or didn't he?' He seemed genuine enough; that was my initial gut instinct. But we didn't have all the facts – and we hadn't heard the girl's story.

I slammed the cell door shut. Then, on an impulse, I turned

and looked back through the wicket. He was sitting there, head in hands, all alone and looking very sober indeed. Yes, I thought, what if he was innocent? I was glad it wasn't up to me to decide.

I walked back with Fordy to the custody sergeant and told him what the prisoner had said while he was being searched. It's all part of the procedure. It's called unsolicited comments – and even those need to be recorded.

Back upstairs they offered me a cup of tea. 'Wouldn't mind,' I said, picking up a statement form and grabbing a seat. I wanted to get my version of events down while it was fresh in my mind.

It took me and Fordy the best part of an hour to write it all down, and there were constant interruptions as PCs came and went, all of them with the usual mix of stories, all the aggravation, sorrow and humour of policing a summer weekend night duty in a busy seaside town.

'I bet you lot love the holiday season,' I said to a weary PC as I signed the last statement sheet and drained a cup of luke-warm tea. All I got was a shake of the head. There comes a time on a Friday night when you run out of things to say. In any case, it was time for me to be on my way. I got on the phone and called the CID. They would be along shortly and could take over from me. Then I rang Chris and briefed him, and at last, at a little after four, we were free to make our way back along a deserted A64 to Malton. I drove slowly, watching the setting moon as it flitted on and off between the trees. There was no need to take risks, and I was tired. Very tired indeed. Fordy and I chatted about the night's events, but only briefly.

'Right,' I said, as we parked outside the station, 'home to bed.'

'Not me, buddy.' He held up his mobile phone. 'Just got a text.'

'Not one of your girlfriends?'

He laughed.

'I just hope she knows about the others,' I said.

'No, it's a mate. Got an invite to a house party.'

'What, now?'

'All-nighter, mate. Y'know what they say, Mike. Live fast, die young.'

When we got inside Jayne was still there, finishing off her statement.

'So how was the girl when you left her?' I said.

'Hard to tell, Mike. She wasn't exactly chatty. But I've got to be honest, I didn't know what to say once I'd finished questioning her. It's not exactly the time to make polite conversation, is it? In the circumstances. Anyway, soon as I got to York I settled her in and handed her over to the experts.'

'Well, yeah, it's what they're trained for, isn't it? Our job's to pick up the pieces, sort things out and move on.'

I waited until Jayne had signed her statement and faxed a copy over to Scarborough. Fordy was away to York to his party, but I was pretty sure Jayne wouldn't want to go straight home. You rarely do after a job like that. I made us a drink, grabbed some biscuits from my locker and sat with her for a while. If she was feeling like I did she'd want some time to unwind, even though it was nearly five in the morning by now. What you don't want after an incident like that is to be taking it home with you. You go down that road and you're never away from the job. But if you don't unload to someone, you can find yourself straight back in the firing line next day with something equally unpleasant, and that's how you build up the sort of stress levels that can make you unwell and impair your judgement. In my Met days it was the norm to sit around and talk about traumatic or unusual events, often over a beer. It's partly a way of off loading stress and emotion, but at the same time you try to learn from what went well and what perhaps could have been done better. Since then they've formalised it. They call it a debriefing. Anyway, Jayne and I sat and had a cup of tea and chewed a few things over.

'Makes you think,' Jayne said, closing her eyes and putting her hand to her forehead.

I waited.

'I mean, that girl . . .' She shook her head and looked at me. 'She made some pretty dreadful decisions, didn't she?'

'Yep. Going off alone with a guy she'd only just met for one thing. And after having a skinful.'

'I mean, don't get me wrong. I'm not blaming her, but looking at her . . . well, her mate looked quite mature. In fact, the pair of 'em did. But then they'd both . . .' Jayne gave a resigned sort of sigh, and I knew exactly what she was going to say. 'It's the booze, isn't it?'

'Exactly. The number of times I've seen girls like that setting off on a night out. They're in a gang, or they're with their best mate, and they're all going to watch out for each other. They have their phones with them, they've booked the taxi for midnight . . .'

'Yeah, bit of spare cash tucked away for the fare home . . . And then the drink kicks in and it's like, inhibitions go out the window. Along with good judgement.' Jayne sighed again. 'Y'know, when you're a girl, your parents spend most of the time holding your hand, escorting you around and telling you that they need to, because there are some "strange people" about. And we all know it, don't we? But, as a woman, you don't really think you're ever going to bump into one of them. Not deep down.' She looked at me, then down at her empty mug. 'Just shows how easy it can happen.'

'Well,' I said, 'you try to tell 'em. I've done talks at youth clubs, and schools. Personal safety. And you really think it's sinking in. But they have a few drinks and they think they're invincible. Then next thing they're alone with some fellow they hardly know and – well, they're in a very, very vulnerable situation. Just two things would help to stop situations like tonight, Jayne.'

'What's that, Mike? Castrate the whole of the male population?'

'Mmm, that'd be a bit harsh. No – number one, if the girls would look out for each other as carefully as they mean to. And secondly, if the lads wouldn't go off with girls they don't know, who are out of their heads on drink or drugs. They're both making themselves vulnerable, in different ways.'

'But I think they set off on a night out full of good intentions.'

'And just to add to the mix, as we all know, there's a small number of women who for whatever reason will cry wolf. Doesn't make our job any easier, does it?'

Jayne shook her head. 'I wonder if they'll convict him.'

'CID have to prove it, don't they? Beyond all reasonable doubt. That's your sticking point.'

'Well, she was raped, wasn't she? Seems pretty bloody obvious to me.'

'We weren't there, Jayne. That's the thing with a case like this, isn't it? There's very rarely any witnesses. Don't get me wrong – I wasn't there and I don't know what happened. But you dealt with the girl and you're convinced she was telling the truth. We dealt with the lad and to be fair, he seemed pretty genuine too. So put yourself in the jury's position. They hear both sides. This is one of the reasons why it's so hard to get a conviction.'

'Yeah, I see what you mean. And we won't know for ages, will we?'

I stood up and got my things together. I was ready for home. 'No, not until the CPS decide whether to press charges. It's a nasty, nasty business, rape. People think it's about sex. It isn't. It's a crime of violence, pure and simple.'

There didn't seem much else to say after that. Maybe I'd gone on a bit, but I suppose I had a few things I needed to get off my chest. We put our things in our lockers and went out to the car park. It was a cool morning with a hint of autumn in the air. The cobwebs on the shrubbery were spangled with dew. A blackbird was singing away in the sycamore trees. Over the road, beyond the old Roman camp and away up on the top of the Wolds, the sky was just starting to lighten.

Jayne paused as she was getting into her car. 'Oh well,' she said. 'As my old man liked to say, another day another dollar. See ya, Mike.'

'Yeah,' I said. 'See you.'

Chapter 9

Dig a Little Deeper

'Not there. You want to be up a bit, lad.'

'What, here?'

'No, not that high. Fetch her down a bit.'

'Just here, you mean?'

'No, not there.' He was getting exasperated now, shoving his cap back on his head. 'I can see I shall 'ave to come up and show you,' he said.

'Walt,' I said, 'you set one foot on this ladder and I'm off home – and I'll be taking this bit of kit with me. I've made a mark, and that'll do me. Now stand right back – go on, by the pond there.'

I pulled the goggles over my eyes and squeezed the trigger through my thick protective gloves. The chainsaw, which had been idling, roared into life. The leaves of the sycamore shivered as the teeth bit into the smooth grey stem a foot or so above my head. I made a neat V-shaped back-cut, then adjusted my footing on the aluminium ladder, brought the saw back to my side, and went for it.

It was like a knife going through butter. There was a shower of sweet-scented chippings, a creak, a sharp crack – and down she went, the whole upper section of the tree thrashing through the lower branches to land with a shudder and a thump.

Walt stood there, shading his eyes from the shower of leaves and twigs that was drifting down onto his upturned face. 'Aye, now tek that last foot or two off and she'll look sommat like.' I did as he asked. 'Aye, then there's a little branch just down by your right knee wants lopping off.'

'Tell you what, Walt, while I'm perched up here twenty foot off the ground on a wobbly ladder, why don't I trim it into fancy shapes for you? How about a peacock? Would that suit you? Or a nice cockerel?'

He didn't answer. He knew better. A minute later I was standing beside him, surveying my handiwork from the other side of his new pond.

'Why, it looks a right dog's breakfast,' I said. 'That used to be a lovely row of trees and now it's . . . Well, it's like a beautiful woman who's had her front teeth knocked out. It'll be years before that recovers.'

'I needed it tekking out.'

'So you keep saying, but you haven't explained why.'

He gave a big sigh. 'It were going to be a surprise,' he said. 'So you've to promise me you'll say nowt.'

'Walt, mate, my lips are sealed.'

He gave one of his grimaces and worked his little finger down his ear, giving it a wiggle. 'You quite sure?'

'Walter, my word is my bond. Scout's honour. Come on, spit it out, then we can get stuck into that pheasant you've got in the oven.'

'It's me barbecue coming up, y'see.'

'Aye, you've been going on about it for the last three months.'

'And I always try to put on a bit of – you know, entertainment like. So this year I'm having . . .' He still seemed reluctant.

'Go on, what you having?'

Walt took a deep breath and puffed out his chest. 'How about clay-pigeon shooting, lad? Does that tickle your fancy?'

'Brilliant, mate. Used to be a dab hand at that. But it's been years since. You got all the gear?'

'Oh aye, don't you worry about that. Just so long as Nick and Algy and suchlike bring their shotguns.'

I looked up at the trees again, and winced at the great gaping hole I'd created. 'But I still don't get it, Walt. What am I taking lumps out of your sycamores for?'

'Aye well, that's like your shooting alley. Your line of sight. I've got it all worked out, d'you see? We get t'machine – set her up just this side of t'pond. And we fire t'pigeons across the gap. It's what you want, isn't it? A sky background. Show 'em up perfect. You just—' He crooked his right arm and peered down an imaginary barrel, his trigger finger twitching. 'Blast the buggers out of the sky. Heh heh heh.'

Walt's barbecue was one of the major social events of the year – along Leavening Brow, that is. All of us from down the Jolly Farmers were invited: Soapy, Algy, Nick the gamekeeper, the other two wise monkeys, plus 'the good ladies' as he called them – although he still hadn't made up his mind whether to invite his Muriel or not. He'd been muttering about her once or twice recently. She didn't approve of shooting wild animals – and that's what Walt liked to serve at his barbecues . . . So the guest list consisted of what you might call his inner circle. The select few. And the date was set for the following Sunday, four o'clock sharp. I'd made sure, weeks previously, that I was on an early turn, and Ann had the weekend off. This was one event in the calendar we were not going to miss under any circumstances.

The Sunday in question got off to a nice quiet start. I came in at six to find Thommo sitting in the parade room, feet up on the table, newspaper spread out on his lap, dunking one of those giant chocolate-covered flapjacks in a mug of tea.

'Sit yersel' down, laddie. Relax. The cells are empty. The radios are silent. The criminal fraternity are all back in their lairs, plotting next week's mayhem. The day of rest is upon us.'

I mashed a mug of tea for me, and another for Fordy. I'd passed him, pulling into the newsagent's, as I came up Castlegate. He wouldn't be far behind me. 'Hey, this isn't bad, is it?' I said, grabbing Thommo's sports supplement. 'I just fancy a nice steady shift. Got a big do on this aft.'

But Thommo wasn't listening. 'Mind you,' he said, 'ye wouldn't have got away wi' it when I first walked the beat. Och no. Back in them days it'd be "Dinnae sit there, laddie, not while the toilets are in that state."'

Fordy had arrived. He slung his copy of *Yorkshire Sport on Sunday* onto the table and looked at Thommo. 'You're not telling us they had you cleaning the bogs out, surely?'

'Aye, unless you could find something better to do – like writing up your reports. I had to scrub the floors, more than once. Then they'd have you polishing the trophies.'

'What trophies?' I said.

'Snooker, darts, bowls ... We were a talented lot in our part of Glasgow. Used to clean up regularly – pun unintended, ye ken. Aye' – he stretched and yawned – 'it was a different world in those days.'

We sat there for a while, supping our tea and skimming through the sports pages, then Thommo got up from his chair and went across to the far side of the room. On either side of the chimney-breast was a tall glass-fronted bookcase, a matching pair. I'd never really done more than glance at them. They seemed to be full of old ledgers and bound volumes of the *Police Gazette*. 'You want tae get a flavour of life in the old days, laddie – aye, and you, Pannett – have a wee peek at these sometime.' He fished out a pair of small black pocket notebooks and put them on the table in front of us. 'Ye're living amid a priceless historical archive, and I'll bet ye never knew it.'

'Can't say I did, mate. How old are these, then?' I opened one of them and read the inscription on the first page, neatly written in black ink. '1 January 1943? Strewth, Thommo, why didn't you show me these before?'

'Because you never asked, you ignorant Sassenach. If ye'd been a Scot now, and benefited from our vastly superior system of education, you'd have grown up wi' a sense of history.'

What I was looking at was a beat copper's notebook dated during the war. There were references to runaway horses on Castlegate, people being bitten by dogs out on the farms, kids caught scrumping at Rillington, people arrested in pubs that had long since ceased trading, like the Black Swan, and the Buckrose Vaults. 'Look at this,' I said. 'He's even logging each lamp-post he walks past. Couldn't have been much of a beat.' I thumbed through the pages. 'Blackout curtains . . .'

'Aye,' Thommo said. 'And ye'll see they noted down every premises they checked, each lock they tried. Good old-fashioned police work in them days.'

We must have sat there for getting on half an hour, reading snippets from the row of little black books on the shelf.

'Listen to this,' Fordy said, reading aloud: '"In pursuing the suspects I inadvertently ran into a clothes line that the boys had hung across the alleyway, throwing me to the ground and allowing them to make good their escape."'

'Nothing new there then. What about these?' I said, taking a large bound volume down from the shelf.

'Now you're into your serious history,' Thommo said as I opened it up. 'Horse and carriage days.'

In front of me was a record of convictions for the Ryedale area from before the First World War right up to 1947, pre-dating the Criminal Records Bureau. Each entry was neatly written in ink and contained the date, name, place, offence and the penalty handed out. In some cases the entry was accompanied by a black and white photograph of the offender, all of them sporting a moustache. Most of the offences were for drunkenness, assault by beating or larceny.

'They were a bit harsh back then,' I said. 'Look at these sentences. Minor theft – a month in prison?' It was all fascinating stuff. 'Hey, and here's a lad done for poaching, out Birdsall way – and look at his name. Same as my mate Soapy. He'll be related. Has to be. Tell you what,' I said, 'this stuff belongs in Malton Museum.'

'Aye, it's a veritable treasure trove, laddie – but here comes our taskmaster, Sergeant Cocks, to drag us away from our pursuit of education and throw us to the mercy of the elements.'

'Give over, Thommo,' Chris said, 'it's a cracking morning out there. And we've got a nice little traffic incident to ease you into the day.'

'No, that'll be for these junior hands, Sarge. I'm on light duties today. My old neck injury, aggravated during that use-of-force training last week.'

'Go on,' Chris snorted. 'There's bugger all wrong with you.'

'Sorry to disappoint ye, Sarge, but the trusty general

practitioner says it'll take a few more days yet to settle down. It's my age, d'ye see . . .'

'Right,' said Chris. 'Looks like this'll be yours, Mike. Birdsall. Tractor blocking the road. Nobody hurt, just a simple case of mechanical failure.'

'Great,' I said. 'No chance of palming it off to Traffic?'

''Fraid not. The only available traffic officer is tied up at Rosedale Chimney Bank. Some clever sod trying a descent without brakes.'

'Aye, go on then. I'll go and get this tractor sorted. Let Fordy here carry on with his history lessons. At least it's a "non-injury". I've had worse calls on a Sunday morning.'

I got in the car and made my way up Langton Road, slowing to pass a line of half a dozen racehorses as they were led out to the gallops. It was a beautiful sunny morning, with a heavy dew on the grass and a thin mist in the folds between the hills. At the gated entrance to one of the farmhouses a huge chestnut tree was already turning a golden brown.

I found the tractor just past Birdsall House on a sharp bend, half turned into the metal rail fence, with its trailer sprawled across the road at an angle and the driver walking towards me in his green overalls.

'Now then, mate. What's the problem?' I switched on the blue lights and got out of the car, putting my yellow jacket on. The last thing you want in an incident like this is some idiot hurtling down the road at forty miles an hour. The least we could do was to make ourselves as visible as we could.

'Blooming axle's gone,' he said. 'Just snapped on me. I'm waiting for a tow back to the yard.'

'Oh aye. Where you from?'

He pointed up the road. 'Over the top, Acklam way.'

'That where your breakdown man's coming from?'

'No, he's from out Scarborough way. Reckons he'll be an hour yet.'

'Right,' I said. A car drew up behind us and I flagged it slowly past. When he'd gone I stood on tiptoe and peered into the trailer. 'Good job that was empty,' I said.

'Aye, I was just off to collect a load of grain.'

'Well, all I can do is keep things moving here till your man shows up.' I went back to the car and took the POLICE SLOW signs from the boot, placing them a hundred yards down the road either side of the trailer. Back at the car I pulled out a couple of portable flashing blue lights. More often than not you find the batteries are dead, but no, these were full of life. But I still wasn't happy. Just my luck to fall for a Mickey Mouse job like this, I was thinking. You can soon lose half a morning if you're not careful – and I was starting to want my breakfast. There was very little traffic, just the odd car every ten minutes or so, but I couldn't leave the scene unattended. Matey wasn't the chattiest either, so I sat in the car and waited. And waited.

It must have been getting on for nine when the tow-truck driver called the farmer from Langton crossroads to get final directions. Ten minutes later he was on the scene, trying to decide how best to drag the trailer out of harm's way while he inspected the tractor. Another half-hour or so, I was thinking, we'll have this lot sorted and I can pop over to Nick's and grab a bite to eat. But even as I started salivating at the thought of that dry-cured streaky bacon and his lass's homemade bread, I heard Julie's voice on the radio.

'Control to all units. Anyone to deal? We've a four-year-old child gone missing at Duggleby. Parents have searched the house and gardens and are now very concerned.'

When you hear a call like that you always listen carefully, even if you're tied up with something else. It's the sort of incident that's likely to require all hands on deck if it isn't resolved quickly. I heard Fordy answer. '*Yes, show me dealing, Julie. I'm still in town, and Mike's tied up at Birdsall.*'

As the farmer and the tow-truck man separated the two vehicles I kept half an ear on what was happening. It seemed the girl had been missing for just under an hour. She was four years old, and her name was Lucy. The parents had been through the house and now some of the neighbours had joined in and were searching their gardens. I didn't like the sound of it at all.

There was hardly any traffic to bother me, and time seemed to be dragging. The breakdown man was one of them who wouldn't be rushed. He drew on his cigarette and walked round the trailer, bending down to look underneath, and then took his cap off and rubbed the top of his head. Then he got on all fours and fiddled about with the linkage.

Come on, I was thinking, just rive the bugger out the way and let me crack on. I looked at my watch. It was getting on for ten already. The breakdown man was emerging from under the rear end of the tractor, where he'd fitted a heavy chain. 'Listen, mate,' I said, 'I've got an urgent job come in. Can you get this shifted sharpish?'

'Shouldn't be long,' he said. 'With a bit of luck I can winch her out the way and free the road up for you.'

'That'd be great,' I said. I wanted to get away as soon as possible and help Fordy. I was concerned that this was potentially serious, and I doubted that he would have dealt with many jobs of this nature. I'd handled a fair few cases of kids going missing, and if there was one thing I'd learned it was that speed was of the essence. A lot of the ones I'd been involved with had been teenagers – thirteen- or fourteen-year-olds getting all temperamental and storming out of the home. Ninety-nine times out of a hundred they show up safe and sound at a mate's house, or come slinking back when it gets dark or they get hungry. Even so, you always have to start out with one eye on the worst-case scenario, particularly with a young child. You have to take into account all the what ifs that you'd rather not think about – because the possibilities are frightening, and they all go through your mind.

I'd just heard Fordy calling Control to say he was going to search the house with the parents, when the breakdown man finally got the trailer off to the side of the road. It was now safe for traffic to pass. 'That's it then,' I said, 'I'm on my way.' I could pick up the POLICE SLOW signs later.

I drove fast, down to North Grimston, up the hill, over the top towards Duggleby. There's always a sense of real urgency when a child goes missing. She could be anywhere, alone, lost, out in the road, trapped in a barn under a machine or something. But where? That's the question. She could have fallen over and be lying in the undergrowth within yards of home, or she could have wandered half a mile away. I was racking my brains trying to remember whether there were any ponds out that way. It all goes through your mind, and all the time you have to consider the other possibilities – that she might have been abducted, either by a stranger or by someone known to her.

I was almost there when I heard Fordy on the radio again. *'I've searched the house – yep, with the parents . . . Yeah, and the garage. No, no sign of her. We need to spread the net wider.'*

That's where these things become really frightening, because once you start broadening the search you never really have enough people. And all the time you're searching you're aware that the clock is ticking – and half dreading that you've walked past something obvious and not noticed it.

I heard young Fordy again. '*I've got the neighbours searching the gardens. Can anyone assist?*'

'1015,' I said, 'I'm just pulling up outside.' Then I heard Chris Cocks's voice. '*Yeah, Control, can I come in on this?*'

'Go ahead, Sarge.'

'*I'm going to get over there and assist. And can you see if a dog section is available, and if there's anyone free to assist from Eastfield?*'

I parked up in the cul de sac just off the road. It was an old cottage, painted white, with dormer windows and a huge rose tree covering the front of it. I saw a group of four or five people gathered outside it, turning to face me as I opened the car door. Further down the lane I could see one or two more poking about in the bushes with sticks. A knot of local kids were standing outside in the road with their bikes. A couple of eager dogs were running loose among them.

'They're inside,' someone said, as I headed towards the gate. The back door was open. I went straight in. I could hear a woman, her voice high-pitched and tearful. 'She's never done anything like this before. Where can she have got to?'

Fordy was in the kitchen with her. She was sitting at the table, running her fingers through a head of dark curls. In front of her was a set of poster paints and a couple of brushes. The table-top and one of its legs were daubed with blue and red. A jam-jar was lying on its side and there was purplish water all over the pale green floor tiles.

'Now then,' I said, 'I'm PC Mike Pannett. I'm sure you've told my colleague already, but can you just spare a minute to fill me in on what's happened, please?'

'She was painting – right here. I was sat helping her. I went to answer the phone, came back and – well, you can see what she'd done. I – I told her off. Sent her to her room. She stamped off up upstairs and I decided to go and hang some washing out, give us both time to cool off. Can't have been gone five minutes.' She covered her face with her hands and started sobbing. 'I came back in, went upstairs to fetch her and she was gone.'

Her husband had come in and was standing in the back doorway in his wellies, a long hiker's stick in his hand. 'I was watching the TV,' he said. 'Lynn thought she was in with me, but . . .' He tailed off and knelt down by his wife, putting his arm around her.

'And what did you do then?' I said. I hated this. They looked a decent couple, and were clearly distraught that their little girl was missing, but at the back of your mind you always have to be aware of the unthinkable.

'We checked the house – everywhere. Looked in the wardrobes, everything, then we went out in the garden. We shouted for her. Then our neighbours next door heard us and came over and – well, they're out there now, looking in the field at the back.' He shook his head. 'Hell,' he said, turning away from his wife and lowering his voice. 'We've not checked that pond.'

'Where's that?' I said.

He was through the door and into the back yard. Fordy and I followed him outside. 'Down there.' He was pointing towards the bottom of the garden.

'Fordy,' I said, 'you say you've searched the house?'

'Yeah – everywhere. She came with me – the little lass's mother.'

Control came on the radio. '*You've a dog section en route from Scarborough, Mike.*'

'Righto, thanks.'

'And, Mike, stand by: the duty inspector's gonna call you on your mobile.'

I turned to Fordy. 'Look,' I said, 'you follow him and search that pond – now.'

I didn't say any more to him, but I was hoping he remembered his training. Every minute was precious, but if it came to it and she was in the water he needed to stay calm and remember that a child can go underwater for several minutes and still be resuscitated, whereas an adult might be a goner.

I watched the pair of them going down the garden while I waited for the inspector to ring me.

'*Right*,' he said, when he came through, '*I'll be covering this from Scarborough. Just bring me up to speed, will you?*'

'PC Ford has searched the house with the girl's mother, sir. He's outside now with the father. There's a pond . . .'

'*Hm – he's very young.*'

'You mean PC Ford, sir?'

'*I mean not very experienced.*'

'That's true, sir, but he's a good officer.'

'*I don't doubt that, Mike. But I want you to search the house again, will you? Thoroughly. I don't want it written off till you have done, you got that?*'

'Yes, sir.'

'*And I don't need to tell you to check everywhere. Cupboards, tops of wardrobes, under the beds, airing cupboards. The garage, inside the car. Even if they say they've done it.*'

There was a moment's silence, then he carried on, '*Mike, you're an experienced officer. You know that if she's not in that house, I'm going to hit the button and organise a full-scale search. I'm going to give the Humberside helicopter the heads-up that we may need them sharpish. That clear?*'

'Yes, sir, as soon as the search is complete I'll get straight back to you.'

'*Now, you've got the dog unit on their way, plus two traffic officers from here, and the early turn coming across from Eastfield. If you get no joy from the house, I'm coming across myself. Sergeant Cocks should be with you shortly as well. Once PC Ford has searched the pond, get him to alert all the neighbours and get them to start searching their own places. Houses, garages and gardens.*'

'Right you are, sir.'

'*Okay then. And good luck.*'

I turned and went back into the house. The girl's mother was on her way out, wiping her eyes with the back of her hand. She looked at me questioningly. All I could do was force a smile. That's the thing in these cases: they look to you for a result. Sometimes it's as if they think you can perform miracles. 'Look,' I said, 'I've dealt with a lot of searches like this. My experience tells me she's not far away – most likely somewhere that's been missed. Now, why don't you and I go back in and check this house from top to bottom. Just to be sure.'

'But I've already done that. With the other officer. She's not here, I tell you. What if she's got out the back? We should be out there in that field . . . I mean, the farmyard . . . the pond.'

'Look, the other officer is down there now with your husband, and the neighbours, and there's another three officers plus a dog handler about to arrive to help out. Let's just make a hundred per cent sure, eh? Just you and me. Won't take long. You never know, she might be panicking at all the upset she's caused and hiding away somewhere.'

I like to think I'm a good judge of character, but once again I found myself looking at this woman and trying to weigh her up.

As a professional I knew I'd be failing in my duty and possibly letting the child down if I didn't ask myself the question: was there any possibility of foul play? Was she just putting on a show for me?

But as I looked at her tearstained face, all I could think was that she seemed utterly genuine. Even so, as we searched the girl's bedroom I checked the edge of the bed, the white melamine surface of the dressing table, the freshly painted windowsill and the area around the door-handle, just to make sure there was no sign of a struggle – like a smudge of blood, a tuft of hair, a rucked-up carpet, a scuff mark, anything that might indicate something untoward. Genuine as she might be, there was the husband to think of – and what about the neighbours? Could one of them have done something?

I pulled the padded headboard away from the wall and looked behind it. Nothing but a ball of fluff and a hair bobble. The room was all very tidy and clean, just a few cuddly toys scattered about on the bed and a pair of pink pyjamas thrown on the floor. Was it too clean? Suspiciously tidy?

I opened up the drawers under the bed and checked them. Empty – just a sheet of lining paper and a sweet wrapper. We went into the bathroom and checked behind the door, inside the shower cubicle, the airing cupboard. But there was no sign of anything.

We went into a little box-room at the top of the stairs. It was all in good order, with cardboard boxes stacked up in one corner, a child's desk and a shelf full of books under the window. There was nothing to be seen, or heard. I went back out onto the landing and called out her name, 'Lucy! Where are you?' The silence afterwards made me shiver, until it was broken by the radio as the Eastfield officers announced their arrival.

Through the window I could see the neighbours – a dozen or more of them now – poking about in the long grass beyond the vegetable patch, and Fordy having a word with them as he walked back towards the house, soaked to the waist.

'What's this room?' I asked. It was the only one we hadn't done.

'She never comes in here,' the mother said, turning the handle and opening the door. 'We keep it for when we have company.'

'Well, come on; let's do the job thoroughly,' I said. I was trying to sound upbeat, positive, as if I really did expect to find her tucked up in bed or something. 'You never know.'

But she wasn't there – not under the unmade bed, not in the tall floor-to-ceiling fitted wardrobes, not buried away under the pile of bedding in the corner. I even checked behind the curtains. It was an old stone-built house and the windowsills were maybe eighteen inches deep – just the sort of place a kid would curl up on a sunny afternoon and nod off. But she wasn't there either. We turned to go out onto the landing again. I was wondering where we'd try next, what I would say to stop her collapsing in a heap and despairing, when I brushed against a round wicker laundry basket. It was about three feet tall, if that. I lifted the lid. It was full to the top. There was a pair of man's underpants and a crumpled towel spilling out over the rim. No matter how ridiculous it seemed, experience told me it needed to be searched. I picked up the first two items, and a paint-covered T-shirt – and there underneath was a mop of blonde curls – and one little girl, huddled in a ball and fast asleep with her thumb in her mouth.

'Oh my God! Lucy, sweetheart!' The mother reached into the basket and dragged the limp child out by her shoulders, hugging her tightly, and screaming to her husband, 'John, she's safe, she's here. John, John!' She was sobbing uncontrollably with the relief – and joy – but the little girl, aroused from her slumbers to find her mother shouting and crying at the same time, and a stranger in uniform peering down at her – well, it was all too much for her. She was now exercising her lungs at full volume, her eyes darting about in panic.

I switched on the radio, holding it tight to one ear while I pressed a finger into the other to drown out the racket.

'Control from 1015 over . . . We've found her. Aye, safe and well. Appears to be anyway. Tucked up asleep with the dirty laundry, over.'

We were on our way downstairs when Fordy came bounding up with the girl's dad. 'What's happening?' he started. Then he saw the mother behind me. 'Oh, thank Christ for that. Where was she?'

'Buried away under the dirty washing,' I said. 'Fast asleep and oblivious to the world and – hey, Fordy, take them mucky shoes off, will you?'

Fordy glanced down at the stairs at the trail of wet footprints he'd left behind him, then at the girl's mother.

'Oh hell. I'm sorry.'

But the mother wasn't listening. She and the husband were both hugging little Lucy, who was now starting to calm down, but staring at me with a frown on her face. 'Who's that funny man?' she asked.

Beside me Fordy was shaking his head. 'I thought I'd searched the whole place,' he said.

'Relax, lad. I nearly missed it myself. If I hadn't half knocked it over . . .'

'Knocked what over?'

'The laundry basket.'

'Laundry basket? What, that round thing – about so high?'

'Aye.'

'But I did check it.' He looked genuinely puzzled. 'First place I looked, Mike. Took the lid off and it was full of all manky – you know, underwear and that.'

'Fordy,' I said, 'years ago an old copper gave me a very valuable piece of advice, which I always remembered: Always dig a little deeper.'

He screwed up his face. 'You're right, but – you know, a pair of grubby old pants . . .'

'Aye, and if you had sommat to hide and wanted to put us off the scent, it'd be the perfect way, wouldn't it?'

'You're right,' he said. 'Hell, I'm sorry.'

'It's all right, mate. Main thing is the little girl is safe and sound.'

We'd found her okay, but now there were the loose ends to tie up. In a case such as this I always like to have a word with the people concerned. They didn't need me to tell them how lucky they were to have such a great bunch of neighbours, but I did go round and thank all of those who'd turned out – and introduced myself to those that didn't know me. And I did point out that an incident like this highlighted the need to be security-aware where young children were concerned. How safe was everyone's house? And garden? And should that pond be fenced off? In the end, yes, it had all turned out okay, but the incident had sent a shudder through the village. It would certainly be the topic of conversation in the area for some time to come, and it would make everyone pause and think about how safe their own homes were and their gardens, their outbuildings – anywhere a child could go.

After I'd talked to the villagers I started thinking about Fordy. Because he and I had a few things to talk about too. By the time we got back to the station and I'd made us a mug of tea he was looking pretty downcast.

'Fordy,' I said, 'don't let it get to you.'

'I just can't believe I never checked that basket,' he said.

'Look, this is how you learn. It's how we all learn. Trust me, mate, you won't ever forget this. And next time you'll double-check every nook and cranny. Or you might be passing the benefit of your experience to another cop. Best way to learn is through your errors and oversights.'

'I know, Mike, but the parents were relying on us. I mean, apart from anything else it's a bit embarrassing. And what must the bloody inspector think of me.'

'Fordy, it's a pound to a pinch of you-know-what, the inspector made the same mistake himself when he was starting out as a copper. I bet that's why he was so keen to send me back into the house to make doubly sure.'

'You reckon?'

'I do, mate. Like I said, it's how we all learn. Young kids like that, it's nearly always the case that they're still on the property. They show up in the weirdest places. In a cupboard, bottom of the wardrobe, blanket boxes, dog's bed. You name it and a kid'll get into it. You just have to use your imagination. Think like a child, Fordy. Shouldn't be too hard for a young lad like you.' I looked at my watch. 'Well, I'd love to sit and natter but it's home time and I've got the main event of the social calendar to attend.' I stood up and grabbed my jacket off the back of the chair.

'Thanks, Mike. Black tie do, is it?'

'Not exactly. We're off to the annual Leavening Brow

Barbecue. My old mate Walt's probably lathering the squirrels in that spicy sauce of his as we speak.'

As I drove out of town I realised I was now starving – and raring to get to Walt's place. I liked to joke about the old fellow and his taste for wild meat. The fact is he'd fed me a few strange bits and pieces in the time I'd known him. We'd had plenty of hare and rabbit, and gamebirds, venison too, but I'll never forget the time I found him in the kitchen with a line of dead crows spread out on his table-top – and serving them to me in pastry the following day. And much as people don't believe me when I tell them, his 'blackbird pie' tasted great. As I've said to Ann more than once, the thing with Walt is, he knows how to make the most unlikely raw material tickle the taste buds. He has a whole row of dried herbs hanging up behind the Rayburn, and a couple of dark, mysterious bottles with cork stoppers that live in his sideboard. God knows what's in them, but whenever he serves you meat, you can guarantee it'll be tender and delicious. The way I look at it, the end result is all that matters.

Ann wasn't so convinced. When I told her the crow-pie story she decided that as far as Walt was concerned she was a vegetarian. And I was to go along with it. 'Saves a lot of embarrassment all round,' she said as we puffed our way up the hill from the village, me with a six-pack of bottled beer under my arm, she with a bottle of chilled rosé wine wrapped up in a damp towel, and a pack of Linda McCartney veggie sausages.

'They're all there,' I said, as we rounded the bend and caught sight of the vehicles parked up along the roadside. There was Algy's Range Rover, Soapy's old Cavalier, and it looked as though the other two wise monkeys had shown up in Cyril's Morris Minor estate.

We made our way in through the old iron gate and round by

the woodshed. 'You never said anything about music.' Ann was cocking her head to one side as the strains of a country-and-western standard wafted across from the garden.

'Neither did Walt,' I said – but there, against the back of the house, was a four-piece band: his brother Cyril on accordion, Ronny the retired RAF fitter on bass, both of them wearing cowboy hats, pearl-buttoned shirts and black string ties with silver fasteners. Walt's lady friend Muriel was there in a blue-and-white-checked frock, her brow furrowed as she scraped away on a fiddle; and out front, teetering about on a pair of Cuban-heeled cowboy boots, strumming a guitar and croaking out the words of the Hank Williams classic 'Your Cheating Heart', was the man himself, his flat hat and green suede waistcoat offset by a red neckerchief and a pair of old blue jeans.

'Why, you're a dark horse, aren't you?' I said as the band put down their instruments and Walt headed for the bar he'd set up on a trestle table by the back door. 'Bit of a country-and-western star on the sly, eh?'

'Why, me and Cyril grew up playing together,' he said, relieving me of my six-pack. 'Just for fun, like. Round the old fireside mostly. Just took it up again this last year.'

'Aye,' Cyril said, 'then we got Ron involved, and now Muriel's decided to join in. We've made a few bob, y'know. Done one or two village hall dances. And we're available for other functions.' He nudged me in the ribs and winked at me. 'Weddings and such-like. Just so's you know.' He glanced at Ann. 'Should you ever . . .'

'I'll let you know, mate,' I interrupted. 'Hey, what about your lass?' I whispered to Walt as he flipped the top off one of my bottles and filled his glass. 'Thought you said you weren't inviting her?'

I felt a sharp dig in the small of my back as the lady in question jabbed me with the sharp end of her violin. 'He didn't, but I decided to come along anyway, to keep an eye on them,' she said.

'Oh, Muriel! Never saw you there.'

'So I gathered.'

'Tell you what, you were playing a pretty mean fiddle, if I may say so.'

'Well, I should do, young man. I was classically trained, you know. We all were in my family. Used to have regular concerts in the front parlour on a Saturday evening. Mother on the piano, myself and my little brothers on assorted strings.' She sighed. 'And Father would sing – even though we begged him not to.'

'Well, it's a treat listening to you, love. But it must be a bit of a culture shock, playing with this shower.' I nodded at Ron and Cyril, who'd pulled their hats low over their eyes and were grinning at me from behind their beer glasses. The better I got to know Walter's lady friend the better I liked her. I decided to wind it up a bit. 'Aye,' I said, 'I bet old Walter here takes a bit of handling.'

'Speaking as a retired teacher, Michael, I can't say I have much difficulty. I treat him like I'd treat a third-year junior.'

'What? A clip round the ear every so often – that what you mean?'

'I mean firm handling and strong leadership; that's all it takes. You should know that, in your line of work. And of course it helps if you can think like a boy – and, having grown up with three of them, that comes easily to me.'

I looked at Walt, and he looked at the sky, as if he was expecting a change in the weather. That's the thing with Muriel; I could never tell whether she was joking or not. And I wasn't sure, in this instance, that Walt did either. I clapped a hand on his shoulder. 'So,' I said, 'you saw sense, did you? Gave up on the old clay-pigeon job?'

'What yer mean, lad?'

'Well, the band – is that our entertainment for the day?'

'No, we're what you'd call the warm-up act.' He pointed towards the pond. 'I've got the main event set up over yonder.'

'Oh. Let's have a look at it then.'

He led me across the garden, through the gate, and over the field towards the pond. I looked up briefly to the far side, wincing again at the sight of the ugly gap in the sycamores. 'Got myself one of them new-style traps,' Walt said. 'Works a treat. Here, what d'you reckon?'

'Bit lightweight, isn't it? Like sommat you'd make with a Meccano set.'

'Aye, she is lightweight. But she's got a little fold-down seat, see? And just you pull on that spring. Go on – cos by heck there's some power in it.'

'Strewth,' I said, tugging at it. 'See what you mean.'

'Aye, I had a practice yesterday and they don't half fly.'

'So who've you got lined up for the contest?'

'He's got me, Michael m'boy!' came a voice from behind us. 'Algy!'

'The very same. Frankly, old chap, I can't see much point in anyone else having a go. I mean, horses for courses and all that. But I dare say I can teach these beginners a trick or two – get 'em up to scratch, so to speak.'

'We'll see, Algy. I quite fancy myself at this malarkey, y'know. Got top marks at target shooting when I was in the TA.'

'Ah, but this is a different animal, old chap. A moving target. Takes more than a good eye to knock those blighters out of the sky. You need a well-honed technique.'

Ann had come across from the garden to join us. 'You say you're handy at this?' she asked him, winking craftily in my direction.

Algy tugged the lapels of his sports jacket. 'If I say so myself, yes.'

'And we don't need to ask Mike whether he fancies himself.'

'Don't you worry,' I said, 'I'll give it my best shot.'

'Best shot, eh? I like that.' Algy laughed. 'Well, look, maybe we should have a little competition. Or two. One for the gentlemen and another for the ladies.'

'Excuse me! Are we frightened of a mere female, boys?' Ann was glaring at him.

I smelled trouble. 'Hey, it's all equal opportunities now, Algy,' I said. 'If we have a competition it's open to all – regardless of race, religion or gender. What do you say, Walt?'

'S'long as you all put your ten quid in it's all t'same to me, lad.'

'You what? Ten quid?'

'Eh, them clays don't come cheap, lad. And then there's rental of t'trap.'

'You're having us on, surely. You never paid for that thing. You'll have borrowed it.'

'Mebbe so, but I'm liable if one of you buggers breaks it, so . . .' He held his hand out.

'Pointless arguing with him, old chap,' Algy said, and delved into his pocket. 'C'mon, old boy, cough up.'

'So who've we got?' I looked around. There were the four of us plus Soapy, who was just coming through the garden gate with a woman on his arm. She was younger than him, and I have to say that even at fifty paces she was – well, presentable.

'Who's she?' I hissed as they approached the pond and he

paused to kiss her. She had long blonde hair, even longer legs, a very short dress and dangerously high heels. And she'd clearly had an effect on Soapy, who'd had his hair trimmed and was actually wearing a shirt and tie. Mind, he still had on a pair of work boots – but by the look of them he'd been at them with a shoe brush.

'She's his intended,' Algy muttered out of the side of his mouth.

'Intended? What – you mean . . .?'

He put his finger to his lips. 'The "m" word, old boy. But that's strictly *entre nous*, as they say in France. And between you and me, if you look carefully at the top of his head you might see a very large thumbprint.'

'Algy,' I whispered. He raised an eyebrow. 'You're gonna have to tell me.'

'Tell you what, Michael?'

'How he does it! How does a scruffy herbert like that find a woman like – well, look at her. You have to say she's easy on the eye.'

I got no further. Algy was sending me signals with his eyebrows, and then the man in question was clapping me on the back.

'Now then, cock-bod. You got them criminals sorted yet? Cos on the telly they reckon there's a crime wave sweeping the country.' He turned to Ann. 'He hasn't been slacking, has he?'

'Hey,' she said, 'we'll have less of that talk. Anyway, why are you dressed for a court appearance? I didn't think you even owned a shirt.'

'Only joking, love.' He let go of the young lady's hand and approached the trap as Cyril and Ron arrived, doffing their hats and bowing elaborately. Soapy ignored them and leaned over the trap, tugging on the release and swivelling the thin metal seat. 'Nice bit of kit, Walt. Who'd you scrounge this off then?'

'Never mind that,' I said. 'How about rescuing your lass from them two old lags and introducing us?'

'Oh aye. Nearly forgot. You won't have met Becky.'

Becky shook hands all round, smiled sweetly, and nodded at us all in turn. Either she was the silent type or she was simply awestruck. It was anyone's guess. After a moment's silence I said, 'C'mon, Soapy, chip in your ten quid and let's get started, shall we?' Poor old Soapy. The idea of parting with a tenner – to Walter of all people – was clearly causing him grief, but at the same time he wasn't going to expose his ingrained Yorkshire thriftiness to Becky. Not yet, at any rate. He dug deep into his trousers and slung a wad of notes at Walter. 'Help yourself,' he said, his face contorted into an agonised grin.

I hate to admit it, but Algy was right. There was more to this clay-pigeon game than just shooting straight. It's all about visual pickup points and break points and quartering your target – as Walt explained to me, patiently, after I kept blasting away at clays that had long since flown across the gap in the trees. And when I thought about it, my last stab at it had been ten or fifteen years ago. No such problems for Ann, though. While I wrestled with the basics, whooping with joy when I managed to hit the odd clay, she was knocking them out of the sky with monotonous regularity. She was soon pushing Algy for top billing, with Walt not far behind. Cyril chalked up their scores on an old blackboard he'd dragged out of the shed.

'Pull!' she shouted. There was a metallic twang as Ron released the trap. Ann swivelled gracefully with the gun on her arm, and as the clay soared across the gap she squeezed the trigger. There was a dull 'phut!' followed, every single time, by the sight of yet another clay shattering into fragments.

'Well,' I said, as she awaited her next turn, 'I guess it's true what they say about an expert. You make it look easy.'

'It is,' she said, grinning at me. 'Once you get the hang of it. You should see my brother, he's one of the best shots in Yorkshire. Anyway, at least you beat Soapy.' She grinned at me. 'I'd say you show promise. Well done, you.'

I put my gun down and sighed. 'Well, I'm not going to make a fool of myself any longer. Looks like this is going to be between you and Algy – once you've seen Walt off. A clash of the titans.' The rest of us could only stand back and admire their skill as they popped away. Soapy got busy ferrying extra beers from the house, and from behind us came the smell of searing flesh as Ron and Cyril went to work on the barbecue. By the time Algy and Ann had agreed to a draw – or 'honours even', as he put it – we were all gagging for our grub.

Walt had done us proud, of course. There were burgers, bangers, meatballs and chops galore. God knows where they came from. I recognised a bit of lamb – or was it goat? – and something that may have been wild boar; as for the rest of it, it could've been anything, and probably was. But the taste – it was out of this world. 'Ann,' I said, 'you got to try this stuff. It's fantastic.'

'How d'you know it's not something he's scraped off the road?'

'I don't, lass.'

'I'll stick to my Linda McCartney if you don't mind.'

'Tell you what, though, I don't see any desserts on display. And you know what I'm like for me sweet stuff.'

Even as I spoke Walt's sister came bustling into the garden from the side entrance, carrying a huge tray covered with a white cloth. 'Sorry I'm late,' she gasped. 'Had a disaster with me apple turnovers, but . . .'

'Never mind about them, lass,' said Walt, whipping the cloth off as she shooed Soapy and his girl off one of the wooden benches and placed the tray on it. 'What about that pumpkin pie you promised me?'

'Too early, Walter. The pumpkins aren't ready yet. You'll just have to wait.'

'These'll do in t'meantime,' Soapy said, grabbing a couple of coconut tarts. 'C'mon, Mike lad, you wanna get stuck in before word gets round.'

'We'll do 'em justice,' I said. 'Come on, Becky, don't stand back or there'll be nothing left.' I handed her a paper plate. 'It's every man for himself around here, love.'

'Ah, at last – a true gentleman,' she purred, as Ann raised her eyebrow at me over the rim of her wine glass.

We made short work of it all: the meat, the corn-on-the-cobs, the home baking, and the wine and beer. As the sun went down in the gaping hole where that sycamore used to be, Walter got the band together for a few more numbers as one or two more locals drifted in from the Jolly Farmers. With Muriel playing a sweet melody on her fiddle and Cyril backing her on the accordion, Soapy and Becky danced around the tables to the strains of 'Home On The Range'. It was a touching sight – so much so that I took Ann's hand and swept her onto the impromptu dancefloor, where we were joined by a beaming Algy and Walt's sister, Hilda.

We left as darkness fell, walking down the hill to our place in the woods with the stars coming out and the lights twinkling across the Vale of York. We were just entering the lane when a barn owl, silent, pale and ghostly, flitted from one tree to the next, right in front of us. Ann squeezed my hand, but neither of us spoke. There was nothing to say. It was the perfect end to an excellent day.

Chapter 10

We'll Meet Again

'I'm in trouble, mate.' Baz kicked his wellies off and slumped into the old leather armchair by his kitchen table. It was a thoroughly nasty day out there on the Wolds. Just walking from the car and across the yard I'd got a good soaking.

'I tried to tell him,' Jackie called out from the stove. 'But you know what he's like. Here, grab a seat and have a cup of coffee, Mike. Warm yourself up.'

'I'll do just that,' I said, shaking the drips from my coat and hanging it on the hook behind the back door. 'Go on, Baz, let's have it. What you been up to, lad?'

'Remember that old Land Rover of mine?'

'Aye, you were working on it last time I came by. Nineteen sixty-six model, wasn't it?'

'Not much wrong with your memory then.'

'No – and you got it for running around the farm in, right?'

'Well, that's t'blooming trouble, mate.'

'Cheers, Jackie.' I took the mug off Baz's missus and reached for the biscuit tin. 'Oh dear,' I said, 'why have I got a bad feeling about this?'

'Cos you know how stubborn he is, that's why.'

'Let me guess. It somehow got out onto the public highway, that it?'

'That's part of it, aye . . .' Baz said.

'And then, Sod's Law – sommat goes and happens.'

'If I hadn't been out numbered by 'em it would've been more than sommat. Bloody outsiders!' Baz was up from his seat. His face was red and he started pacing the floor in frustration. I could see that, deep down, he was seething.

'Steady on,' I said. 'Just take a deep breath and tell us the tale. It's not like you to be so wound up.'

'I'll tell you all right. And you make sure you're sitting comfortably, cos it's a bloody saga, mate, that's what it is.' He reached down, peeled a thick woollen sock off his foot and held it up for inspection. 'Now look – me bloody welly's sprung a leak. If it ain't one thing it's another.' He put the dripping sock over the rail of the stove, and sat back down in his comfy chair. 'There's a new lad in the area, comes from Selby, somewhere over yonder. Comes over with dogs and does a spot of poaching. He's a nasty bugger, and he thinks he's a hard case, all dressed up in army paraphernalia. You know the sort. Camouflage trousers and them big black paratrooper boots, forage cap – aye, and a great fat beer belly on him.'

I pulled out my notebook. 'I believe I may have heard about this one,' I said. Only the previous week I'd been talking to one of my oppos in Hambleton, and he'd mentioned a notorious criminal type from down that way who'd been spotted out and about in the Easingwold area. 'Is it him who goes around asking you if he can walk his dogs? And then you can't get rid of him?'

'Sounds like the same youth,' Baz said. 'Comes over all "yes sir, no sir" till he gets the nod, like, then he starts knocking off your game bods and taking hares. And if you challenge him he threatens you wi' destruction. It's like he's running one o' them protection rackets, Mike. You say yes to t'bugger and you're lumbered wi' him; you say no and – why, he teks no bloody notice. Just does as he pleases. He wants sorting.'

'So where do you stand with him? What you been up to?'

'I'll tell you. It was about eight, eight thirty last night. I was out in t'Land Rover. I've just turned some sheep out into a field of turnips and I went out to check on 'em. First thing I saw was this old estate car – one of them big Peugeots – parked up alongside t'woods. So I got out. Had a little nose around. Soon spotted him, across t'far side of me rape-field, what I planted about a month since. Lamps, dogs, the bloody lot.'

'On his own, was he?'

'No, he had a couple of other fellows with him. Anyway, I could see three or four hares darting about, and them all flashing their lights at 'em, like. So I says to meself, "Right," I says, "we'll cook your bloody goose for you." I get back in t'cab, swing her about, and give it full beam, right across t'field. I've fitted a couple of right powerful lamps on since you saw her. Halogen jobs. One of them's on a swivel. Doesn't half cast a beam.'

'I bet they loved that.'

'Well, they shouldn't be tekking advantage, should they? Anyway, the hares soon scattered, and next thing I see is Fatso, loping across t'field like, bold as brass and trampling me crop, and his mates trotting after him. Right, I thought, it's time old Baz was out of here. But by the time I get back in me cab he's across t'road in front of me, shaking his fist, effing and blinding, and t'dogs snapping at me window.'

'Nasty.'

'Aye, and there's more to come. Soon as I've driven past him they pile into their vehicle, and next minute they're right up behind me, headlights on full beam. Well, the last thing I want is him following me into t'yard, so I swing off down the lane.'

'Ah, that's your problem. You're on the public road, Baz.'

He paused and rubbed his chin with his open hand. 'Mike lad, I'd no choice. Anyway, you know that lane. Never sees a car after dark – apart from a courting couple now and then. But he was coming at us like a mad thing – right on me tail, flashing his lights and leaning on t'horn. Had me bloody rattled, I can tell you. Anyway, there's worse to come.' Baz was breathing heavily, as if he was reliving the entire episode.

'You got his number, I presume?'

'Oh aye, I got that all right.'

'Go on, then. What happened next?'

'Well, it ended up where the buggers . . . You aren't goin' to believe this, Mike.'

'Try me.'

'Well, they drove me off the bloody road. They were that close I lost control and ditched it.'

'Hell. Any damage?'

'No – apart from an odd scratch to t'Landie she's right as ninepence. They're built like bloody tanks, them old ones. Anyway, soon as they saw me go off the road they was away. I tried to back out, but she wasn't having it. Front wheels were in a foot of muck. Had to abandon ship and walk home.'

'He was in a right state, weren't you, love?' Jackie had sat herself down on the chair arm and put her hand on his shoulder.

'Hmm – nasty business,' I said. 'So when did you say this was?'

'By the time I got back here it must have been about nine o'clock.'

'And where's the Land Rover now?'

'In t'ditch where I left her.'

I looked out of the window. 'Well,' I said, 'it ain't much of a day, but I s'pose we'd better take a look.'

'Aye, go on then. Just let me find a dry pair of socks. I'll go down on me tractor if you want to follow me. I want to get her pulled out, but I thought I'd best wait for you to come by.'

It was still chucking it down when we got outside. A proper, old-fashioned autumn day with the wind swirling around the yard and water splashing out of the gutters onto the concrete.

I dived into the car and when Baz set off in the tractor I followed him, hanging back a bit to avoid the muck he was throwing up. The Land Rover was only a few hundred yards from the house. There was a pair of deep gouges in the verge where it had slewed off into a shallow ditch and come to rest with its front end wedged into a thorn hedge.

I stayed in the car till Baz had pulled it out; just wound the window down to watch him at work, his yellow waterproof coat almost luminous under the darkened sky. 'Now,' he said, as he stowed the chain in the cab, 'let's see if she's still running okay.' He got in and turned the key in the ignition. It fired up all right, ran for about thirty seconds, and then started spluttering. 'Eh oop,' he said, his brow furrowing as he turned again and pressed the accelerator pedal. There was an explosive sort of cough, followed by an eruption of black smoke from the exhaust, then silence. He turned the key once more.

'She's not having it, is she?' I said, as he swung the door open and stepped out, the rain bouncing off his bare head.

'Aye, and I can tell you why.' He was unscrewing the diesel filler cap. 'Cos I've seen this before. The bastards.'

'What? What is it?'

He was bending over, wiping a raindrop off his nose before sniffing at the filler. 'They'll have put sommat in t'tank. Might be sugar . . .' He sniffed again. 'Sand, more likely. God help 'em if I get hold of 'em, Mike. This'll cost me an arm and a leg, this will.'

There was nothing to be done except let Baz haul his crippled vehicle back to the yard and then deal with the paperwork. This wasn't as simple as it sounds. The case was complicated by the fact that Baz was making allegations of dangerous driving and – if something had indeed been put into his tank – of criminal damage. But at the same time he was making an admission of driving his vehicle on a road with no insurance or MOT. Still, I thought, at least he didn't need a road fund licence. The trusty Land Rover was too old to need one.

Once I'd finished taking all the details I explained to him that I would be investigating the matter. 'But you do realise,' I said, 'that your own offences will have to be taken into account?'

'Aye,' he said. 'I s'pose they'll have to.' He'd come in out of the weather and was sitting in my car, the raindrops running down the lines of a very anxious face.

'Try not to worry, mate. There are reasons why you did what you did, and I'm sure they'll go in your favour. Anyway, I'll let you know what happens.'

By the time I set off for town the rain had eased and the clouds were lifting. It was still blowing hard, but away towards the west the Pennines stood out as a clear grey line, and above them there were one or two patches of brightness in the sky. That's good, I thought, because we've a big weekend coming up and we could do with some decent weather.

One of the great advantages of having your own rural beat is that you're free, in theory at least, to go where you see fit.

Of course, you know you'll be required to help out in town on a Friday and a Saturday night; and you'll respond to calls as and when they come in, even if they're outside your area. However the following morning, which was Saturday, I was posted to take an hour or two patrolling around Pickering. Not because there was a crime wave there or anything, but I was certainly expecting to find a few colourful characters.

They started the Pickering Wartime Weekend back in the early 1990s. Whoever thought of it can't have had any idea just how popular it would become. It certainly filled a gap in the market, as they say, because it's grown, year on year, to become an absolute phenomenon, one of the great gatherings for nostalgia buffs and re-enactors around the country. They take place right through the season, but this one is the last – and one of the most popular. I'd heard plenty about it since I came back to North Yorkshire, but for one reason or another I'd always missed it, and I was determined not to let another year go by. So, next morning, after I'd tidied my paperwork and made a couple of local calls, I set off up the A169.

The road into town was lined with men, women and children walking in from the car parks. I'd never realised that quite so many people would take so much trouble over dressing up. Whenever I've heard people talking about re-enactment I've always imagined those burly fellows with beards putting on armour and wielding swords to revisit Civil War battlefields, or marching through the streets of York dressed as Vikings. But here were scores, well, more like hundreds, of authentic-looking soldiers, airmen and sailors representing the British and American forces of sixty or seventy years ago. A few were dressed in German army uniform, and there was even a Norwegian group carrying skis and all dressed in white. And everywhere you looked were land girls, civil defence volunteers, air raid precaution officers, French Resistance fighters, nurses, kids with little suitcases acting the part of evacuees, and of course the good old Home Guard, or Dad's Army as we like to call them now. On top of that there were hundreds of people dressed as civilians from the period. It really was a fantastic spectacle.

There was no way I'd get the car into the town centre; it would be absolutely chock-a-block. Instead I parked in the yard at the police station and went for a stroll. Well, I'm saying I strolled. As I made my way down towards the station I had to squeeze through tightly packed crowds, all gathered to watch the parade of vehicles and personnel that was due to start at around ten forty. And I hadn't gone far when I found myself face to face with a couple of fellow police officers – or so I thought. It was a second or two before I realised they were in period costume.

'Keeping busy?' I asked. They were both in their fifties, by the look of them, and making a big thing of acting the part – even down to the measured walk, the trimmed moustaches and the hands clasped behind their backs. They were really into the role, although the one who answered my question seemed distracted.

'Oh . . . yes, Officer. Plenty to – ah, plenty to keep us on our toes.' I soon saw what was on his mind. A tall blonde lady wearing a silk dress, a pillbox hat and a pair of stockings with seams up the back of her shapely legs was posing for photographers while her partner, dressed in an RAF officer's uniform, stroked his handlebar moustache, pulled out a silver case and lit up a cigarette.

'Never mind the talent-spotting,' I said. 'You wanna concentrate on the job. Round up a few of them black marketeers.'

'Don't worry,' his mate said. 'We're keeping our eyes peeled. Might have a look at the station next. Always plenty of dodgy characters hanging around up there.'

'Right,' I said. 'I might go up there myself. Be nice to see the old steamers in action.'

But right now the parade was about to start. I have to say it was pretty impressive: first came those on foot, some of them actual forces veterans, proudly displaying their banners, flags and medals. Then came the vehicles. First a tank came rumbling down Potter Hill, followed by an assortment of Jeeps, motor-cycles, scout cars and lorries, some pulling artillery pieces or anti-aircraft guns, and all heading towards the marketplace where the veterans were taking the salute. The air was filled with the smell of exhaust and the streets echoed to the rumble of V8 engines as a whole cast of characters from the pages of history rode past. Winston Churchill, sitting up on the rear seat of a staff car, puffed on his cigar and waved two fingers to the crowd. Field Marshal Montgomery sat impassively, dark beret in place and a thin smile on his lips, while ahead of him a trio of gorgeous-looking women clung to the Free French fighters as they swept by in a sleek black Citroën.

As I stood there, taking it all in, I felt someone prodding my back. ''Ere, wanna buy a pair of genuine silk stockings, guv?'

Turning round, I saw a thin, weaselly figure in a dark blue pinstriped suit with wide lapels. He had a scarlet tie, matched by a handkerchief in his top jacket pocket. On his feet he had a pair of what they used to call co-respondent shoes – part brown and part white – and on his head a dark trilby hat with a white band, pulled down over the upper half of his face. He looked every inch the classic wartime spiv. With his thin, greasy moustache and the flashy rings on his fingers – not to mention the Cockney accent – it took me a moment to realise who he was.

'Ronnie bloody Leach!'

'Aye, but you had to think about it, didn't you?' He shoved the hat back on his head and grinned at me. 'What d'you reckon, then? Got it all from the Salvation Army shop in York. And me gear, like.' He unbuttoned his jacket and showed me what he was carrying in the lining. 'See – I've got watches, stockings, razor blades, chocolate: you name it.' Then he grinned, reached up and stroked his moustache. 'How d'you like this, then? Bin growing it specially. Part of me new image.'

'Which is what, exactly?'

'I'm gonna be an actor.'

'You what?' I ducked as I was hit on the side of the head by a packet of chewing gum, hurled into the crowd by a party of Yanks in a Jeep. Ronnie bent down to pick it up and slid it into his pocket.

'No, it's right,' he said. 'They were filming one of them historical things up at Castle Howard for t'BBC, and I got taken on as an extra. There's a website where you can get jobs all round the country. Some people make a living at it.'

'Ronnie, anyone can get taken on as an extra. So long as you can stand there and cheer when the director shouts "Cheer!"'

'Aye, but they picked me out specially for a scene of me own. Said I was just the sort they was looking for. That was the director himself. Told me to walk up to that actress – what's her name? Her dad was in films – and her mum.'

'They all are, Ronnie. They're all related to each other. They call it keeping it in the family.'

'Hey, right classy woman she is. Anyway, I had to lift her

purse out of her handbag and then "melt into t'crowd". You wait till it comes on t'telly. You'll see.'

'They call that typecasting, Ronnie. Horses for courses. If you want my advice, lad, don't give up the day job. If you still have one. Hey, mind your back, there's a couple of fellows there want a word with you.'

The two period policemen had sneaked up behind him. One of them grabbed his arms while the other took out a notebook. 'Now then, young man,' he said, 'I'm arresting you for trafficking in rationed goods under Section . . .'

I left Ronnie protesting his innocence, much to the amusement of several passersby, who were snapping away with their cameras.

The newspapers reckoned there were as many as 10,000 visitors to the town that day – and with a crowd that size it was no surprise that I bumped into one or two more familiar faces. I spotted Nick the gamekeeper queuing up outside the baker's shop for a bite of lunch, and as I finally made my way to the station there was Soapy on the front step of the pub with a pint pot in his hand, surveying the row of pre-war cars and vans that was parked along the roadside. 'So where's your girlfriend?' I asked.

'Becky? She'll be about somewhere.'

'Aren't you worried?'

'Worried about what, cock-bod?'

'Why, that one of these handsome lads'll whisk her off in a vintage Austin or some such? You know how some girls are when they see a fellow in uniform.'

Soapy just snorted.

'No, take it from me, lad. You wanna be careful. They don't like you going off on your own, y'know.'

'She knows where to find me.' He raised his glass, which was almost empty. 'I'm going to need a refill, cock-bod. I'd buy you one – only you're on duty.'

'Very thoughtful of you. And where's the man himself today?'

'Algy?' Soapy shook his head. 'In his own words he has . . . declined the offer.'

'What offer?'

'Didn't he tell you?'

'I haven't seen him for a while – not to speak to anyway.'

'Ah, well. He's been upsetting people.'

'That makes a change.'

'Aye, told the organisers he was going to turn up as Winston Churchill.'

'Is that right? Well, if anyone can impersonate our great war leader, Algy can. I'll never forget the time he sat me down and recited the "blood, sweat and tears" speech off the top of his head. Word perfect, he was.'

'You're lucky that's all you got, cock-bod. I've had 'em all. And more repeats than t'bloody BBC. Even the Iron Curtain one. Drives you nuts.'

'Mind you, I've just seen Winnie go by, giving 'em all the two-fingered salute.'

Soapy nodded, and drained his glass. 'That, my friend, is the point. That is what they told him. Said they already had someone lined up. Said could he come as a spy – but only if he agreed to be arrested on t'station trying to board the train.'

'I see – and he didn't like that, eh?'

'Didn't like it? You should've heard him, Mike. He went right up in t'air. If they wouldn't have him as Winnie they certainly weren't having that 1938 staff car he's doing up. And as for being a spy – well, he said it was a slur on his character and he'd see 'em in court. He was not happy, mate. No, Algernon is mounting a one-man boycott this year.'

'I see. So he's at home, is he? Sulking?'

'I wouldn't say he's sulking, Mike. Not any more. No, he's got other things on his mind now.'

'Oh dear. What is it this time?'

'That hunting ban they're on about.'

'If it happens.'

'Oh, it's gonna happen, cock-bod. At least, in his mind it is. And he's making plans.'

'Which you're not at liberty to tell me, I suppose?'

'I promised I'd keep schtum. But what I can say, Mike' – he glanced around and stepped towards me – 'What I can say is, if he drops in on you over the Christmas holidays – well, you haven't to laugh. Cos that would upset him.'

Before I could get anything else out of him, Soapy had put a finger to his lips and gone back inside.

I made my way across the road and into the station, where I was greeted by a sign written in big bold letters:

WE ARE SORRY BUT ONLY TICKET HOLDERS AND RE-ENACTORS
DRESSED IN 1940S COSTUMES ARE ALLOWED ON THIS PLATFORM

'And police officers in pursuit of their duties?' I said to the ageing squaddie who was guarding the entrance.

'Yes, *sir!*' he shouted, standing smartly to attention, his rifle upright by his side.

The platforms, the booking office, the waiting room and the snack bar – even the footbridge – were heaving with people, all craning their necks and peering through their viewfinders to get a snap of the *Sir Nigel Gresley* as the legendary locomotive, gleaming like a kingfisher in the autumn sunlight, puffed its way towards the buffers, hauling a string of maroon-coloured coaches. One or two had video cameras set up on tripods. One had succeeded in getting a particularly elegant young woman in a mink stole up on the footplate, much to the delight of the grizzled old driver and his mate, who stood there, faces blackened by coal dust, grinning through a haze of white fur and perfume.

I watched the venerable old steamer manoeuvre its way round to the front of the train, and then, as the passengers loaded up for the run to Grosmont, I headed back to the police station to collect the car. I drove to Malton by way of Low Marishes, where somebody had reported a bonfire out of control. By the time I got there the fuss – and the fire – had died down. It had been more smoke than flames, and it was well away from any buildings. With luck, I was thinking, it would be that sort of day: all quiet on the western front. Because, to tell the truth, my mind was elsewhere, thinking about Baz and his problems. He'd left a message with the front desk at Malton saying that the garage had found a quantity of sand in the fuel tank of his Land Rover.

I knew very well who this poacher was who'd had the run-in with Baz. I'd had another chat with my mate in Hambleton, and learned that they called him Michelin Man, or Mitch for short. And I knew, from several reports, that he spelled nothing but trouble and would continue to do so, given a free rein. He was one of those individuals you'd really like to see put out of action. As Baz had said, he needed sorting. But of course, as a police officer you can't act on what you'd like to see happening. However, I had taken that statement off Baz, and he was still insisting that our friend had forced him off the road. So there was no reason why I shouldn't ask the Selby police to pay a call on this Mitch, arrest him, and quiz him about his movements on Thursday night – and the damage to Baz's vehicle. Depending on what he said they would at least tell him that he'd been reported for dangerous driving.

As soon as I got through to Selby the desk sergeant there knew who I meant. Oh yes, he said, we know him of old. Clever as a cartload of monkeys. Poacher, petty thief, several convictions for breaking and entering. And he's suspected of nicking red diesel: there's been a spate of theft from farm tanks the last month or two – all of them in areas where he's known to take his dogs. Yes, he said, when he'd got that lot off his chest, they would gladly send a couple of PCs round to bring him in.

The officer assigned to the task called me back a few days later. 'Nice fellow,' he said. 'Threatened to do me for harassment, and denied any involvement. Then when I pressed him he said, yeah, he did recall going out that way to walk his dogs the other night.'

'So did you ask him about running a Land Rover off the road?'

'Oh, I asked him okay.'

'And?'

'He turned the tables on your mate. Says he was like, and I quote, "a madman on speed", unquote, and he was forced to take evasive action. And he's every intention of going back to exercise his dogs there whenever he feels like it, because he has the farmer's permission.'

'Used to have it, you mean.'

'I'm telling you what he said, Mike.'

'What about the sand in the Land Rover's tank?'

'Oh, he just laughed. Said your mate deserved it but he knew nowt about it. I wouldn't have expected anything else from him, would you?'

'No. Thanks for your time anyway. If you can send me the paperwork I'll put the file together and see what the CPS make of it all.'

You have to be impartial as a police officer, but when it comes to a case like this, when you know someone's deliberately causing trouble – and when they tell you to your face that they're going to carry on stirring it – well, that's when you set your stall out to try to nail them. What he was saying was, you can't touch me. And I was gritting my teeth and saying, oh yes I can. We were talking red rags and bulls now. And it was probably a question of waiting for him to show his face. Because that type always do, sooner or later. They just never know when to stop.

Meanwhile I went back to Baz and laid it on the line to him. He was not to get involved. At all. Any aggravation, any hint of it, and he was to come to us. Right away. This time he meekly accepted it.

The break came on a Sunday morning a week or two later. In fact, I can pinpoint it precisely, because it was the day the clocks went back and for the first time in years I was on the early shift. I actually set my alarm for five thirty, then turned over and nudged it on, just so that I could relish every extra minute in bed. But when I looked through the curtains about half an hour later the sky was a beautiful pale blue, the trees were still, and a fox was making his way stealthily across a lawn turned white by the first frost of the season. I was about to wake Ann up to show her, but she looked so cosy I thought better of it.

We'd had a long spell of wet and windy weather since the time I visited Baz and Jackie and this whole business kicked off, but now, suddenly, you could feel winter on its way – I mean the good part of winter, the crisp, cold, sunny weather that energises you and perks up your appetite. As I took Henry down the lane for his morning run I revisited my childhood, stamping on the frozen puddles and throwing shards of ice for him to fetch. Daft as a brush, that dog. He'll chase anything, and if it doesn't contain nails or barbed wire he'll eat it and come back for more.

At the station the day got off to a quiet start. After we'd had a cup of tea, there were the usual drunk and disorderlies to release from overnight detention. It was the same old faces and the same old story: hung over, full of remorse, reeking of tobacco smoke and stale booze and wondering where they were going to get a breakfast at seven o'clock on a Sunday morning. It was just a matter of doing their fingerprints, photographs and DNA swabs before they were charged or cautioned and then released. It's not the best job, not in the fetid atmosphere of an unventilated custody area. But someone has to do it. Following that, it was the usual Sunday-morning checks – making sure all the patrol vehicles had all the equipment that they should have on board: signs, first-aid kits, shovels, brushes, blankets and the rest. When that was sorted and I'd polished off another cuppa I took a drive along the A64, coming off at Kirkham to cross the Derwent before making my way up to Walt's by way of Westow. I wanted to check how the weir was running and see if I could spot the odd salmon jumping. I'd just pulled into the car park by the ruined priory when I heard Julie from Control on the radio.

'*Had a call from a farmer out near Duggleby. He's seen poachers on his land, shooting hares. Any unit to deal, over?*'

I doubled back to the car. '1015, show me as dealing. Who is it, Julie? Who's the farmer?'

She gave me a name. I knew the man, and I knew he wasn't one to bother us unnecessarily. I also knew that he didn't allow any unauthorised shooting on his land.

'I'm on my way.'

'*All received, Mike. I'll see if I can get any further details and organise some backup for you.*'

I drove up the hill, swinging onto the road that would take me over to Langton and onto the Beverley road at North Grimston. 'Julie, have you got any vehicle details for me?'

'*Yes, Mike. Peugeot estate . . .*'

Aha. I could feel the surge of excitement as she read out the number, adding that the registered owner was none other than our friend the Michelin Man from Selby. 'Right,' I said, 'can you let me know when you've got some backup sorted, cos this guy isn't Mr Friendly. He has a serious attitude problem, over.'

Fordy came in right away. '*I'll be on my way from town, Mike. Be free in a few minutes and with you soon as I can.*'

'*Control to 1015, over.*'

'Go ahead, Julie.'

'*Yes, I've also got a single-crewed traffic car on its way from Pickering.*'

This was just what I wanted to hear. People like Michelin Man try to rely on their demeanour – their sheer physical presence – to intimidate you, especially if you're alone. It doesn't work with me these days, although I dare say it did when I was new to the job. Just because you have the uniform it doesn't mean they won't have a go at you, as I found out many a time in London, and of course just recently with the Sunset crew. It can be unnerving when you're out in the middle of nowhere and you encounter a bloke like him, with his mates. You have to be switched on at all times; show him that you mean business. Basically they're sounding you out, testing your confidence, so – of course it helps you if you know you've got backup on the way. It just puts the odds a little bit more in your favour.

As it happened, I almost caught our man with his trousers down. When I got to him he'd got his vehicle stuck in a gate-hole, and there he was gunning the engine and shouting at his mates, who were getting showered with mud from head to toe as they put their shoulders to the rear and the wheels spun and the car sank ever deeper into the mire. Behind them, you could see where they'd skidded about, chewing up the ground and leaving dark scars on the frost-whitened winter barley.

'Now then . . . just turn it off, will you?' I shouted above the roar of the engine.

He saw me okay, but he ignored my request and kept his foot down. The lads – there were two of them, dressed in identical camouflage jackets, their trousers tucked into army-style boots – stopped pushing and stared at me.

'Now!' I shouted. 'Let's have that off.'

One of them went and tapped the driver on the shoulder.

He pulled a cigarette from his lips. 'Wass your f***ing problem then?' he snarled.

'Just turn it off, will you?'

He spat on the ground, and did as I asked.

'Now, what are you doing here?' I said.

'Shooting rabbits. You got a problem with that?'

'If you're on private property, yes. D'you have permission to shoot on this land?'

'Course I 'ave.'

'Oh aye? Who off? Who gave you permission?'

He gave me a name. 'Well,' I said, 'you've got a problem right away, because that's his land over there.' I pointed across the field to the east. 'What you're on here doesn't belong to him. And the man who does own this, he won't allow shooting hares. Or shooting full stop.'

'Who says we were shooting hares?'

'You've been seen, within the last hour.'

'Well, buster, whoever told you that was a lying f***er. You see any hares here?' He was out of the vehicle now, standing up to his full height and staring me right in the eye. I can't say I liked it. Some people just give out unbridled hostility. You have to be very careful how you handle them – and yourself. I could feel my own hackles rising as he drew on his cigarette and exhaled smoke in my face. 'You show me the evidence,' he said. 'Go on.' He stood there, the corners of his mouth turned down, his arms extended by his sides in a classic posture of defiance.

'Tell you what,' I said, 'let's have a look in there, shall we?' I motioned to the hatchback door. 'Then we'll discuss the criminal damage you've caused.' I nodded at the field where they'd chewed the crop up with the car.

'F*** off! It was like that when we showed up.'

I wasn't going to get involved in a debate about that now. Knowing the landowner, who was an upstanding Yorkshireman – and principled at that – I was pretty sure he would back me up with a statement and press charges if needed. Especially with this guy's reputation as a bully.

He opened up. The inside of the car was, as I suspected it might be, empty. Just three pairs of trainers and a couple of raincoats. His mates stood there grinning.

'You say you were shooting rabbits?'

'You've got a hell of a memory, copper.'

'Where are they?'

'Never said we hit any, did I?'

'What are you shooting with?'

'Air rifle.'

'Let me have a look.'

'There's no law against air rifles, y'know.' He turned to his mates. 'Told you, lads. We're dealing with one very thick copper here.' They laughed, nervously. They weren't quite as cool as he was.

He turned to me, a sneer on his face. 'No law against air rifles, my friend. Didn't they tell you in that coppers' school you went to?'

'Let me see the gun,' I said. I learned years ago not to rise to the bait. It doesn't get you anywhere. And it riles them.

He reached into the car and pulled it out from beside the front seat. I could see right away that he'd modified it, and I reckoned straight away that I might just have got him – not that he had any idea. Yet. He was still posturing for his friends. They were younger than him, and by the look of them they weren't the brightest pebbles on the beach.

What he'd done was to take a standard air rifle and adapt it by adding a canister of compressed gas to give it more 'poke'. I'd learned about this on my wildlife course a year or two earlier. Until then I'd never come across it. The law is very strict about the power of an air rifle if it is to remain within the bounds of legitimacy. For an air pistol the kinetic energy at the muzzle must not exceed six pounds per square inch; for a rifle the limit is twelve. Beyond that – and I reckoned this could well be beyond it – they're classifiable as firearms, which require a firearms licence. And since I knew that Michelin Man had a criminal record, I knew that he was barred from possessing one. There he was, smirking at his mates while I examined the gun – and I was about to deflate him, big time.

'I'm not happy with this,' I said.

'Nor me, pal. Sights are crap. It's like I said, I haven't shot owt yet.'

'Well, I think this needs to be examined by the firearms team.'

'You what? A bloody air rifle?'

I tapped the gas cylinder. 'With this on, lad, it could well be a firearm – for which you need a firearms licence.' At this point I had enough to arrest him, but experience told me to wait until my backup arrived. Just to be on the safe side.

Matey was on the back foot now. He dropped his cigarette on the ground and trod on it. He was about to speak when the traffic officer arrived.

'Now then,' I said. 'Just the man I want to see. You got the sampling kit for this gentleman's fuel tank? He's already in a bit of bother, but I just want to make sure we get everything sorted.'

'Sure.' The officer opened up the back of the car and pulled out a dip sampling kit. 'Right, sir,' he said. Michelin Man shifted uneasily on his feet as the traffic officer made his way towards his car. 'Hey, I never filled that up. My mate had it all week, and—'

'We'll just take a look in here, shall we?' the traffic officer cut in. 'Make sure you're not breaking the law. We don't want that, do we now?'

While he assembled his kit, I took the names and addresses of all three men and passed the details to Control to run checks on them.

'Well, well, well. Amazing what you find.' The traffic officer was holding up the little paper test strip. 'That's red diesel in there, mate, to be used by farmers and the like for running agricultural vehicles.'

'1015 to Control, over.' This felt good. It felt very good indeed. It's always pleasing when you know someone's an offender and you manage to collar them. That's what the job's about, after all. Law enforcement. But when you have someone like this, who you're pretty sure is breaking the law but looks to be wriggling out of it – yes, it's a source of real satisfaction when you find something to nail him with. 'Aye, can you inform Customs and Excise we are going to be bringing in a vehicle that we suspect is running on red diesel. We're going to need recovery for it too. Just needs a front-end lift, over.'

'*All received, Mike, confirm the vehicle is the Peugeot, details as given earlier? And is it going to Malton?*'

'That's a yes, yes, over. As well as one prisoner.'

Michelin Man and the boys were looking pretty glum by now. They were leaning against the car with their coats wrapped around them, their shoulders hunched. They knew they were in trouble, and they weren't looking forward to meeting the excise officer. Those fellows are unrelenting in their pursuit of offenders, and savage in the penalties they can impose.

I now had the great pleasure of arresting Michelin Man on suspicion of possessing a section one firearm without a licence, of criminal damage and of tax evasion. And, yes, I may as well admit it, I couldn't resist mentioning to him that my gang was bigger than his.

I'd no sooner got that wrapped up than Fordy arrived in the van and Michelin Man was duly handcuffed and placed in the cage.

'How we gonna get back to Selby?' one of the others asked.

'I'm afraid that's your problem, not mine,' the traffic officer said.

I said nothing. Of course we would give them a ride back to

Malton, but I wasn't going to tell them that until I had to. Let 'em squirm, I thought.

It was a week or two before we got the results from the firearms unit at York. The humble air rifle that our friend had been using packed quite a punch: a muzzle energy of fifteen to sixteen pounds per square inch, in other words well over the limit, which meant that we now had two charges to hit him with.

More important than that, in a way, was the fact that word would get out about what had happened. This man had been cock of the walk – for a while. Or so he thought. And now we'd nailed him. Don't get me wrong: this wasn't victimisation. But the fact is that if you think someone's taking the mick, it gives you an added incentive: one, to put a stop to it, and two, to send out a message to others of his type. It also gives a boost to your standing within your community – it shows that you can get a result, even if it does take a little time.

We eventually charged Michelin Man with being in possession of an unlicensed firearm. For the fuel tax evasion, Customs imposed an instant fine that far exceeded the value of his vehicle. What that meant, in practice, was that they seized his vehicle to pay the penalty. We never did find any hares, even though Fordy and I made a pretty thorough search of the hedges up there on the hilltop. But, as I said to him later that day when we were tidying up the paperwork, remember Al Capone.

'What, the gangster?'

'Aye, that's him – and racketeer, extortionist, peddler of illicit alcohol. You name it, he was into it. You know what they got him for in the end?'

'I dunno. All of the above?'
'No. Tax evasion.'

There was still a loose end to tie up. I mean Baz, of course. I went to see him a week or two later, and he had good news. The CPS had decided that it was not in the public interest to prosecute him for taking his vehicle on the public highway with no insurance or MOT, given the mitigating circumstances of the case. 'But I got this,' he said, handing me a letter.

I unfolded it. It was a formal warning. 'That'll maybe make you think twice another time,' I said.

Baz took the letter back from me. 'Don't you worry, Mike. I've already had her tested and put her on me insurance. Just in case, like.'

'Good lad,' I said.

'By the way,' he said, 'been meaning to ask you sommat.'

'Fire away.'

'This Country Watch business.'

'Yeah?'

'When's your next meeting?'

'Oh, it'll be after Christmas I should think. Why d'you ask?'

'I was wondering if I could join up, like.'

'I'll give you a bell, mate.'

Chapter 11

Tracked Down

'Jayne, you ever wondered how a conspiracy theory starts up?'

A full moon was shining over Spaunton Moor. It was so bright that it almost hurt your eyes to look at it. As I sat there I saw a dark shadow move out from behind a rock and merge with the clumps of heather silhouetted against the skyline. There'd been a lot of talk recently of the Ryedale Panther, and for a brief moment I was tempted to wonder . . . but when I rolled my window down to have a closer look the faint purring of the engine was interrupted by the bleating of an old ewe, its breath forming clouds in the frosty air.

I shivered, and wound the window back up. 'I mean, Elvis is still alive,' I said. 'Who started that one up?'

'Wishful thinking, innit? People who just can't accept that he's dead. Anyway, it sells newspapers.'

'Aye, and records.' I reached for my flask. 'Okay then, how about the moon landings? You heard that one?'

'What, that they never happened?'

'Aye, that's it. NASA mocked them up in an MGM studio. Where did that come from?'

'God knows, but it always makes me laugh.'

'And what about Harold Wilson? Don't they reckon he was working for the KGB or something?'

'Who the hell's Harold Wilson?'

'You what? Oh, never mind.' I poured a half cup of coffee from my flask and looked at the clock on the dashboard. Two forty-eight. It had been a quiet night – too quiet for me – and the time was really dragging. Jayne took a bite out of her sandwich. 'Smells good,' I said. 'What's in it?'

She passed me the plastic box so that I could read the label. 'French brie and sun-dried peppers on a bed of rocket.' I laughed. 'D'you know what my mum used to pack us up with when I was a lad?'

'You mean before she sent you crawling up them chimneys with your brush and your ragged trousers?'

'Don't be daft now. You're talking about a proud woman and a good mother. She wouldn't send us out to sweep chimneys in a frayed collar, never mind ragged trousers.' I drained my cup and shook the flask, wondering whether I'd get another cup out of it. 'No, I'm talking about when I went off for a day's fishing with a bottle of pop and a brown paper bag.'

'Hang on, let me guess.' She chewed for a moment, then said, 'I know . . . bread and dripping. No, I forgot – you ate all the dripping at breakfast. How about a nice banana sandwich? That's what my grandad used to take when he was down the docks.'

'Oh aye? What docks was that then?'

'Rotherhithe.'

'I thought your lot came from Peterborough.'

'Nah – my dad did, but Grandad was a Londoner. He grew up in New Cross, just down the road from the old Den. Big Millwall supporter.'

'Oh, hell. Saw some right nutters down there when I was in the Met.'

'Yeah, well, he wasn't one of them. He was a very nice man. Your original gentle giant.'

'So how did he end up in Peterborough?'

'Had an accident and did his back in. Never worked again. Then they knocked his street down and moved everyone out to the sticks.' She wiped her hands on a paper napkin and tilted her seat back. 'Go on then, put me out of my misery. What did your mum put in your sandwiches?'

'Fish paste. God, it used to stink. But if we'd been very good we'd get jam for afters.'

'No wonder you grew up like you did. She spoiled you.' She closed her eyes and folded her hands across her lap. 'So anyway, tell me about this Wilson geezer.'

'Harold Wilson. Surprised you haven't heard about him.'

'It sorta rings a bell. Wasn't in the team that won the World Cup, was he? 1966 an' all that.'

'D'you know, Jayne, I reckon he shoulda been. Tricky left-winger, always ducking and weaving. Played for the opposition for most of his career.'

Jayne snorted. 'West 'Am? No wonder I never heard of him.'

'Ooh dear . . . let's change the subject, shall we?' I unscrewed the lid of my flask and tipped it over my mug. It just about covered the bottom. 'Anyway, you've got me off the subject. I was going to tell you about the latest conspiracy theory.'

'What's that?'

'Haven't you heard? It concerns us.'

'What, us as in you and me?'

'Calm down, lass. We're not talking romance.'

'I should bloody well hope not.' Jayne laughed. 'Go on then, what's it about?'

'Big cats, mate. Somebody's written in to the *Gazette and Herald*. Reckons the panther's on the loose again, rampaging through the countryside, slaughtering sheep . . .'

Jayne yawned. 'So – keep your kids indoors, eh?'

'Oh hell aye, according to the paper nothing's safe. Cats, dogs, kids, even the occasional unwary copper. And this is the best bit, Jayne – are you listening?' She grunted. 'The story is that we – North Yorkshire Police – have got our heads together with the Yorkshire Tourist Board to do a whitewash job. They reckon we're denying all knowledge in case it frightens the visitors off.'

'Yeah, but it wouldn't, would it? Think of the Loch Ness Monster. Best scam they ever came up with for boosting the hotel trade.'

I didn't have an answer for that, but I didn't need one.

'*Control to 1015.*'

'1015, go ahead, over.'

'*Mike, we've just had a burglary reported. A farmer. Says he's had his Land Rover stripped. Will you take a look?*'

'Yeah, all received, pass details.' I belted up, threw my flask into the back and waited for Julie to come through with the name and address. 'That's a strange one,' I said. 'Stripped.'

'Wassat mean then?'

For a moment I wondered whether this was another Baz and Jackie drama, but it turned out it was nowhere near their place. In fact, it was a farm I'd never visited – at the top end of our area, up near Hutton-le-Hole.

It was just turned half past three when we got there, but the guy was waiting for us, pacing up and down the yard in his overalls and one of those caps with earflaps, an alert-looking Labrador by his side. 'By, you're here smartish,' he said.

'All part of the service,' I said. 'Anyway, I'm glad you're out to meet us.'

'I'm up at four anyway,' he said. 'Do me milking. But I heard this noise about an hour since and – well, just come and see what the buggers have done.'

He took us across the yard, round a frozen puddle, and into his garage through a side door. There was his Land Rover – or rather the shell of it. The bonnet was missing, both doors, various electrical parts including the headlights and indicators, and all four wheels – plus the spare. 'They've even taken the bloody windscreen wipers, look.'

'Hell,' I said. 'Right mess, isn't it? I've never seen anything like it. Why've they stripped it down like that? Why not just drive it away?'

'They've tried the front entrance and couldn't get it open, that's why. I got broken into a few years back.' He squeezed down the side of the vehicle and showed me the main door, festooned with big brass padlocks and chains, some of them attached to iron rings set into the concrete floor. 'Lashed out on this lot. Never entered my head they'd break through the side door and take it away in bits.'

'What about your dog?' Jayne said. 'Didn't it make any noise?'

He took off his hat and ruffled his hair. 'Tell you the truth I did hear her bark – or thought I did. But it was just the once. And I went back to sleep. There's been a fox about . . . Then when she started again about half two I came to check.'

I cast an eye over what was left of the vehicle. To think they'd gone to such lengths, more or less dismantling the vehicle and removing everything of value. 'Must've taken 'em long enough,' I said. The farmer didn't reply. I was briefly reminded of the Sunset Gang, taking all those bricks out from the supermarket wall, one by one. Was this the way we were going, with crim-inals becoming ever more brazen? 'Well,' I said, 'how much d'you reckon it'll cost to put right?'

'Thousands.'

'And they'll get a decent price for all the bits, will they?'

'Aye, they'll have someone lined up. Some dodgy back-street garage. You want to see the price of Land Rover parts.'

'Right,' I said to Jayne, 'we need to get the SOCO in on this.' I turned to the farmer. 'That's the scene of crime officer. He'll be with you sometime after eight, depending on how much he has on. But he'll ring first and give you a time. Let's just hope he can come up with something. Meantime, don't disturb anything in here, will you?'

We went outside. Jayne and I had a good look around with the torches. With a bit of luck they'd have dropped one of the items they were trying to steal, or one of their tools. I searched for footprints, tyre marks, anything that might give us a starter for ten. But as far as we could see there was nothing.

Back in the house we took a statement from the farmer, then headed to the station. By that time our shift was almost over, and on the way home I thought over what we'd seen up there. It was an unusual sort of burglary, and I assumed at first that it would be a one-off, but in fact it heralded a spate of similar incidents that would have us chasing our tails for some time to come. Over the next couple of weeks there were three or four reports of farm buildings being broken into and vehicle parts taken, along with sundry tools and equipment. Then a sheep farmer called in to say he'd had his quad bike stolen from his yard. It's hard enough to make a living with sheep these days, and the loss was a serious blow. Quad bikes are a regular sight in our part of the world, bouncing over the pasture with a shepherd at the controls, a few bags of feed or a bale of hay in the back, and a black-and-white border collie perched on top. With a secondhand value of two or three thousand pounds, they're very attractive to thieves.

By now it seemed more and more likely that all these thefts were the work of a single gang, most probably coming in from outside the area. But who were they, and where were they from? It was all very worrying – and of course it got everyone on their toes. Even the chief superintendent was taking an interest, according to Birdie, and that set him on edge. I decided it was time to call a Country Watch meeting, get everyone together and bring them up to speed with what was happening – as if they didn't know already, because the bush telegraph was throbbing with rumours. I planned it for a Tuesday evening, and booked the usual room at the Dawnay Arms at West Heslerton. I sent out word that this was an emergency of sorts, but just to reinforce the message I made a point of attending the livestock market that morning. It would be a good chance to spread the word, and to pick up any titbits of information. A lot of country people will tell you things face to face that they wouldn't ring up and talk about. But when I bumped into Bob Easton outside Fox the butcher's he had something else on his mind.

'You know me,' he said, pausing to look at the rabbits and pheasants that hung in pairs outside the shop. 'I mean, I've always been as sceptical as t'next fellow. Feet on the ground, that's me. But I saw something last week, and to tell you the truth it had me wondering whether there's not some truth in the rumours.'

'Bob,' I said, 'if there's one thing I don't need right now it's one of me stalwarts telling me they've had aliens landing in a barley-field. Or are we talking crop circles?'

'Just wait till I've had me say before you start taking the mick.'

'Go on then, let's have it.'

'Well, something's been scratching the bark off an ash tree, not a hundred yards from the house. Something big and powerful.'

'Deer,' I said. 'They like to eat bark.'

'Aye, they do, but this isn't a deer. A deer gnaws at a tree, doesn't it? You can see the teeth-marks. This is more like – well, I can only say it's been torn at. By some beast with claws – right sharp ones an' all.'

'I think I hear the "P" word coming.'

He shrugged. 'Mike, if you could see it for yourself that's exactly what you'd think. I did, anyway. And then I remembered all them rumours. You know, about a panther.'

'Get away with you, Bob. There's no bloody panther out there.'

'Mike, I'm telling you what I saw with me own eyes. And I'll show it to you if you want to come by.'

'Tell you what I'll do,' I said. 'I know a vet. He's as level-headed as they come. Helped me out over a dead otter a year or so back – and he doesn't live very far from you. I'll put it to him and see if he'll take a look.'

We'd strolled up the Shambles and were in the market proper now. Bob was starting to cast an eye over a consignment of young bullocks that was being unloaded from a trailer. 'Anyway,' I said, 'Dawnay Arms, seven o'clock tonight.'

'I'll be there,' he said.

I made my way around the market premises, spreading the word, listening to bits of gossip and, in the background, the auctioneer's voice as he sold off the first of the cattle. 'Seventy? Do I hear sixty? Let's have fifty then. Come on now, forty to get us started. Forty . . . and two . . . forty . . . and four . . . forty-six at the back now . . .'

'*Control to 1015.*'

'Yeah, go ahead, over.'

'Can you make your way down to Wentworth Street car park? We've a report of a four-by-four being stolen.'

I got down there straight away and was met by the owner. 'Can you bloody believe it?' he said. 'Parked the bugger half an hour since, popped back to get me hat and it's gone.' He pointed to a row of estate cars, four-wheel drives and the like, most of them mud-spattered, many of them with dogs sitting inside. It was a typical Tuesday-morning scene. 'Left her right in that spot there, where that Toyota is.'

'Okay,' I said, 'let's have the details and I'll put the word out. It can't have got too far, surely.' The fact is, there are a hundred ways a vehicle like that could have made good its escape. And if the thief had got out of town he could be away down the A64 and on his way to Leeds by now. But I had little chance to speculate, let alone follow it up. No sooner had I got his details down than in came a report of a second theft from the same car park, this time of an Ifor Williams trailer, the type a farmer would use to carry a couple of bullocks or half a dozen sheep. They'd unhitched it from the vehicle it had been attached to – which contained a pair of agitated border collies. I soon realised what had happened.

'Cheeky buggers,' I said to Chris when I got back to the station. 'They've nicked the four-by-four, then hitched it up to the trailer and made off with that. Mark my words, Sarge, we're dealing with another organised team here. Tuesday – it's easy pickings, isn't it? Car parks full of unattended vehicles. The buggers have targeted us. And if I were a betting man I'd say there'll be more bad news before the day's out.'

I was right. When I got to the Dawnay Arms that night the place was heaving. There must have been thirty-five, forty of my regulars, including Bob Easton, Nick and his lad, and of course the Colonel, and they were queuing up to tell me about more bits and pieces that had gone missing the previous week: items of machinery, a trailer – and another quad bike.

So in between taking notes I talked to them and reminded them about the simple things, like making sure that their locks were secured at all times and their lights and alarms were working. And I stressed the need for vigilance. 'If you see owt or hear owt,' I said, 'pass it on: to the control room and to each other. Any problems with getting through to Control, then give me a ring on my mobile.' That's half the point of Country Watch. Intelligence and information-gathering; and, most of all, co-operation. 'We're here to help each other,' I told them, 'and to make it harder for thieves like these to get away with it. So, any unusual movements, take a note of the registration number and ring the details in. So far we've nothing to go on. We need to build up a picture. And that can only be based on information, of which we have very little. Now, I propose we start gathering information by a tried and trusted method.'

The Colonel immediately pricked his ears up. 'Ah, you mean an operation, like we had last year – or was it the year before?'

'It may well come to that, but for the moment, I'm just wanting observations. They'll be back, don't you worry. And we need to be ready for them. So we watch the roads, and we log movements. I'm asking for volunteers to be ready to go out, round the clock if necessary, and report back on what's moving and when. But just remember, your job is to observe and record. Nothing more.'

Good old farmers: they may spend a lot of time grumbling, about the weather, the price they get for their produce and the unfair competition from abroad, but I can only say that my lot

– if I can call them that – were always onside. A forest of hands went up, and I was able to start taking names and planning a campaign immediately. There was a determination in the air, a willingness to do what it took. Everyone wanted to be involved in getting a result. We had a crime wave on our hands and we were not going to sit there with our fingers crossed, hoping something showed up. It's at times like this that it comes home to you just what you're up against in trying to police an area the size of Ryedale. A lot of big empty spaces, a labyrinth of single-track roads, plenty of quiet ways in and out, and any number of places to hide, unseen. Still, I had a gut feeling that these criminals were from outside our area, and that meant that their vehicles would be conspicuous. They'd be on the move at dead of night, when my Country Watch members would be parked up in gate-holes, on hilltops and behind hedges, watching, listening and reporting in.

The thing about this kind of work is that you know you're waiting for that little slice of luck. It may be someone you've pulled over for having a defective brake light, or for speeding. It may be a chance encounter on a lonely road at dead of night, or it may just be that a copper on his beat sees something that doesn't quite make sense, and decides to probe into it. Which is what happened to Ed.

A week had gone by since the Country Watch meeting. I was off duty, but Ed was very much on the case. 'Tell you what happened,' he said, when we met up a couple of days later. 'I was out on the A64.'

'Our infamous "crime corridor", eh?'

'Yeah yeah yeah – are you listening?'

'Sorry, mate.'

'I was over by Whitwell and I saw this van, parked up on the roadside, facing towards York. Just something about it, you know? What's it doing there at one in the morning? So I pulled up and had a look. It was in quite good nick, a Fiat Ducato.'

'Anybody in it?'

'Nah. And the engine was cold. So I checked the number – and guess what?'

'No, you tell me.'

'It's from the Pontefract area, and it's suspected of involvement in a number of burglaries.'

'Ponte? Interesting . . . And was there anything going off that night? I mean around Whitwell?'

Ed shook his head. 'Bugger all, mate. Could be they saw me and I scared 'em off, of course. Who knows? I sat up watching for a bit, then I got a call. Checked back an hour later and it was gone.'

'Still, bloody good spot, Ed. Gives us something to feed into the Intelligence Unit. Yeah, nice one, mate.'

We got onto the computer before going out on patrol that night, and dug up a few more details on the van. It was thought to be used by a travelling gang who were, in the time-honoured phrase, 'of interest' to West Yorkshire police regarding a number of thefts from outbuildings – of machinery, electric gardening equipment and, most interestingly, quad bikes. 'Tell you what,' I said, 'let's do a TE. Find out if anyone else has registered it.'

A TE, or Transaction Enquiry, draws on the Police National Computer and gives details of any check made anywhere in the country in relation to a particular vehicle. You key in the number and it brings up the date, the place, the officer conducting the check, and the reason for it, no matter how minor. It could be worn tyres, suspect tax disc, anything. Two months earlier this van that Ed had spotted had been seen at Scarborough, late at night, unattended. And a few weeks before that in Malton. Nothing untoward, except that in each case the officer had thought it a bit odd, and noted it.

'What d'you reckon? Were they out doing a recce?'

'Can't think what else,' Ed said.

'But why take a van? Why not a car? It'd be a lot less conspicuous.'

'Time will tell, mate.'

It was about a week later. I was out on a night shift with my old mate Thommo. We were well into November now, the cold and flu season. Ed and Chris Cocks were both off sick, leaving us a couple short, so Thommo had been called in for an extra shift; and if there was one thing that was guaranteed to put a sparkle into PC Greg Thompson's eyes it was a bit of overtime – or 'a wee bit of plus' as he called it. Especially on a nice quiet night such as this, when we'd delivered a couple of prisoners into custody at York and were taking a leisurely ride back along the A64 in the Transit. I was riding shotgun and he was at the wheel rhapsodising about the blood sausage he'd brought in his pack-up, then reminiscing about the good old days in Glasgow.

'Aye, laddie, it was no place for shrinking violets. It was all gangs, see? Pull a knife on you as soon as look at you.'

Here we go, I was thinking. Story time. 'On a weekend, laddie, it was twice nightly. They'd call ye out to a fight in a pub and next thing it was bottles, glasses, chairs; all heading in your direction. Once had some nutter rip the dartboard off the wall and hurl it at me. Aye, and a silver salver loaded with canapés. It was a wedding, see, and the bride's ex-boyfriend turned up with his pals. Afore ye knew it, it was the OK Corral all over again.' He laughed. 'Aye, but when the dust settled, guess who had his pockets full of delicacies, eh? Salmon, crab, caviar. You name it.'

'That was the old days,' I said. 'You'd be on a charge now.' We were just passing Barton crossroads, making our way towards Whitwell hill at about sixty, and Thommo wasn't listening. 'Course, I got stabbed twice, ye ken.'

'Aye, I believe you have mentioned it,' I said. If he'd told me once he'd told me a dozen times, but the thing with Thommo was he was always ready with another version of the story. With one hand on the wheel he unzipped his fleece jacket and tugged at his shirt.

'Did I ever show you where they got me? Upper intestine – just round the side here. Ye can still see the scar if you look closely.'

'Er – how about concentrating on the road, eh?' My head was still full of images of his blood sausage.

'There's another one down here.' He reached forward and pulled up his trouser leg.

'Thommo!'

'What is it, laddie? What's happening?'

'I'm trying to tell you I know what a stab wound looks like, okay? And watch the bloody road!'

He fell silent. I was just starting to worry that I might have hurt his feelings when he braked sharply, and jabbed his forefinger towards the passenger window.

'Christ, mon!' He stopped pointing and grabbed the wheel again. 'A bloody invalid carriage? On the A64?'

'You what?' He'd brought the Transit to a stop, half on the road, half on the footpath, and was slinging it into reverse.

'I'm telling you, laddie—'

'Don't be daft. They don't have invalid carriages these days.'

But he wasn't having it. I wound down the window and leaned out into the chill night air. We were going backwards in a perfect straight line at somewhere between fifteen and twenty miles an hour. I had to hand it to the man: he could drive.

'We'll see, shall we?' Thommo put it into first, swung the wheel, and headed for the entrance to Whitwell village. 'There y'are!'

Ahead of us, moving rapidly, was a set of red tail-lights, lighting up brightly as the vehicle swerved around the left-hander. 'I tell you what that is,' I shouted. 'It's a bloody quad bike. And he's gone into a dead-end there, mate! Get after it!'

I grabbed the radio. '1015 to all units. Any units to assist. Suspects on possible stolen quad bike just entering Whitwell from the A64.'

We were in the village now, our headlights illuminating the entire length of the street. Above me I saw a bedroom light come on and someone pulling back a curtain.

'Okay, Mike. The good news is the dog section's on its way from Malton. Should be with you in ten minutes. Jayne and Fordy en route to you from Staxton.'

'Where the hell have they got to?' Thommo was cruising slowly, the pair of us peering up every side entrance and gateway, our Dragon Lights flashing off the walls and windows.

'There. What's that?'

Ahead of us in a private driveway was the quad, its engine still running.

'They cannae be far,' Thommo shouted, climbing out of the van and flashing his torch up and down the street. I jumped out, switched the quad's engine off and put the keys in my pocket.

We both stood listening in the silence of the night, hoping to hear footsteps, a dog barking, anything that might give us a clue as to where our suspect might be. While Thommo watched the front of the house and shone his Dragon Light up and down the street, I made my way round to the back garden.

'What on earth's going on? Who are you?'

Looking up, I saw an elderly male at a bedroom window. 'It's the police, sir. PC Mike Pannett. Someone's just left a stolen quad bike on your drive and run off.'

'Excellent.' He sounded a little bit like the Colonel. 'So what are you waiting for? You get after him. I'll be right down to help.'

'No, don't you worry. It's best if you stay inside. We've a police dog on its way.'

'Right you are, then. I'll keep an eye out through the window.' He leaned back inside and shouted, 'Audrey, get the kettle on, old girl. Spot of bother outside, but don't worry – the police are here.'

We started on a quick search of the village. There isn't much of it, so it wasn't going to take long. Then the dog handler showed up, and for a few minutes we thought we might get a result. At first the dog seemed to have picked up a scent but, whatever it was, the trail soon went cold. Meanwhile, Thommo had given up on his search and was standing beside me on the drive, breathing hard.

'I bet it's sommat to do with that Fiat Ed reported,' I said. 'Maybe we should put out a circulation for it.'

'Aye, good idea.'

Just as I was getting on with that Jayne arrived with Fordy. 'Wass going on, then?' she asked. I filled her in, briefly, and sent her to sit up at Crambeck, the next village along the main road, just in case matey had made it across the A64 and hidden there, or gone looking for a vehicle to get away in.

When the owners of the quad bike showed up they couldn't believe their luck. They only lived a few doors down from where it had been abandoned. Once they'd had time to think about it they remembered that, yes, they had seen a stranger out and about a week or two back, late at night – which was unusual in a tiny village like that – but no, they didn't have any further details.

'Listen,' I said, 'any time you get something like that just call us. It may not lead to anything directly, but it's all useful intelligence. At the very least we can try and keep an eye on the village. You haven't seen a Fiat Ducato van in the last week or two, have you?' I added as an afterthought. But no, they hadn't.

A couple of hours later, having searched the village thoroughly, Thommo and I made our way back to Malton. He was uncharacteristically quiet. I could tell he was down, and I was feeling pretty deflated myself. To have actually seen the thief and then have him slip away – it's something you really hate. But you can't afford to let it get to you. 'Listen,' I said, 'they got lucky. That's all there is to it.'

'True, but it still smacks of failure. And I don't like that. One moment we have them in our sights, and the next they've slipped through our fingers. It's awful frustrating.'

'I tell you what I reckon. I reckon the bloke on the quad was waiting at the side of the road to be picked up by the van that Ed saw. It makes sense, doesn't it? I mean, how else do you get the quad back to Ponte?'

'You could be right.'

'I just hope we get another crack at them. Because they'll come again.'

'Aye, they will, laddie, they will. These people are gamblers. A gambler keeps going till he runs out of money; a criminal keeps going till he runs out of luck.' He tapped his head. 'Psychology, d'ye see? The delinquent mind. I did a course on it, ye ken.'

*   *   *

After my night with Thommo I had a couple of days off. Ann was down south visiting an old friend from her Met days. It felt odd to be on my own for the first time in getting on for a year, and I really missed her. Missed her support as much as anything, and having someone to unload to after a bad shift. But at least I had Henry for company, and I had a couple of outside jobs to see to, which pleased him. There's nothing he likes better than to follow me about and chew lumps out of any tools or clothes, or anything else I happen to leave lying about. A large oak tree in the woods had shed a couple of limbs in a recent gale, so I borrowed Walt's chainsaw and spent an afternoon adding to my pile of logs. By the time I finished I reckoned we had a full winter's supply. Next day I was out early, stacking them up against the side of the garage, the new ones at the rear, the seasoned ones close to hand. Back in the house I was just thinking about a nice fried breakfast when the phone rang.

'Now then, lad.' It was Walt. 'I've just got back from t'post office and there's all hell on in the village.'

'Why, what's happened?'

'Been a spate of break-ins, they reckon. There's one of your lot down there now, tekking details. Young lad. You'd best get yourself down there, help him out. Only looks about fifteen.'

I turned the grill off, grabbed my wellies, put Henry's lead on him, and set off. In a professional sense I had no need to get involved, but the way I looked at it anything that was going on in my own community was my business.

It only took a few minutes to get to the pub car park where I found Fordy with Stuart, the SOCO.

'What's the score?' I asked.

Fordy shook his head. 'You aren't going to believe this, Mike, but there's been five burglaries overnight. Five.'

'Bloody hell. What we talking about? Not house-breakings, surely?'

'No. Outbuildings, garden sheds, garages. Seems they all took place in the early hours, but—'

'Let me guess: nobody heard anything?'

'Yep.'

'Apart from me,' I said. 'I can't believe it!'

'What do you mean?'

I banged my fist into my hand. 'Last night. Ann's away and I wasn't sleeping well. I'd forgotten, but I woke up about three and heard a diesel going by. Real slow it was, rumbling along.'

'Didn't you think of investigating?'

'You know what it's like. I was half asleep. Yeah, I remember now. Quarter past three it was. I thought it was odd, going so slow. I was going to have a look, and then next thing I knew the alarm was going off at seven thirty. So what time was the first report?'

'Seven o'clock. A guy just up the road here. Went to collect his milk and found his shed door off its hinges. Mower, strimmer, rotovator – all gone.'

'I don't believe it,' I said. 'You know who it'll be, don't you? It'll be those bastards who've been plaguing us the last few weeks.'

'Has to be,' Fordy said.

'So you're saying nobody saw anything?'

Fordy shook his head. 'Nah. Another guy, like you, thought he'd heard a vehicle crawling by, about two thirty, but . . .' He shrugged.

'Well,' I said, 'you're in charge, Gary. I'm off home for me breakfast. Make sure you fly the flag, and make sure everyone's on the ball with their security. This is a first for this sort of thing – round here at any rate.'

'Somebody's already gone down to Yates's. Buying a job lot of padlocks, he reckons.'

'Good. And don't forget the shed alarms, eh?'

'Don't worry, mate. I'll see to it.'

'Right, I'm off home. Why don't you pop round for a coffee when you're done?'

'Will do, thanks, Mike.'

I left him and Stuart to it, but instead of going straight home I walked up the hill to Walter's. It was either that or have him on the phone quizzing me about what had happened. I found him on the roadside with his electric trimmer – not that his hedge needed anything doing to it: he'd already had his autumn tidy-up. But if there was any sort of excitement he had to be out there to keep tabs on it, and oil the wheels of the rumour mill.

'It's a bad going-on,' he said, shaking his head. 'Nowt safe these days.'

'Well,' I said, 'let's hope lightning doesn't strike twice, but you never know with people like this. They may just decide it's easy pickings round here and go village to village.' I glanced at his hedge trimmer. It was a brand-new, heavy-duty thing with about forty feet of cable trailing back to his shed. Plenty of thieves would think it was worth nicking for that alone. 'You make sure you've all your gear stashed out the way,' I said. 'Under lock and key.'

'Aye well,' Walt said, 'my chainsaw's as valuable as owt, and that's in your safe hands, isn't it?'

'I'm telling you nothing's safe at the moment, mate. Not till this lot are put out of business.'

I thought it best not to mention to Walter that I'd probably heard the thieves' vehicle. I felt bad enough as it was, and if he knew what had happened I'd never have heard the last of it.

I popped into the Jolly Farmers that lunchtime, just to catch up on things. I learned that all the victims had the same tale to tell, with minor variations. Sheds and garages broken open, and all the high-value equipment taken. Everyone was shocked by what had happened: not just the people who'd suffered losses, but the whole village. According to the landlord this was the first actual crime to take place in Leavening in five years. It was certainly the first I'd encountered. A siege mentality had descended on the village, and the general consensus was that the thieves had better not come back. I did my best to reassure everybody, but as I walked back home that afternoon I had visions of night-time mobs armed with pitchforks, lighting the way with burning brands.

The burglaries in Leavening were a jolt; a reality check, I suppose you'd call it. Not just to us in the village, but to everyone at the station as well. And the shock waves had reached out well beyond the bounds of Old Maltongate. When I got into work the following day Birdie was waiting for me in the parade room.

'Do you mind telling me what the hell is going on, Pannett?'

I hated it when he called me that. He only ever did when he was seriously ticked off. 'I've had the chief superintendent onto me twice this morning. And she is not happy. You know what she's like for stats.' He gave me the hard stare. 'Don't you?'

'Yes, sir.'

'According to her figures there's been a one thousand per cent rise in burglaries on your patch over the past three months. One thousand per cent, Pannett. That's a hundredfold.'

'Tenfold, sir.'

His eyes narrowed. 'I beg your pardon?'

'Er – I was going to say it's a tenfold increase, sir. A thousand per cent is ten times a hundred.'

He measured his words carefully. 'Call it what you will, Pannett, but it's a massive increase, and it's unacceptable. We're looking at an explosion of criminal activity in isolated village communities, so' – he pointed to the window – 'get out there and put a stop to it. Or our chief super will be coming at you wielding a large pair of scissors. And it won't be your hair she's after.'

Steady on, I was thinking. This isn't the Great Train Robbery. We're talking about a few mowers. But of course I kept schtum, and took it on the chin. Like you had to. Even so, I felt doubly aggrieved. I lived out there. I was feeling the effect of it the same as everybody else.

When Birdie had stormed back to his lair I got on the blower and contacted all the Country Watch members who'd volunteered to help me that night at the Dawnay Arms. It was time to mount a proper operation. But even as I rang round, rallying the troops, I was aware that we would be shooting in the dark. We could have people at every road junction, in every farm entrance, parked up in driveways all over the beat, but at the end of the day, what you need more than anything is that lucky break. I didn't say that, of course. I told them I wanted as many of them as possible on standby. Because when the opportunity presented itself we were not – repeat, not – going to waste it.

We'd got round to Sunday, and nothing had happened. When Ann came back from London in the early evening, I was getting ready for work, and had wound myself up like a watch spring. 'It's these bloody burglaries,' I said. 'I'm really fed up about them. And I'm kicking myself. First I miss the chance to nab 'em at Whitwell with Thommo, then I hear their van go by the night they hit the village. At least, I'm assuming it was them. Now my phone's red hot. Everybody's after a result, and I'm supposed to deliver. And I've been missing you, big time. So come here and give us a hug.'

Ann folded her arms round me. 'You're not having a very good time, are you?'

'No, I'm not.'

She was silent for a moment. Then she said, 'Listen, Mike, when do they seem to be hitting? I mean, is there any pattern?'

'I was thinking about that. Spoke to the crime analyst. The only thing we could see is, they appear to take Friday and Saturday nights off.'

'Not much new there then. I've not known many criminals work a seven-day week.'

'Probably out celebrating. No, if you're wondering where they'll strike next, the only thing you can say with any certainty is, it'll be a quiet little spot somewhere within six hundred square miles.'

Ann sighed. 'I see what you mean.'

'What we need is a break. People are always saying I'm lucky, but . . .'

'Mike, you know as well as I do: you make your own luck in life. If you get the Country Watch out you'll cut the odds straight away.'

'Let's hope so.'

I set off for my night shift about half past nine. I was doubled up with Jayne again. I was starting to enjoy working with her. She was less inclined to get over-excited now, and was learning to rein in her earlier impulse to hand out tickets right, left and centre. But she was still eager to get out on patrol.

'Right, Mike. You ready to hit the streets?' She put down her empty mug on the table in front of me.

'Hang on,' I said. I was flipping through the almanac, a

buff-coloured book containing the phone numbers of all the police stations, courts and other organisations we liaise with. 'I just need to phone a friend.'

The friend I had in mind was a sergeant over at Pontefract. Dave, his name was. I'd met him when we did the wildlife course together a couple of years back. And, as luck would have it, the lad was on duty, on the desk and answering calls.

'So what can I do for you, Mike?'

'I need a favour. We've had a Fiat van – one of them Ducatos – prowling about the countryside. I'm pretty sure it's been involved in a spate of burglaries over our way, and it's from out your neck of the woods.'

'Go on.'

'Well, I'm trying to keep tabs on it, so if I give you the address could you . . .?'

'You mean, can I get one of my cars to swing by?'

'Aye, see whether it's parked up.'

'How d'you know it's not in a garage?'

'I don't. I just have a feeling me luck's in tonight.'

'Are you now? Does your missus know?'

'Enough of that. Look, if I give you me mobile number—'

'Go on then. It's pretty quiet down there. Thieves all waiting till the Christmas presents are stacked up under the trees. Yeah, I'll get someone on the case and pass your number to them. That okay? Then they can speak to you direct.'

'Thanks, mate.'

Within a couple of hours I'd received two phone calls from a Pontefract unit. They'd spotted the van, parked up, not too far from the address I'd given Dave. Better still, they told me that the users of the van had access to a couple of lock-ups on the estate nearby. 'So why's the van out in the open?' I asked. 'Is that usual?'

'No,' they said. 'It isn't. They never leave it out.'

'Brilliant,' I said. As far as I was concerned, this pointed one way and one way only: our suspects were planning something. Tonight.

Town had quietened down, and we'd just pulled up by the primary school in Sand Hutton to have a bite of grub. It was one of the villages that hadn't been hit and, as I said to Jayne, you never know . . . Jayne had pulled out the books she was working through in preparation for her sergeant's exams. I had to hand it to her: she'd set her stall out and was sticking to the task.

'Y'know what?' I said. 'I always reckon Sunday night's perfect for thieves.'

'How's that work, then?'

'Well, think about it. New working week coming up. People get themselves off to bed nice and early. And they don't want to be disturbed. We've had a decent weekend, weatherwise, so a lot of them have been out in the garden, raking up leaves, having bonfires – and you mark my words, there'll be all sorts of bits and pieces left outside, or slung into sheds and the doors not locked. It's amazing how people will make their houses secure and leave thousands of pounds' worth of gear in a garage with a cheap old padlock on it.' Jayne didn't say anything. I wasn't sure that she was even listening.

Just then my mobile rang, it was the Ponte crew again. 'Mike. Still no movement on the van.'

'Oh.'

'Mind, it's no surprise is it?'

'What d'you mean?'

'See, down here, mate, we police our patch properly. The buggers don't dare take us on.'

'Yeah yeah yeah.'

'That's why they're sneaking off to places like Ryedale, cos it's a soft touch.'

'Get out of it. You know bloody well why they travel up here.'

'Do I?'

'Aye, cos there's nowt worth nicking down yonder. Or if there ever was, they've had it while you lot were asleep on the job.'

It was all a bit of fun, and when push came to shove I knew they'd help me out if they could. And sure enough, an hour or so later as we were crossing the river at Kirkham, they were back on.

'Mike, the eagle has landed.'

'You sure about that?'

'Er – maybe I mean the bird has flown. Anyway, we went by at – let's see . . . one twenty-five, and your van is on the move.'

'You sure about that?'

'Well, it's gone.'

'Any idea where?'

'That'll cost you extra, my friend. No, no idea. Just went by and it was no longer there.'

'That's great, mate. Cheers. Catch you later.' I was almost quivering with anticipation as Jayne put her books away and belted herself in. Could this be it? It was a long shot; it was the proverbial needle in a haystack job, but at least I felt we were in with a shout.

'Well, Jayne. Let's hope they're heading our way.'

'Right – then all we have to do is find them.'

That was indeed the point. Finding them. 'This is where we need to call up our eyes and ears,' I said.

It took a while to rouse all the Country Watch team. Nick the gamekeeper and his lad were already up – they'd been out looking for poachers on the estate – but all the others were in bed, and took some waking. While I rang them on my mobile Jayne got onto Control.

'Just for information, we've had intelligence from West Yorkshire about a white Fiat Ducato. The vehicle is of interest in relation to non-residential burglaries in the Ryedale and Hambleton areas. We're requesting observations and sightings only at this time.'

'*Yes, all received. We'll put a general circulation out.*'

The question we were now pondering – always assuming they were actually coming our way and hadn't just popped out for a late-night curry – was what route would the suspects take? Surely they wouldn't come sailing up the A64, which they would expect to be well patrolled. It was the various back roads into our district that we needed to be watching. But then again, you can never be certain.

'Tell you what,' I said, 'let's park up at Buttercrambe. That's the sort of route I'd take if I was looking for a nice sneaky way into Ryedale. Up the A166, and nip in through Gate Helmsley.'

We parked under the trees, within earshot of the old mill-race, and swapped seats. It was my turn to drive and I knew these roads like the back of my hand.

'This is a bit like fishing,' I said, as the bare branches clicked and clacked in a gusty northeasterly wind.

'You mean sitting here by a river in the freezing cold, bored out of our skulls?'

'I mean having everything in place. The Country Watch at their posts, all those sheds and garages piled high with bait. Just waiting for the big fish to come swimming by.'

'I always hated fishing.'

'Can't imagine you out there on the river-bank with a rod and reel.'

'Used to get dragged out by a boyfriend I had, years ago. To watch.'

'Ah well, it's not a spectator sport, is it?'

'That's what I told him when I dumped him.'

It was beginning to look as though it'd be a long cold night – and a frustrating one. By the time it got to about three o'clock I was convinced it was all going to fizzle out. That's when it all kicked off.

'*Control to 1015, over.*'

'Go ahead, over.'

'*We've got one of your Country Watch people called in. Colonel somebody. Wants to talk to you.*'

Jayne was watching me, and grinning like a kid. 'Lost his balls again, has he?' she said.

'Great time for my mobile signal to give out,' I said, putting the car in gear.

Half a mile up the road I managed to get a three-bar signal. I pulled over and called the Colonel.

'Ah, Mike. Good man. I've just had a report from the Neighbourhood Watch Co-ordinator. You'll know Edith. Lovely gal. Her mother rode to hounds with me, you know . . .'

'Yes, I'm sure she did – now what have you got?'

'Ah yes, well d'you know, she's seen the most extraordinary thing. You'll never believe this. Had to go down and look for myself. And there he was on the main street, bold as brass . . .'

I braced myself for another Ryedale Panther sighting.

'This is in Wintringham, mind you – and there's a chap putting mowers and rotovators and such things out on the verge. Looks for all the world like one of those bin people putting out the refuse on a Monday for the lorry to pick up. D'you know, Mike, I think this could be the fellow we're after.'

'Where are you now, Colonel?'

'I'm down a driveway, tucked away behind a hedge, up at the end of the village.' He went quiet for a moment, then dropped his voice to a stage whisper. 'Well, would you believe it? Here it comes now!'

'What, the van?'

'Yes, by Jove. One of those Fiat things. A Ducato, if I'm not mistaken. Isn't that what we're after? It's making its way up the village.' I could hear the excitement in the Colonel's voice, and his rapid breathing. 'It's stopped. And they've started to load the goods. This is dashed exciting, Mike. What do you want me to do?'

'Wait there. Keep on the phone, don't get involved and make sure you don't show yourself. I'll hand you over to Jayne. You keep her updated while I drive.'

I passed Jayne my mobile. 'Right, you get the updates from the Colonel. Try and establish how many suspects we're dealing with. He never said.' I pointed the car towards Bossall and the A64, and got my foot down. With any luck we'd be in pole position to intercept them.

'1015 to Control. Active message.'

'*1015 go ahead.*'

'Information from Country Watch. A white Fiat Ducato in the village of Wintringham, concerned in burglaries currently in progress.'

It took no more than five minutes to get across to the main road. I turned right and headed towards Whitwell-on-the-Hill. Jayne was listening intently as the Colonel kept her up to date. 'They've loaded the last of the stolen goods into the van and are now leaving the village at speed. Just the two suspects as far as I could see. And they're heading towards the A64.'

'Right, Jayne, pass that to Control,' I said. 'We want all the backup we can get. Tell 'em we're heading in that direction.'

'Will do.'

It was barely two minutes before Control came back to us. They'd got a double-crewed car from Eastfield making its way from the Staxton area; Fordy and Ed were on their way from a job out at Hovingham, and York was sending a traffic car from Tadcaster.

'Typical,' I said to Jayne. 'The one night when you need units to box an area off, and where are they? Scattered to the four corners of the earth. Staxton, Taddy and bloody Hovingham. Still, better than nowt.'

As I sped east we clocked the handful of vehicles that were heading towards us. We were making our way up the dual carriageway at Whitwell when we saw the trees illuminated by a pair of headlights.

'This could be it. It's about the right time over the distance,' I said.

'Looks like it!' As a van shot by us down the hill Jayne turned to check the rear number-plate. 'That's the one okay. And I don't think he's seen us – yet.'

By the time I'd driven to the next gap in the central reservation and turned around, the tail-lights of the van were a mile ahead, passing the Barton crossroads.

'1015 to Control.'

A familiar voice came across the radio. '*Go ahead, Mike.*' It was Brian, the most experienced control-room civilian in the force.

'Brian, just to let you know, trying to get behind this van believed concerned in burglaries. I don't intend to try and stop it until we have backup. Heading towards York on the A64, just passing Flaxton Lane end. It's about 500 yards ahead of me.'

'*All received, Mike. The Taddy car shouldn't be too far away.*

I've also dispatched a double-crewed car – making their way to you from Haxby.'

'Cheers, Brian.' I was concentrating now on keeping a decent distance from the van. Close enough not to lose him, far enough not to panic him. 'Jayne, you got your CS handy?'

She leaned away from me and pulled it out from her belt. 'Yeah.'

As we approached the lights of the Hopgrove roundabout the van slowed down. The driver was well aware of us now. He seemed to hesitate, swerving out into the right-hand lane before swinging onto the roundabout. His tyres squealed as he feinted to come off on the Leeds turn-off, then lurched back towards the ring road, leaving two black scars on the surface.

'Come on, matey, decision time, I think!' He was hugging the inside of the roundabout, screeching his way round a second time. On my left I caught sight of a pair of headlights coming from Leeds direction. As the van rocked its way towards the outside lane the car braked sharply and swerved.

'They don't know what to do,' Jayne said.

'No, and they're going to endanger themselves, and anyone who comes by.' I decided it was time for the blue lights.

'Listen, Jayne, if these buggers do pull up we need to go in hard and dominate them. And any trouble – don't be afraid to gas them.'

'Don't you worry, Mike. I'm not gonna let them get away. Not after all this.'

'And if this bugger thinks he can throw me off he can bloody well—' The van swayed to left and right as the driver tested his tyres to the limit, and I wrestled the wheel to stay hard on his tail.

'Where's our bloody backup?' Jayne shouted.

'Eh oop, here we go!' The van driver had made his mind up. 'Back to Malton, is it? Big mistake, sunshine.'

'Whoa! Hold tight!'

As suddenly as he'd made the one manoeuvre he executed another, the rear lights glowing red as he slammed his brakes on and pulled over.

'Now what's he up to?' I waited. Was he about to put his foot down and take off again?

'Right,' I said, opening my door and grabbing my CS canister. 'Me to the driver's side, you take the passenger, okay?'

'Got you.' Jayne opened her door and ducked into the icy wind.

'Let's go then.' We walked forward side by side, peeling off to go one each side of the stationary vehicle. In a situation like this you always approach with caution. We knew nothing about these people, other than that they were highly suspect. Had they pulled over because they knew the game was up? Were they preparing to fight, or do a runner? Could they be armed?

Holding my CS gas in my right hand where it was plainly visible, I rapped on the driver's side window with my Asp. There were two men inside, both in their thirties at a guess, and both dressed in black T-shirts with cigarettes in their mouths. The driver wound his window down. He didn't speak, just stared at me and shivered as the wind blew the smoke out of the cab and into my face. At the same time his mate was winding his window down and backing away from Jayne's gas canister.

'Right,' I said, 'you mess me about, you're gonna get a faceful of CS gas. Now take the keys out of the ignition and put your hands on the steering wheel, because you're under arrest on suspicion of burglary.' He passed me the keys and did as I told him. His mate did the same. Neither of them said a word. Then I heard the sound – the very welcome sound – of sirens, two of them; one from York direction and one from Scarborough.

I unhooked a set of cuffs from my belt. 'Okay, I'm going to

ask you to step outside and put your hands on the bonnet; then I'm going to place you in handcuffs.'

By the time we'd done that the backup had arrived, lights flashing, the cars angled across the road to block any escape route. With six officers around the van the suspects were now handcuffed, and very subdued. They'd clearly weighed up the odds and, in that immortal phrase, decided that discretion was the better part of valour. We put them in separate cars.

'Jayne.' I beckoned to her before opening the rear door of the van.

'Stone me!' She just stood there, staring. It was crammed to the ceiling with a tangle of mowers, strimmers, hedge trimmers and loops of cable. There was a mountain bike, a small diesel-powered generator, an electric chainsaw and a whole stack of other miscellaneous items.

'*Control to 1015.*'

It was Brian again. He'd been talking to the Colonel, who'd gone round the village knocking on doors. I looked at my watch. 'What, at three forty-five in the morning?'

'*Now, don't go complaining about their enthusiasm, Mike. Anyway, just so as you know, he's come up with six householders who've had their sheds burgled – and he's still got the other side of the street to check. We'll send someone off the early turn to get the details.*'

As I closed the van door I felt my shoulders relax. I turned up my coat collar. For the first time since we'd left Buttercrambe the cold was really penetrating. I went over to where Jayne was standing talking to the traffic lads. 'C'mon,' I said, 'let's get them back to York custody.'

She yawned. 'Yeah, and let's hope they're not too busy over there.'

We left it to the traffic officers to bring the van back while the Haxby lads acted as prisoner escorts for the run into York. When we got there I had a word with their night inspector. I told him I'd been liaising with West Yorks Police at Pontefract, and asked him to authorise an immediate Section 18 search of the prisoners' addresses and lock-ups so that I could get Dave to send someone out and look for any other stolen goods. He agreed, leaving Jayne to grab us a cup of tea while I got on the phone to Dave. Then it was time to ring the Colonel, bring him up to speed and thank him for his efforts. Finally, exhausted as we were, Jayne and I sat down to write our statements.

So we were feeling thoroughly shattered but pretty pleased with ourselves as we drove back along the A64 into the face of the early-morning commuter traffic. We went over the night's events and how the extended team – Country Watch, the York lads, the traffic officers and so on – had co-operated in a tight and successful operation. Jayne wanted to know about Brian, the lad in the control room who'd done such an excellent job of getting backup for us. 'He used to be a police officer,' I said. 'Over thirty years in uniform, and now he's racked up twenty-odd as a civilian.'

'Blimey, he must be due his pension.'

'I think he's already drawing that,' I said, 'but if you ask me he deserves a bloody medal. No substitute for experience.' Jayne sighed and tilted her seat back. 'All we need now is a decent result from Ponte,' she said.

Next night, when we showed up at half past nine, we got it. Chris Cocks, back on duty after his dose of flu, was full of it.

'By heck,' he said, 'it's a good job you two weren't in earlier or you'd have been gagging.'

'Why, what's been going off?'

'Birdie, mate. Singing your praises. And it was sickening. It really was. He used words you only get on *Countdown* – or do I mean *Call My Bluff*? Anyway, watch out next Valentine's Day, Mike, because you'll be on his list; and as for young Jayne . . .'

'Well, Chris, I always say when push comes to shove the cream rises to the top.'

'Sure it ain't the crap that floats?'

'Yeah yeah yeah. So what's he so extra-specially chuffed about?'

'That search you asked for at Pontefract.'

'Oh aye? Any good?'

'They only uncovered three garages full of gear that belongs up here. And they got full confessions from your two prisoners – plus a stack of TICs.'

It turned out that our two lads in the Fiat Ducato had admitted to no fewer than sixty-seven burglaries. Several they would be charged with; the others would be taken into consideration. Among the swag that was found were all the Land Rover parts from our friend up on the Moors, and what sounded like the proceeds from the break-ins at Leavening. It was a staggering result, giving us the biggest clear-up of unsolved burglaries we'd ever had in Ryedale.

But if Jayne and I thought we were going to get any credit for it we had another thing coming. As Birdie explained to us over a cup of tea the following week, it was the CID who'd taken the confessions. And they would be claiming the clear-ups.

'Hang on a minute,' I said. I could feel Jayne holding her breath. Any second now and she'd be blurting out something she might live to regret. 'That was our job and my Country Watch that nailed those buggers. With respect, sir, you know what the chief superintendent's like for statistics. If I got those clear-ups I'd have a hundredfold reduction in crime on my patch.'

'Sure you don't mean tenfold, Mike?' He couldn't help laughing, and I have to admit I was grinning myself. 'Listen, Mike, I see what you mean, but we're all in this together, one big policing family, and after all you can only have one name down for the clear-up.'

'Yeah, but why does it have to be the CID? If the "modern police service" wants me to be judged on my "performance indicators" then why can't I have the result and put my name in the box?'

'Now, Mike, don't you go worrying yourself about the detail,' he said. 'I asked the pair of you in here to congratulate you, not to argue the finer points. Have a chocolate biscuit. And here, take the rest of the box too. You deserve it. That was a terrific effort.'

Just as we were leaving, Birdie called us back. 'By the way you two, I've had a memo through about that rape case you dealt with.' We paused, half in the office and half out. 'Just so that you know,' he said, 'there will be no charges brought.'

I opened my mouth to speak, but Jayne got in before me. 'Why's that then, sir?' Birdie had picked the memo up from his tray and was scanning it. 'It appears the girl didn't want to go through the trauma of giving evidence in court – and the possibility of seeing him get off.' He shrugged. 'It was basically going to be her word against his.'

Jayne raised her eyebrow. 'So, we'll never know what really happened.'

'There you have it.'

Chapter 12

Count Your Blessings

I must have been eight or nine when I found a copy of *The Hound of the Baskervilles* in my Christmas stocking. It was a beautiful book, hardbound, with lots of illustrations, but I'm not sure I ever read it. At that age I would never have sat still long enough to plough through two hundred pages. I was too busy chasing a ball around the garden. Later, I was too busy chasing girls; but I still took it down off the shelf from time to time and flipped through the pages to look at those pictures. There was Sherlock Holmes in his trusty fore-and-aft hat, pursuing criminals across a rugged hilltop, pacing his study as he tried to make sense of the thickening plot, or inspecting mysterious objects for clues as to who had committed the latest dastardly outrage. But the image I always came back to, the one that first made me think about a life of fighting crime, was the ace detective, crouching down in the woods, holding a magnifying glass to a set of enormous footprints.

So I had to laugh, as I took out my digital camera, got down on my knees and edged my way forwards through two inches of crusty snow on the fourteenth green of Ganton golf course.

Seriously, I actually did laugh out loud, despite the fact that I'd been called in to work an extra shift thanks to an outbreak of flu, and despite the fact that Ann and I had just found out that we were going to be spending most of Christmas Day apart. It was like a sketch from *Monty Python*. The sun was going down, a bitter wind was blowing through the gorse bushes and a bank of yellowish clouds was about to bring a fresh shower of snow off the North Sea to cover what might or might not have been the tracks of a large animal. Could it be a cat? Or was it a dog? I suppose if I'd paid closer attention when I was on that wildlife course a couple of years previously I might have had a clue – but I seem to remember I had Ann on my mind back then, and not a lot else.

With the snow under my knees melting and seeping through my uniform trousers and then the thermal long johns that were an essential part of my rural officer's kit, I got ready to snap the first picture of a vague impression that was rapidly being obliterated. As I steadied myself, a gust of wind blew a large, wet flake down my right ear. Sod it, I thought. If I could learn to keep my mouth shut I might have been back at base now supping tea and munching Ed's wife's homemade Christmas shortbread. Instead of which . . .

'It's your own stupid fault,' was Ed's opinion when we spoke before briefing that day. 'You know what the press are like.'

He was right. But when the man from the *Gazette* rang in to say that someone – of course he couldn't reveal the identity of his source – claimed to have spotted a police officer loading a large, tranquillised beast into a Ministry of Defence Land Rover up on Fylingdales Moor, under the very shadow of the early-warning radar station, there was no way I could take him seriously. When he added that the animal in question was thought to be a large cat, possibly a panther, the temptation to play along with him was overwhelming.

What I was supposed to say – the official wording, if you like – was that we'd had no such reports and had no knowledge of any confirmed sightings of large cats in the Ryedale area. Which was the truth. But it's a bit of a mouthful, and besides, I've always had this mischievous streak in me, and in this case there was no middle ground. People were either believers or non-believers. The temptation to stoke the fires of rumour was too great. So, being me, I gave our intrepid reporter the Pannett line: 'I can neither confirm nor deny the rumour,' I said, my tongue planted firmly in my cheek. I thought I was being funny, or clever, or both, by doing this, and I delighted in telling everyone what I'd said. So, a week later when a copy of the paper was thrust into my face by Inspector Finch, there was no point in denying anything. We were all sitting around the table, having the usual pre-shift cuppa, and Ed had produced the familiar biscuit tin, prising it open and peeling back the clean white napkin his wife always wrapped around her annual Christmas treats.

'What have you done now, Pannett?' the inspector hissed, jabbing at the page with his forefinger.

'Oh dear,' I said. Under a banner headline I saw my name; and there, highlighted in big bold letters, were my words. 'Police wildlife officer PC Mike Pannett's remark,' the piece read, 'has lent weight to local suspicions that some kind of wild beast has indeed been trapped up on the Moors and spirited away. Has it gone to a secret research establishment? And are Ryedale Police involved in a cover-up?'

Birdie stood there, staring at me. Ed was holding the napkin over his mouth, smothering a grin. Jayne, watching them both like a hawk, was reaching a hand out towards the tin.

'Thanks to your indiscretion, Pannett, I've been deluged with letters, phone calls and emails. Do you think I've got nothing better to do than deal with this kind of thing?' He held a printout towards me. 'Addressed to me personally. A lady from Ganton.' I reached out to take it from him but he snatched it away. 'No, I'll read it to you, shall I?' Without waiting for an answer he put on his glasses and started. 'Several times this last month I have seen a large black creature prowling the golf course. After Monday's snowfall a set of huge footprints, with claw-marks, appeared in the snow on the fourteenth green.'

'Blimey,' said Jayne, shrinking back in her seat with a piece of shortbread in her hand.

'Yes, blimey indeed.' Birdie glanced at Jayne, then turned to give me the hard stare. 'I suggest, Pannett, that it's time we stop treating this as a bit of a lark and start taking the public's concerns seriously. I further suggest that it's time for you to investigate, don't you agree? Now!' he said, as I got up from the table. 'Before it gets dark!'

So there I was, clutching my camera with numb fingers and snapping away, even as the footprints filled with fresh snow. If Birdie wanted pictures I'd give him pictures, even if they did show nothing more than a vague smudge. And if I came down with pneumonia – well, it would be on his head. You get like that some days. Cursed, you might say. However, as I said, I have a mischievous streak, and I suspected that – deep down – our inspector had a sense of humour. So I spent a few more minutes out there on all fours, creating my own paw-prints in the snow with my outstretched hand. And then as an after-thought I picked up a twig and added a bit of definition, a few 'claw-marks'. Then I plonked my wellie down next to it, to give a sense of scale, and took a few more snaps. If the press wanted a big cat, I thought, well, how about a lion, rampaging over Ganton golf course?

Packing the camera away in my pocket, I trudged back along the fairway to the car, my knees wet through, cursing as a lump of snow fell into my right boot and melted. What am I doing? I thought. How did I end up out here, chasing phantoms, when I should be at home decorating the Christmas tree and laying in the wine? Well, if I'd gained nothing else, I'd got myself a new year's resolution. From now on I will be a model police officer. I will give the press what I'm supposed to give them: a humourless, boring, formulaic response.

It's a good job I'm an optimist. Mr Cheerful, that's me. Ask anybody. Even as I negotiated the rush-hour traffic along the A64, my wet trousers sticking to my thighs and a nasty little tickle at the back of my throat, the sight of all those Christmas trees that seemed to illuminate every porch and window in Norton lifted my mood. But it was only temporary.

Back at the station I found a deserted parade room. All that remained of our Christmas treat were a few crumbs scattered across the table and my mug of tea, now stone cold.

'Thanks a bunch, team,' I muttered as I threw my coat over the back of a chair, 'and bah humbug to the lot of you!' To cheer myself up I downloaded and printed my 'lion' paw-prints and slipped a copy into Birdie's in-tray.

It was going to be a difficult first Christmas for Ann and me. Every year you try to work it so that you have a couple of days off over the holiday period, but when there's two of you, working different shifts at different stations and hoping to have a bit of time together, it doesn't always work out. The way the cards were dealt this year, Ann had three days off on the run-up, but was down to work the early turn on Christmas Day, meaning that she would be leaving the house at five in the morning. I was down for the late shift and wouldn't finish until ten at night. We tried to arrange swaps here and there but everybody had their arrangements in place. Nobody was going to give up what they had, not the single officers, certainly not those with young families who would normally be glad of a spot of over-time. In the end we had to give it up and revert to Plan B: the old days. I'd go to my mum's for an early roast turkey and pudding, like I did when I was single, then scoot off to work. Ann would finish her turn and shoot round to her mum and dad's for tea before coming home and getting Keeper's Cottage warm and cosy for our own late-night festivities. And to make up for it all we'd invite everyone over to ours on the thirty-first and see the new year in with a bang.

The snow that had fallen on Ganton golf course – and on me – didn't last long in the Vale of Pickering. It didn't even amount to much on the Wolds; but it was several inches thick on the Moors. A week before Christmas, when I drove down towards town for my night shift there they were, a line of white to the north under a moonlit sky, making me shiver in my seat. I was doubled up with young Fordy that night, and our first call was out Farndale way, where someone had reported seeing a car off the road. It turned out to be a false alarm, but at least it got us away from town and any possible aggravation down there. Rather than go straight back I decided to take a look along Blakey Ridge in case anybody had got into difficulty there. The ploughs had been out but there had been a fair wind earlier, which had driven the fresh, dry snow back onto the roads.

'Tell you what, mate, I like it like this,' I said. With the moon shining through a veil of cloud, an old stone barn, its roof covered in a tangle of ivy, took on a ghostly appearance.

'Reminds me of the old days,' I added. We'd reached the top now, and on an impulse I turned towards the Lion Inn, the pub that stands all alone and provides such a welcome refuge to hikers and bikers, as well as families out for their Sunday drive. I pulled off the road and circled the parking area, the frozen puddles popping and cracking under our wheels. It was almost empty, but there were still a few people kissing each other goodbye, lobbing party poppers and shouting the compliments of the season to each other as they got into their cars, taxis and hired minibuses. I pulled up on the verge, took an apple from my pocket and started munching.

'What d'you mean, old days?' Fordy said.

'Eh? Oh, you wouldn't remember. I'm talking thirty years ago, when we used to get proper winters. Snow up here used to be feet thick, back then. People were always getting snowed in or stranded. Cars failed, roads blocked.' I pointed towards the pub. 'Had to stay there overnight sometimes.'

'That must've been, like, really harsh,' Fordy said. I looked across at him, but he never cracked his face. 'I mean, miles from home, no chance of getting away. Nothing to do but sit by the fire drinking beer till the emergency services showed up. Yeah, tough old life. Specially with the grub they serve.'

'You been in there?' I asked, nodding towards the pub just as the coloured lights around the entrance were turned off section by section.

'Yeah. Couple of times. I was there the other week, as a matter of fact. Bloody good it was.' He was trying to smother a grin. 'Came up with me girlfriend.'

'Which one's that then?'

'The latest, of course.'

'Does she know that's how you refer to her?' I wound down

the window, threw my apple core into the heather and relaxed in my seat. ' "The latest"?' He didn't answer. 'So, where's she from?'

'Leeds. She's at uni there.'

'Hey, you wanna watch that, lad. Lot of competition for you. All them bright young students. They've nowt else to do but party, y'know.'

'Never mind the fatherly advice. Anyone tries it on with her I'll handle it. No worries.'

'Tell you what, why don't you bring her round to our place, New Year's Eve? Me and Ann are having a bit of a gathering.'

'You know what, that would be great. She's been on at me to see a bit of country life. She's lived in towns all her life.'

'Well, just the job then. There'll be some right characters there. Bring her along and show her the real Yorkshire, eh?'

'I will. Thanks, Mike, count us in.'

We didn't stay long up there. It wasn't doing much for our mood, watching people come out of the pub in their glad-rags, going home for a good night's sleep. I put the car into gear and drove steadily back towards Hutton-le-Hole under a clear, starlit sky.

We cruised around the village, but there was nothing to see. The pub there had long since closed its doors, and the only sign of life was a solitary dog-walker, shoulders hunched, puffing on a cigarette while his dog sniffed at the frost-whitened grass and made its way along beside the beck that tumbles down through the village.

Out on the main road we cruised back to Pickering, then made our way to Malton for a quick cup of tea. It was gone two o'clock by now, and everything was quiet. 'Tell you what,' I said to Fordy, 'we'll take in one of my favourite viewpoints.'

'What, in the pitch dark?'

'You wait and see,' I said.

We drove out to Thorpe Bassett Wold, which rises above the A64 between Scagglethorpe and Rillington. On a clear day you can see for miles around the vale and the Moors beyond. At night it's a great place to sit up, as we say, watching for the sweep of headlights as an occasional car comes up from Settrington or along the tops from Mowthorpe.

'I've had a fair few results up here,' I said.

'I bet you have,' Fordy chuckled.

'From sitting and watching,' I said. 'Villains, I mean. Bloody hell, you've got a one-track mind, you have.'

He settled back in his seat. 'Only joking,' he said.

'I should hope so. Well, with a bit of luck we should be in for a nice, uneventful shift now,' I added.

Fordy laughed. 'Steady on, Mike. You told me never to say that, remember?'

'Aye, I did.'

'Tempting fate. That's what you told me. First time I ever went out on patrol with you.'

He was right to correct me. The call came bang on cue.

'*Control to 1015. From the fire brigade. We've got a house fire, persons reported. Address given as . . . rural farm, Hanging Grimston. Tender en route. Can you attend?*'

'On our way, Brian.'

'*All received, Mike. Fire Brigade Control are having difficulty in pinpointing the location. It's right on the Yorkshire–Humberside border.*'

'That's all received, making my way from Thorpe Bassett Hill. If the fire brigade are struggling, Brian, I think I know where it is. It's a really isolated spot. If they need me to guide them in, let me know.'

'*I'll get onto fire Control.*'

'Persons reported?' Fordy said. 'Does that mean there are people still in there?'

'Sounds like it, mate. What a bloody place for it to happen. Couldn't be further out on a limb.'

'You know where this place is though, don't you?' he asked. I could tell by his voice that he'd realised just how serious this could be.

'I do. I've been to it once before. Pretty sure I have, anyway.'

'Well, let's hope Trumpton find it okay. Quicker they get there the better chance we'll have.'

The fire brigade would have got the call before us, but they'd need two or three minutes to get their men to the base at the bottom of Sheepsfoot Hill, and once they did get going, like us, they'd be feeling their way along the icy roads.

As soon as we set off from Thorpe Bassett I put my blue light on. The chances of passing anybody were remote, to say the least, but it was instinctive, automatic.

'Better take it steady,' I said. We'd barely gone a hundred yards down the hill towards Settrington when I started to feel the black ice.

Fordy pointed at the temperature gauge. 'Minus four,' he said.

I could feel the ABS kicking in as I braked to negotiate the bends. In conditions like these, it's a fine balance between getting there as fast as you possibly can and not getting there at all. You can't help but push yourself, even while your head is telling you you could be off the road any moment.

'*Control to 1015.*'

'Go ahead, Brian.'

'*Fire brigade making their way out along the Birdsall road and are asking if you can guide them in to the location as their system is playing up.*'

'That's a yes. We'll be at Birdsall in a couple of minutes. Is that any good?'

'*Stand by.*'

'Bloody hell, Mike, I was hoping they'd be ahead of us.'

'F***ing hell!' I shouted as the ABS kicked in and the car juddered. I caught a fleeting glimpse of red as my lights caught a pair of eyes, followed by the silhouette of two roe deer leaping across the road in front of us.

'Christ, Mike.'

'What's up with you, Fordy? Thought you fancied rural policing.'

'I do, but . . .'

'Missed 'em by – ooh, several inches, I'd say.'

'Is that Trumpton ahead?' Fordy was leaning forward as the familiar blue light pulsed across the sky.

'1015 to Control, have met fire brigade, now continuing.'

'*Brilliant, also two Humberside fire tenders en route. Humberside Police are also dispatching a rural unit, as it might be their patch.*'

I gave the fire brigade the thumbs up out of the window and drove warily past them, allowing them to pull out behind us. We were soon climbing, steeply, out of Birdsall, hitting a really icy stretch. For a moment I thought I felt the front wheels spinning. I moved as close to the verge as I dared to gain a bit of purchase. I had to keep the momentum going, otherwise the fire crew wouldn't make it up the hill.

'Soon get lost out here,' Fordy said. 'Not many signposts.'

'Why d'you think I carry all them maps in the back seat?'

The road was a bit better at the very top, and I soon spotted the turn-off to Hanging Grimston.

'Fordy, you need to be out and get that gate open sharpish.'

'Will do.'

He was soon back in the car, rubbing his hands. 'What the hell are those gates for, out there in the middle of nowhere?'

'To keep the sheep in. Whaddayou think?'

We had about a mile and a half to go along narrow, single-track lanes. In my rear-view mirror I could see the tender's back end swinging out to one side then the other as they struggled on the treacherous surface. With several hundred gallons of water on board they were carrying a huge weight.

'Well, if they thought that was difficult . . .' I said, and left the remark hanging as I caught my breath. We were now descending steeply, and I could feel the ABS kicking in again as I braked all the way down the hill. I didn't say anything to Fordy, but this was as treacherous as I'd known it. I could see us or the tender going off the road at any time. I held my breath, my hands gripping the wheel tightly. How they were managing to drive the tender down there at all was a miracle.

'Christ! I hope they've got out,' Fordy said. We were within fifty yards of the farmhouse and there ahead was a column of thick, pale smoke rolling into the night sky. Flames were clearly visible through one of the ground-floor windows and smoke was seeping out around the wooden frame. Our headlights flooded the white façade of the house. On the lawn, with thick coats over their pyjamas, were two children, turning to watch their mother as she came towards us wearing a dressing gown and a pair of wellington boots.

I braked sharply and stepped out. She was already shouting at me. 'He's gone back inside! You've got to get him out!' The blue lights of the tender exaggerated the look of panic on her face as they flashed on-off-on-off. It was a vivid scene, everyone's breath coming in clouds, the air filled with the shouts of the firemen as they got a ladder towards the house and started unwinding the hose.

'Who has?' the station officer shouted above the noise of the tender. 'Who's gone inside?'

'My husband – he went back for the dog.' She pointed to an upstairs window. 'In there.'

'Anybody else inside?'

'No, just my husband. The kids are here.'

Behind me the firemen were latching the hose into the tender and throwing the reel out across the garden. Two others were putting on breathing apparatus while their mates worked on the ladder. There was a sudden hiss as a stream of water arched across the garden to burst against the front of the house.

Wisps of smoke were starting to curl up under the eaves. The two little lads, gazing intently at the scene before them, were walking slowly backwards towards their mother, right by where Fordy and I were standing. One looked to be about seven, the other one couldn't have been more than four or five. 'Barney ran upstairs,' he said, turning to face me. 'Daddy's gone to rescue him. He always runs upstairs when he's frightened.'

I looked at the mother. She knew there was only one thing that mattered right now.

'Right, Fordy, let's have these lads in that car. Jack that heater up and keep the engine running.'

I turned to the mother. 'These fire brigade lads know what they're doing,' I said. 'They'll soon have him out, don't worry.' Inside I was praying I was right.

Behind her I could see a fireman knocking aside the plastic Santa that stood on the front step as he carefully opened the door. The fresh air rushed in and the flames seemed to feed on it, flaring up hungrily and spewing black smoke out in an upwards wave.

The ladder was in place now, and two of the crew were climbing towards an upstairs window.

In the distance I heard the sound of sirens as the Humberside crews approached, together with an ambulance.

'Listen,' I said, as the woman shivered and drew her dressing gown tighter around her, 'come and sit in the car with the boys. You'll catch your death out here.'

But she wasn't having it. All she was interested in was her husband – and the dog. She stood and watched as two of the firemen played a jet of water in through the front door, trying to douse the flames in the living room.

I took my jacket off and placed it over her shoulders. 'Mummy, what'll happen if the chimney burns down?' the little lad called from the open car window. 'How will Santa get in?'

'Never mind that for now,' she said. 'Look, here comes Daddy.'

I had my torch shining on the ladder as one of the firemen reached out and helped to open the bedroom window. The waves of smoke parted and a man with tousled hair, a blackened face and wearing a T-shirt and pyjama bottoms clambered out to be guided backwards, rung by rung, onto the lawn.

As his wife hugged him, the station officer was asking, 'Are you absolutely sure that everyone is out?'

'Yes, there was just the dog,' he gasped, turning to look as yellow flames licked at the curtains in the room he'd just escaped from. I glanced up at the fireman who'd brought him down. He shook his head. The hoses were playing through the door and windows into the house itself, but the flames seemed to have the upper hand.

At incidents like this a police officer can feel a bit like a spare part. The family were now in the back of the ambulance getting checked out and the fire brigade units were absorbed in fighting the blaze. It would be they who would determine the cause. Our job was done – unless something suspicious came to light. For the moment, all we had to do was watch and wait as they brought it under control.

While we stood there the Humberside rural officer arrived. I'd come across Neil a few times at jobs on the borders of our respective beats, and would sometimes meet up on a night duty to catch up on what was going on. We'd often get poachers operating on land that reached into both of our beats. I walked towards his car to bring him up to speed. As we were chatting we had it confirmed by the control room; the farm was in fact within the Humberside police area by approximately fifty yards. 'So,' I said, 'looks like it's yours, mate.'

I left him to it and went to find Fordy. He was outside the ambulance speaking with Mum and Dad.

'The only thing I can think of is the front-room fire,' the dad was saying. 'The guard was up when we went to bed. I'm sure it was. Christmas-tree lights were off.' He glanced back towards the house. 'What a mess. All t'kids presents an' all.'

I could see he had a tear in his eye. 'Listen,' I said, 'the fire brigade will work out what happened, but the main thing is that your family are all safe and well.'

'Except the dog,' he said. 'That'll break the kiddies' hearts. We got him last Christmas. They even made him presents at school. Border collie he was. Daft as a brush, but . . .'

'I know,' I said. 'It'll be heartbreaking for them, but . . .'

Back at the farmhouse they were just about on top of the fire, dousing what remained of what, an hour ago, had been the family's home. It was a shocking sight. The downstairs doors and windows were gone, the outside wall was streaked black, and from inside the furniture and carpets were giving off dank, evil-smelling fumes as the water dripped down from sagging ceilings. Now that the fire was out I was able to poke my head in through the front-room window and flash my torch around. There was the skeleton of a tall Christmas tree, leaning against the hearth, the bucket it stood in melted and shapeless, and underneath it a charred mound of what must have been the family's Christmas presents. My thoughts were interrupted by the sight of one of the fire crew emerging from the door carrying the dead dog in a blanket. He carefully laid it on the lawn.

The station officer approached me. 'The seat of the fire seems to be in the living room, near the hearth,' he said. 'Most likely a stray ember got past the guard. But we'll have to await confirmation on that.'

It was clear that there was nothing more that Fordy and I could do. We left Neil to see that the family were taken over to a relative's house.

'Makes you think,' I said to Fordy as we drove back to town.

'Yep.'

'Those poor people, a week before Christmas. Home out of action for God knows how long, kids' presents up in flames and then poor Barney the dog. Absolutely awful.'

'They've lost the lot.'

'But on the positive side, they all got out safe and well.'

'Yeah, that's the main thing.'

'Tell you what though, we were lucky. When you think about it.'

I could see him turn to me, unsure as to what I meant. 'Those roads going in,' I said. 'So icy. I don't mind telling you, I wasn't sure we'd make it. Just think if the tender had come off the road.'

'Could have been a different story for their dad.'
'It could indeed.'

I was in a sober mood when I got home that morning, slith-ering my way down the lane to Keeper's Cottage. That fire could so easily have proven fatal, for the family as well as their dog. Part of me knew just how lucky they'd been, but another part of me was gutted for them. I couldn't stop thinking about what might have happened. I suppose it was seeing the family gath-ered on the lawn there in their night-clothes. They looked so vulnerable. As indeed they were. If the fire brigade had been a couple of minutes later the outcome could have been very different indeed.

Before I tiptoed up to bed I double-checked our own fire-place. Ann had been home the previous evening and would most likely have lit the fire I'd laid for her before I went off to work. But the guard was in its proper place, just a pile of warm ashes in the hearth. Everything was as it should be.

Even so, I didn't find it easy to get off to sleep that morning. In fact, I was still half awake when Ann got up to go to work. By this time it was getting light and all sorts of things were going round in my head. I was thinking about the up-and-down nature of our work, and the unpredictability of it. I was telling myself that I'd had my share of emergencies for a while, but of course I knew better than that. Somehow things like house fires, serious road accidents and sudden deaths seem to come in clusters. Like the time I had to deal with two fatalities in a single shift – although that's a story for another time.

So in the end I didn't sleep well at all, and when something set Henry off, barking and yowling in his kennel, I gave it up as a bad job, had a drink of tea and took him out across the frozen fields, amusing myself with the thought that maybe it was the Ryedale Panther that had started him off. I enjoy those walks with him – when he's not trying to escape into the wide blue yonder, that is. I find it's a good time to mull things over. Not for the first time in my career, I found myself thinking about my decision to be a copper. Did I realise I was letting myself in for Christmases like this? No, I'd just had my heart set on serving the community, trying to make a difference – and of course there was a young man's thirst for adventure, excitement, anything rather than the dull routine that seemed to be the lot of office workers, for example. Some of the lads I joined up with were in it because they wanted to drive fast cars – and they soon worked their way into traffic. Others wanted to get into intelligence, or tackle organised crime. Me, I'd had my fair share of excitement in London and now I'd settled for being a rural police officer, out and about on my own most of the time in glorious countryside; but at times like this it didn't seem to be the brightest decision I'd ever made. I thought of Jayne. Hadn't been in the job any time at all and was already working towards her sergeant's exams. And then I thought of the paperwork that Ann complained about now that she'd taken the promotion in York. Swings and roundabouts, I suppose. Pluses and minuses.

I started to make my way home, lost in thought. Henry was still tugging away on his lead, desperate to chase the rabbits that had come out to graze before the frost came down again. We passed a neighbour of mine who'd been out shooting. I only knew him by sight, and we didn't stop to talk, other than a brief exchange of seasonal good wishes, but by the time I got home I was feeling a bit better.

As it turned out, when Christmas Day arrived it wasn't so bad after all. I had my dinner at my mum's place and then went into a quiet shift at work, and when I got home at just gone ten Ann was back from her parents' and had the place all ready for our celebrations. The candles were lit, the fire was glowing, the red wine was warming on the hearth and our presents were under the tree. Dressed in her fur-trimmed Santa hat, Ann looked gorgeous.

'Why don't you go and grab a quick shower?' she said. 'I've got a few nibbles to sort out in the kitchen. Then we can sit in front of the fire and open our pressies.'

Ann had done me proud. I'd dropped a few subtle hints to her over the past few weeks that I was still a big kid when it came to Christmas. I like to have a lot of presents to open, even if they don't cost a lot. So as well as the socks, the woolly jumper, the aftershave and the chocolate orange, there was a beautiful wooden fly-box.

'Where did you get this from?' I said. 'It's perfect.'

'Well, you were wittering on last summer about not having enough room for all your flies. I spotted an advert in the back of your *Salmon and Trout* magazine. Had it delivered to my mum's to keep it secret. Glad you like it. Now, what have you got for me?'

I passed over an armful of presents. She was just as excited as me. After opening the smaller gifts of slippers, silky knickers, chocolates and books, she finally came to a small but perfectly formed box.

'Let me guess,' she said. 'Perfume?'

'Better open it,' I said.

She carefully peeled the paper off. 'Ooh, Coco Chanel,' she purred. 'Oh, that's brilliant, Mike. Thank you.' She reached over and kissed me.

'That is the right one, isn't it?'

'Oh yes. I love it.'

'Yeah, me too . . . but can you explain something to me?'

'What?' She was only half listening, too busy dabbing the perfume onto her wrist.

'What on earth do they put in it to make it so . . . expensive?'

She looked at me and shook her head. 'Mike,' she said, 'you've been spending too long with Walter. The cost is immaterial. The result, my dear, is everything.' And she moved across the hearth towards me.

Next day it was back to work for both of us, but at least we had the prospect of our party to keep our spirits up. New Year's Eve, and my early shift, didn't get off to the best of starts. The weather was still icy, the roads treacherous, and there had been numerous incidents around the county overnight. I kicked off by helping to rescue a motorist trapped in his car after crashing into the bridge at Howsham. Mercifully – miraculously, I should say, because his car was a total mess – he was uninjured. So I was pretty well exhausted when I got back to the station some time after half past nine, plonked my sandwich on the table, then made my way to the front desk. 'I'm gonna have a brew, Chris,' I began. 'D'you fancy—'

But he was on the phone, holding his hand up to me. 'Yes,' he said, 'yes, I've got that, Julie, Mike's just arrived, if you show him as dealing. Thanks.'

'No rest for the wicked then, Sarge. What you got for me?'

'Another bloody Ifor Williams trailer gone from a farm at Leppington. I thought we'd got this lot sorted, Mike?'

'Well, I always thought those Ponte boys were more into the quads and garden machinery.'

'They did Land Rovers, didn't they?'

'Parts, yes, but there was no way they could have taken all the trailers and horseboxes too. I'll go and find out what the SP is.'

I headed back out to the yard, thinking. It had been quite a year for organised teams hitting us hard. And here we were again, perhaps; just when we'd had a really good result, it seemed there was some other lot ready to take their place.

'Mike, just the man I wanted to see!' Inspector Finch was shouting to me from across the yard.

'Oh hello, sir. Good Christmas?'

'Wonderful, thanks, Mike. Make sure you have a great New Year's Eve. You deserve it.'

'Thank you very much, sir, and you.'

He walked towards the back door of the station, then stopped and turned towards me again. 'Oh, and, Mike?'

'Yes, sir?'

'Interesting photographs you sent in.'

'Ah. Those.'

'Yes, those. I take it that the beast in question has been disposed of?'

'Er, yes, sir. I saw to it myself.'

'I hoped you had.'

I had a quiet enough shift. There was no lead at all on the missing trailer. That would have to wait until the new year, I suspected. My last job of the old year was to drop a Christmas newsletter off at Barry and Jackie's. I didn't linger – just stayed long enough to catch up, sup my tea and make an impression on the biscuits. About midday I went back to the station. The clouds had thickened, the snow was falling steadily, the roads were suddenly deserted, and it seemed as if the whole town had gone into hiding. By ten to two the late shift were in and I was on my way home via the supermarket, where I filled the back of the car with a few extra bits and pieces for the party before sliding my way out of a slushy car park and making my way home to Keeper's Cottage.

'Had me worried,' Ann said when I showed up about three o'clock.

'What, about the weather?'

'You know what people are like. You get an inch or two of snow and they decide they don't dare leave the house.'

'Aye, but our friends are made of sterner stuff,' I said, picking up the yard brush and sweeping the slush off the back step. I looked up at the sky, the broken clouds already flushed with gold as the dying sun glowered at us through the bare trees. 'Anyway, they were out gritting when I came home, so it shouldn't be too bad. Even if it freezes. Nobody's coming that far, are they?'

For the next few hours we busied ourselves getting the place in shape. I laid a fire, and made sure we had plenty of nice dry logs stacked up in the hearth. Ann beavered away in the kitchen producing salads, dips, nibbles and sandwiches – although Walter, Muriel and Ed's missus had all promised us they'd bring some food. At about seven I put a match to the fire. While Ann sorted out the drinks I went through our combined music collection and arranged a playlist. If I say so myself, I did a pretty good job.

'Right,' I said, proudly displaying a neat stack of CDs. 'All in order. You've got your nice gentle mood music for when they all show up, right? Then a few rock classics to get everyone a-moving and a-grooving, couple of disco favourites that even I can dance to, and then some seriously cheesy romantic stuff to drive everyone out the door at one o'clock.'

Ann wobbled on a chair, her hands full of balloons, streamers and drawing pins. 'Don't you dare put that Shania Twain on!'

'You can talk.' I flipped through the pile. 'Pavarotti? Gangsta rap?'

'Listen, I have an open mind,' she said. 'And a wide-ranging taste. Eclectic, that's me. Anyway, I bet you've forgotten the national anthem.'

'What do we want that for?'

'To see the new year in, of course.'

'Ah. Good point.' I looked at the pile. 'Nope, we haven't got it.' Then I saw Ann grinning at me. 'All right, all right – I fell for that one. Back in the kitchen, you! Where you belong.'

In any case my musical plans lasted as long as it took Walt's lady friend to breeze in and take charge. They were first to arrive, and by way of breaking the ice I greeted her with, 'Now then, Muriel, packed your fiddle, have you?'

'I most certainly have,' she said, looking at me over the top of her steamed-up glasses as if it never entered her head not to bring it. She started unbuttoning her fur coat, paused and turned to Walt. 'Well, where are your manners, young man? Help me off with this, then go and fetch our instruments from the car. And that baking too.' Across the room Ann, wine glass in hand, was adjusting the sound system. Muriel marched across to her, Walt following along behind as she shed the coat one arm at a time. 'Oh, we shan't be bothering with that thing,' she announced. 'Surely not. There's quite enough piped music in the world, don't you think? Shops, bus stations, restaurants? There's no escape. It's all just mindless drivel, most of it. We can surely converse politely until the band members are assembled?'

'I'm sure we can,' Ann said. She grinned at me, shrugged and swallowed half the contents of her glass. Even she wasn't going to argue with Muriel.

'What about the rest of the band?' I asked. 'When are they coming?'

'They're on their way,' Walt said, as he folded the coat over his arm and walked towards the door. Then he turned towards me and lowered his voice. 'Little detour at t'Farmers, like.' He nodded at Muriel, who was now busy inspecting the fire and placing a guard over it. 'They find her a bit – y'know – daunting.'

'Well, what's up with them?' I said. 'Are they men or mice?' There was a rap on the back door and in came a familiar face. 'Eh up, here comes my man Soapy – and the lovely Becky. Now then, you two, how are you doing?'

'Mustn't grumble, cock-bod.' He looked around. 'Where's the pop, then?'

'Just there.' I pointed to a stack of bottles to one side of the sink.

He paused, glanced at Becky, then said to me, 'Have I to tell him the good news, sweetheart?'

'You're surely not—' I blurted out, but mercifully he stopped me in time.

'Aye, we're getting wed. Next April. Whaddaya reckon to that, eh? Me, a married man?'

I stood there for a moment with my mouth open, until Becky saved me any further embarrassment by filling the silence. 'It's all right,' she said, laughing. 'We're not what you'd call under pressure.'

Soapy laughed. 'She means she ain't in t'family way or owt.' He flicked me in the stomach with the back of his hand. 'We're talking serious romance here, cock-bod.' He rubbed his thumb and forefinger together. 'Cost me plenty of this, I can tell you.

You shoulda seen us. Lord and Lady Muck, riding down to t'Stone Trough at Kirkham in Algy's Frazer Nash, with himself driving. Candlelit table for two, bottle of champers, starters, main course . . . We went right through t'card, then had a couple of brandies to finish off.' He beamed at Becky. 'We had the full monty, didn't we, love?'

Becky laughed. 'D'you know, he even put a suit on,' she said. 'Now if that isn't dedication . . .'

Soapy shrugged. 'Aye well, you've to do things right, 'aven't you? Where a lady's concerned, like.'

'By heck, you're full of surprises, you are,' I said. 'Tell you what, I wish I'd been there to see it. Did he go down on his knees, love?'

'He did when he got the bill!'

Soapy looked at Ann as she went by on her way to open the door. 'So anyway, when you two planning to tie t'knot? We could do a double wedding if you like, save a few quid. I can soon talk that vicar into a "bogof". Buy one get one free, like. What you reckon?'

'Ann and me?' I said. 'Let's just see what next year brings, eh?'

'How's that, cock-bod?'

'It wouldn't do to steal your thunder, would it?' I turned to see Ed and his missus arriving. 'Anyway, let me get Becky a drink, eh, seeing as you can't be bothered, and I'll find out what Ed's wife has been up to in her kitchen.'

'Spanish omelettes,' she said, holding out a huge metal tray. 'We can eat them cold or heat them in the oven. Up to you.'

'Nice one,' I said. 'I think Ann's left the oven on in case. By the way, Cath, did Ed tell you how I missed out on your shortbread?'

'Only through his own daftness,' Ed said. Then he prodded me in the ribs with his forefinger. 'So the answer's no: she is not going to bake you a fresh lot. You got that?'

As the rest of the guests arrived – my mum, Ann's mum and dad, my sisters Christine and Gillian, Ron and Cyril with their instruments, Jayne, Fordy and his girlfriend – it occurred to me that there was a significant absence. Muriel and the boys had just struck up and the younger guests had exited to the kitchen, when I took Soapy aside and asked him, 'Hey, where is Algy boy, anyway?'

'The gaffer?' he said. 'Good point, cock-bod, good point.'

'Well?'

'All I can reveal, matey, is Algy told me I can have as much pop as I like cos he'll give me a ride home.'

'But what about your car?'

'Becky's in charge of that.'

''S right,' she said. 'I'm on the fruit juice.'

'You wanna watch it,' I said. 'He's crafty that way – handing responsibility to other people.'

'Delegation, cock-bod. Teamwork.'

'But Algy's not driving down, is he? He likes a drink at New Year.'

'You'll see,' Soapy said, winking at Becky. But before I had time to question him further, young Fordy was introducing me to his young lady. 'This is Katy,' he said. 'Katy, my colleague Mike.'

'Pleased to meet you,' I said, leaning forward to be kissed. 'Gary's been telling me all about you. You're a student at Leeds, that right?'

'That's right,' she said.

'He seems very keen on you, Katy.'

'You mean, as opposed to one of his other girlfriends?'

I couldn't tell whether she was joking or not. 'No,' I said. 'No, that's not what I meant. He was – er, he was talking about you the other night. On our night shift . . .'

'Oh. Saying nice things, I hope?'

'Naturally. He was being very protective.'

'Excuse me?'

'Oh, just laying out his plans for any of them students, if they tried it on with you. Dangerous fellow is our Gary.'

Before she could respond Fordy whisked her off for a dance, and I was cornered by my mother.

'So, Michael . . .' She looked around. 'This is really lovely. Your Ann's done the place up beautifully. Y'know, you really are a very lucky boy.'

'I did help,' I said, but she ignored the comment.

'I've been chatting to your friends, and I was just saying, you have a lovely home and Ann's doing ever so well at York.'

I had an awful feeling I knew what was coming.

'Don't you think you should be thinking about . . .' She took a sip of wine, and looked at me.

I braced myself. Go on, I was thinking, spit it out. The 'm' word. Why does everyone want to get us spliced?

'. . . well, about promotion? You know, you could have done ever so well at school. If only you'd *applied* yourself.'

'Yes, Mum.'

'Your father was such a clever man, and everyone else has done very well. I blame that old headmaster of yours. You should have gone to grammar school, you know. You passed your eleven plus, but there was only the one place left, remember?'

It was a story I'd heard many times over the years, and it always embarrassed me.

'And he gave it to his own son, you know.'

'Yes, Mum, I know . . .'

'Well, anyway, it's all very nice, dear.' She raised her glass. 'Onwards and upwards, Michael. Now, if I can just get some more sherry for your Aunty June.'

I escaped to the kitchen where I found Ann huddled in the corner, wolfing down a handful of miniature sausage rolls.

'What you up to?' I asked.

'I'm absolutely starving,' she said, coughing into her hand. 'I couldn't resist them.'

'Well, it's our party, love. You can do as you please.'

'Yes, but what about Walt?'

'Eh?'

'He thinks I'm a veggie.'

'Oh, that was ages ago,' I said. 'He'll have forgotten all about it.'

'Yes, but I don't want him to. Imagine us showing up at his place and he pulls one of his badger steaks out of that Rayburn. No.' She dusted the flakes of pastry off her hands. 'As far as he's concerned I do not eat meat.'

Ann drained her glass, grabbed a bottle of red and refilled it.

'Steady on!'

'Well, it appears that our party's about to be hijacked by a bossy retired schoolteacher and your hillbilly friends with their country-and-western band. I can cope, but not if I'm stone-cold sober. That's what I say.'

We clinked our glasses together. 'Okay,' I said. 'But on your own head be it. Any more of these and I may get the urge to dance. And then you will be in trouble.'

As if on cue, the band went into their own unique version of 'Come on Eileen'. 'Mike,' she said, putting both of our glasses on the table and slipping a hand around my waist, 'if you can't dance to this it's time to get on eBay and find yourself a Zimmer frame. Now let's get out there and show these people how to party.'

So there we were: me and Ann, Fordy and his lass, Ed and Cath, bopping away in one corner, while Becky and Soapy got down to some serious smooching in the other. With Muriel giving it everything on the fiddle, and swaying her hips as she scraped the bow across the strings, Walt put his guitar down, whooped like a cowboy and grabbed hold of Jayne.

'C'mon! Can't have you sitting this out on yer own, can we now? Bonny lass like you.'

'Cheers. Nice to see there's still one or two gentlemen about the place,' she said, casting a glance in my direction as her partner swept her clean off her feet.

A moment later Walt was cupping his right hand to his mouth and calling out, 'And . . . *change* your partners, please, ladies and gentlemen!' and before I knew it he'd swung Ann away from me and somehow manoeuvred Jayne into my arms.

'Now then, Jayne. Enjoying yourself?'

'Too right,' she said as I grabbed her hand and twirled her round. 'Always wondered what sort of place you and Ann had out here. Proper countrified, innit?'

'And . . . *change* partners again!'

'Watch yourself, lass. I think he's after you,' I shouted as Walt came by and whisked her away once more. But it was Ann he was after, and Jayne was left lumbered with Ed, who is not the world's greatest mover.

I looked at my watch. Only ten minutes left before midnight. I was just about to tap Fordy on the shoulder and steal his girl off him when there was a loud bang on the window.

'What the hell was that?' Ann was already across the room, reaching behind the curtain for the cord.

'Bloody hell!' The curtains had parted, one by one the band had stopped playing, and there, behind the glass, nostrils flared and eyes wide, was a huge white horse's head.

'Musta got loose from somewhere,' I heard someone say as I stumbled through into the kitchen, tripping over the pile of wellies and boots, and opened the back door, with Ann and Ed behind me.

As we stepped into the darkness a familiar voice boomed out from the side of the house. 'Greetings, my boy! I bring good cheer in a bottle and good fare in my saddlebags.'

'Algy! I should've known it. What the hell are you doing, mate?'

'Well, the fact is . . .' His voice was suddenly a lot less noisy, and a note of uncertainty had crept into it. The lad was gasping. 'I was all right getting up on the damned beast. But I can't for the life of me see how a chap's supposed to get off again. Do give me a hand, won't you?'

Ann pushed past me, strode into the garden and round the corner. We followed; me first, then Ed, Walt and the rest of them.

'It's easy enough,' Ann said, but I didn't hear the rest. Everybody was cracking up at the vision that was Algernon. He had on a pair of fawn jodhpurs, a tight-fitting red jacket with gold buttons, a pair of long dark motorcycle gauntlets, a brass hunting-horn tied around his middle, and a pair of goggles covering his eyes.

'What the hell's all this about?' I said, as he slithered off the horse's back onto the snow-covered grass.

'Remember what I said, months ago, in the Jolly Farmers?'

'I do, but I never thought—'

Algy wagged a gloved finger at me. 'Ah, well that's where people underestimate Algernon, you see. I'm a man of my word. I believe I said that if this hunting ban thingy gets up a head of steam I'd be straight out to get a horse and ride to hounds.'

'Well, good on you,' I said. I peered past him at the horse. It was a magnificent creature, all of seventeen hands and beautifully groomed with a tightly plaited mane.

'But anyway,' Algy continued, 'the midnight hour is upon us. If you'll help me fetch the saddlebags inside I have vintage port, chilled champagne and some rather tasty little snacks from Fortnum and Mason. Oh – and any chance of some oats for Lord Nelson here?'

We left Ann and my sisters to tether the white gelding to my log-seat and coo over him. The rest of us piled inside, Algy opened his bottles, and a few minutes later we were all toasting the new year as Lord Nelson snorted and stamped outside the window. Muriel's band played 'Auld Lang Syne' and a couple of other numbers, then packed up their instruments. And as I slipped my all-purpose dance CD on, Algy popped outside for one last item from the saddlebags, a piece of coal. 'To bring you luck,' he said, placing it ceremoniously on the hearth.

'Great night,' Soapy said as he and Becky helped themselves to a trifle my aunt had brought.

'Fantastic,' I said. I looked around. It was just great to see everyone having a good time in the home Ann and I had put together. Even though I'd been up since five thirty I felt full of energy and very much awake.

By the time the last guests had gone and we had the place to ourselves it was three o'clock. We sat by the hearth watching the fire die down around Algy's lump of coal and sipping a last glass of wine.

'Oh, nearly forgot.' Ann reached behind the settee and pulled out a large brown envelope. 'Got one last present for you.'

'Oh aye, what's this then?'

'Only one way to find out,' she said, as she kicked her shoes off and settled back in her chair.

I opened it up, and laughed. Inside was a new set of *Blackstone's Police PC to Sergeant* study books.

'This a hint, is it?'

She looked at me. 'New year, time for a new endeavour,' she said. 'I just thought, if you're tired of people taking the mick about me being a sergeant, maybe you'd like to surprise them.'

'D'you know what, Ann, you must be a mind reader. I didn't want to tell you, but I've just applied to sit the next set of exams. These books are just the job. Thanks.' Then I reached across and kissed her. 'I can tell you now,' I said, 'we're in for a great new year.'

Acknowledgements

A special thank you to: Phil Pelham for his dedication to the cause; Liz Earl and James Prentice for tea and more; everyone at Welcome to Yorkshire for their continued support.

Finally, thanks to the great characters of North Yorkshire, without whom this book could never have been written.

And finally . . .

Since my first book, *Now Then, Lad* was published, I've had letters from readers all over the world wanting to know more about my patch – the Yorkshire Moors, the Yorkshire Wolds and all that lies between. I've included some of the places in the map at the beginning of the book and if you'd like to know more, have a look at www.yorkshire.com or www.visityork.org.

And if it's a proper cup of tea you're after there's www.yorkshiretea.co.uk. Twenty years ago Yorkshire Tea pledged to plant a million trees around the world. By 2007 they'd actually planted 3 million. Now, with an acre of rainforest being destroyed every second and half of the world's rainforest already lost, there's a new commitment. They've joined forces with the Rainforest Foundation UK to save an area the size of the Yorkshire Dales in the Peruvian Amazon – one of the most threatened rainforests on the planet. To find out more visit www.yorkshirerainforestproject.co.uk.

Now read this exclusive extract from
Mike Pannett's next book:
Just the Job, Lad,
available soon from Hodder & Stoughton.

Chapter 1

'Walt! Where are you, mate?'

All I could hear was the cawing of the rooks as they busied themselves high up in the sycamores. For a moment I stood and watched them, shielding my eyes against the sunlit sky. The way they keep airborne while being buffeted this way and that always fascinates me. Their wings, struggling with a gusty southwesterly, looked like broken umbrellas. I half expected to see them crash to the ground at any moment, but somehow they held themselves aloft and managed to keep working their way to and fro with sticks in their beaks. Spring was here, their young were hatching, and they were busy repairing their nests, rickety, fragile things perched amongst the topmost branches.

'Walt!' I pushed the wrought-iron gate open and squeezed into the yard. 'Come on now, let's be having you.' I knew he was there – somewhere. The car was parked in its usual place with the lid of the boot wide open, and the door of his shed was creaking as it swung this way and that.

'Come on out. It's no good hiding, mate.'

From inside the shed I heard a dull rumble, followed by

clattering, as if a pile of loose slates was falling off a roof. A moment later a cloud of dust rolled out, followed by Walter, clutching a grubby red handkerchief to his mouth with one hand and holding a coil of frayed hempen rope in the other. It was quite a warm afternoon, despite the wind, and the layer of grime that covered his bare forehead was streaked with sweat.

'Good job you're here, lad, cos I'm at the end of me tether.' He paused to flick a cobweb off his waistcoat and mop his face. 'I've had it up to here, lad.'

'Oh,' I said, eyeing the rope. 'Decided to end it all, have you? Just because me and Ann took off for a few days in the sun?'

''Tisn't a laughing matter, lad.' I'd never seen Walt scowl before. He nodded towards the kitchen window, where I could see Henry's head bobbing into view as he hurled himself at the steamed-up glass. 'That blooming dog of yours, why, he's led me such a dance.'

'Aye, he's a challenge. Bit of a slippery customer is our Henry.'

'Slippery? He's like a blooming little eel – and crafty with it.' Walt was shaking a tangle out of the rope. 'Why, there's no controlling him. Pulled t'lead right out of me hand this morning. Shot off across t'field and come back two hours later without it.'

'So is that for me?' I said, holding my hand out.

'I'm goin' to lend you this rope, that's what I'm going to do. While you buy a new lead – a strong 'un. If you want my advice you'll get yourself down to Yates's and treat yourself to one o' them chain-link jobs.' He led the way to the back door, and kicked off his turned-down wellies. 'And I'll give you another tip while you're here. You want to get that dog properly trained before you go traipsing off abroad and dropping your friends in the mire. Why, he's three sheets to t'wind.'

'He's a character all right.'

'A character? He's bloody cracked, that's what he is. You wanna get him to one of them – them pet psychics.'

'You mean psychiatrist, Walt.'

'You know what I mean. One of them as sorts his mind out.' Walt handed me the rope and opened the back door. Henry leapt out, almost taking me off my feet as he jumped up at me, licking my face.

'Right then,' I said, threading the rope through his collar and trudging towards the gate, 'I suppose I'll see you later.'

I had my hand on the latch when he called me back. 'Now then, don't be tekking it personal, lad. Let's not be falling out.' I turned around to see him forcing a resigned sort of grin. 'Tie him up to t'post yonder and come in the house. We'll have a cup of tea and a bit of a catch-up, shall we?'

'Good man.' I followed him inside, hung my jacket on the back of the door and sat myself down at the scrubbed wooden table. Walt filled the teapot from a simmering kettle and put two mugs and a plate of rock buns on the table. 'Them's me sister's,' he added. 'Fresh out of her oven this morning. Dig in, lad. They want eating.'

'I tell you what,' I mumbled through a mouthful of crumbs, 'that sister of yours can't half bake.'

'Aye well, she used to do it professionally. Still does a turn for family and friends. Weddings, christenings and suchlike.' He sat down and started drumming his fingers on the table. And whistling. Then he winked at me. 'How was your trip?'

'Oh. Grand, mate, grand.' I was looking at the teapot, still on the stove. I fancied another cake but my mouth was dry as a bone.

'I hear they have good weather over yonder.'

'Fabulous, Walt. Eighty degrees; nonstop sunshine. You can't beat it.'

'Ower warm for me. Don't suppose I'd fancy the grub either.'

'What, all that barbecued lamb? You'd love it, mate.'

'They drink a lot of wine, according to them travel programmes.'

'They do, Walt.' I was twiddling with my mug, wondering when he was going to get up and pour the tea.

'And right cheap, they reckon.'

'Half price, mate. Less than that. We got through a glass or two, I can tell you.'

'Aye, cos they don't pay the duty we do. My sister always fetches me a bottle or two, y'know.' He was drumming his fingers and whistling again.

'Oh hell, Walt!' I went over to the door and reached inside my jacket pocket. 'Here,' I said. 'Almost forgot.' I handed him the duty-free Ann and I had brought back for him.

He tore the wrapping paper off and stared at the Greek writing on the bottle. 'Why, what sort of concoction is this?' He unscrewed the top and sniffed at the contents.

'It's all the rage over there, mate. Ouzo.'

'Ouzo, you say? Smells like blooming aniseed balls to me.'

'Aye, it does. And you wanna go steady with it. Just a little splash in the bottom of your glass and top it up with water. Treat it like medicine. Like the doctor says. One spoonful at bedtime – or as required. It'll calm your nerves after all the excitement.'

Walt just grinned and put the bottle in his cupboard. 'Aye well,' he said, 'I suppose I shall have to forgive you now. But don't forget what I said about a lead. Chain-link, that's what you want.'

As I walked back down the hill half an hour later, with Henry tugging away at his rope, I still felt a twinge of guilt, but I knew Walter wasn't one to bear a grudge. We'd had a really good holiday, me and Ann. And we needed it. We'd timed it to perfection. The end of April had seen a cold wind sweeping down from the north, and we'd grinned smugly all the way to Cyprus, supping our duty-free; and as we lazed away the afternoons on the beach we scanned the papers, day after day, relishing the reports of record low temperatures, and the familiar photographs of snow-covered daffodils. How lucky can you get? By the time we arrived home the sun was shining, the fields were greening up, and the birds were singing. Spring was in the air, and the best of it was, I could look forward to another day off before I was due back at work. No such luck for Ann though: she was starting that same night, ten o'clock, and wasn't feeling like it. At all.

'Tell you what,' I said, as we strolled along the brow above Wharram Percy with Henry tugging at Walter's rope. It was getting on for teatime, and I was thinking about food. 'I'll make you a nice pack-up to take into work tonight, something to look forward to. Then maybe this evening I'll pop over to my mum's. Catch up with her, show her a few holiday pictures. I'll download 'em onto a CD for her.'

'Just mind your mum doesn't keep you nattering till the small hours,' Ann said. 'I know what you two are like, once you start reminiscing.'

'I'll be all right,' I said. 'I don't have to be up early.'

As ever, Ann was right. Mum and I chatted long into the night. We talked about everything under the sun, as we always do, and I never did get to show her the photographs. It was past midnight when I set off for home. Tired as I was, I was already starting to think about work, and what might be in store for me after a ten-day break. You try and switch off when you're away from the job, but of course you never manage to tidy all the loose ends before you sign off. I'd left a few unresolved problems, one of which was a series of thefts that had plagued our area over the winter. This wasn't small-scale stuff. It was trailers, horseboxes and the like, with the odd four-wheel-drive vehicle thrown in. We'd had bits and pieces of intelligence but no substantial leads, and our inspector had got on the case, demanding that we come up with something – soon.

Some people say you shouldn't take your work home with you, but I've never really seen the sense in that, certainly not for a rural officer. The people I socialise with are the same people I 'protect and serve', as we like to say – unlike in London, where you tended to live outside of the area you worked in. So anything my friends complain about when we're out at the pub on an evening, or when I pop into the village shop, even when we're out fishing – it all goes into my own personal database. Much as I like my time off, a part of my brain is always on duty. Always has been. As far as I'm concerned, if you're a police officer that's what you are. An upholder of the law, twenty-four seven. There's no getting away from the job. You expect people to confide in you – the same as they would if you were a doctor, I dare say. You may not always be conscious of it, but as a copper you're always absorbing bits and pieces of information. And I'm always observing, taking mental notes. I don't mean to. It's just the way I am. In fact, thinking back, I sometimes wonder which came first – an observant, inquisitive nature or the ambition to be a copper. Because I was always interested in what was going on around me. Always will be. Besides, I joined up to catch criminals. Don't get me wrong, I don't go around looking for it off duty, but if something happens I'm not one to turn a blind eye.

I'd made my way onto the A64 and was just approaching the Little Chef, near the lane that takes you down to Claxton, and there, parked up next to the filling station, I spotted a little yellow Datsun. I wouldn't normally have taken much notice, tired as I was, but as I passed it a match flared up in the cab and illuminated three faces, all male. Now, if it had been a car, and if they'd been youngsters, I might have assumed they were on their way home from a night out, maybe on their mobiles trying to find out where the party was. But this was a rusty old pick-up, and they were all grown men, in their thirties at least, maybe older. They didn't look like lads on a night out. And the petrol station was closed. Closed at half ten as far as I could recall. So the thought sort of skittered across my mind: what were they up to? No question about it: they looked dodgy.

Even as I hesitated, and then drove on towards the dual carriageway, I remembered something Ed had mentioned just before I went on leave. Something about a pick-up truck that had been seen in the vicinity of a recent trailer theft. As I thought about what he'd told me my foot hovered over the brake. He'd said it was a yellow one. And a Datsun.

To tell the truth, at that moment I clean forgot I was off duty. I went onto automatic pilot. I checked the rear-view mirror. There was nothing behind me. I drove on a few hundred yards until the road curved and I was sure I would be out of sight, then turned around and headed back towards York. I slowed as I approached the filling station, hoping to get a better look at the truck and the occupants, and maybe get their registration number. But they'd gone, and in the distance I caught just a brief glimpse of their rear lights before they disappeared from sight.

It was at this point that I realised the position I was getting myself into. One, I was off duty. Two, I was in my own car, which wasn't the nippiest. And three, I had none of my equipment with me. No handcuffs, no CS gas – and, of course, no uniform to identify myself as a copper, although as always I had my warrant card in my wallet. All I had was an unreliable mobile phone – and here I was out in the country where the signal came and went on a whim. This was not the type of situation you would want to be in when you were on your own, not even if you were on duty.

I drove on, at speed. A mile further, at the junction where I'd joined the main road, I saw the pick-up signalling right for Flaxton and Sheriff Hutton. I slowed instantly. I had been surveillance trained in the Met, and had a fair bit of experience involving following suspect vehicles. I'd learned to be cautious. The last thing you want is to alert a driver to the fact that they're being followed. As often as not it'll panic them and your cover will be blown. They end up spooked, and that's the end of the job. So there was no way I was going to telegraph my intentions by switching on my indicators and following them down the lane. Instead I would drive on past the junction totally naturally, give them time to get ahead and out of sight, then turn round and pick them up somewhere down the minor road. But as I watched them swing off to the right I saw two cars approaching me from the direction of York – and both of them slowed, signalled, and turned towards Flaxton.

Perfect, I thought. Cover for me. I signalled, pulled to the right, and braked as they made their manoeuvre. I noted that the first was an old Mondeo, with a single male occupant. The second was a battered Cavalier. I followed it into the lane. I could clearly hear that its exhaust was blown. That's when I started to get the feeling that there was something wrong. Something in my gut – something about the type of vehicles and the look of the occupants – was telling me that the three vehicles were actually together. I picked up my mobile from the seat beside me and punched the autodialler, hoping that the night duty staff in the control room weren't too busy.

I was in luck. The control-room staff responded quickly.

'Mike?'

'Yeah Brian, it's me.'

'Thought you were on leave.'

'I was. Still am, in fact. But listen, I'm out and about and I've just spotted sommat.'

'Fire away.'

'I've got three vehicles in front of me heading from the A64 towards Flaxton. There's something not right about them. Can you get somebody out here?'

I gave Brian the number of the Cavalier, which was barely fifty yards ahead of me and travelling at a steady 30 to 40 mph, which, given the time of night, seemed slow.

It didn't take Brian long to come back. 'Yeah, we've had intelligence reports on this one, Mike. Owned by a known associate of . . .' The name he gave me sent a shock wave through me. It was a member of a notorious gang, an extended family from one of the York estates. They were into a wide range of criminal activities and had a record of vicious and violent assaults.

My hands tightened on the wheel. 'Right,' I said, 'he's in a convoy of three vehicles, and I'm pretty sure the first vehicle is also suspect. It's a yellow . . . '

I got no further. The familiar whine from my phone told me I'd lost my signal. I dropped it onto the seat beside me and concentrated on keeping a safe distance – a discreet distance –

from the vehicles ahead of me. Maybe I should have turned round and gone back to where I was getting reception, but I was determined not to lose this lot. If they were up to something perhaps this was a chance to collar them in the act and put them out of circulation for a while. The area would certainly be a safer place. Besides, by this time the adrenaline was flowing through my veins and I could smell a result.

We were approaching Flaxton now, and I'd relaxed a little. I expected them to carry on to Sheriff Hutton or beyond, but suddenly they pulled in at a gated entrance to a field, one after the other. I wondered whether they suspected me and wanted to get me out of the way. If I'd had any doubts up to now, this at least confirmed that the three were operating together. I drove on past at a steady speed, looking straight ahead all the way. That's another surveillance tip: never show any obvious interest in the suspect. What you need to do is act as normal as possible.

The question was, what should I do now? I got to the village, passed the first few houses and then, as the road curved, I stopped, backed into an empty driveway and switched off the engine. Then I lowered the window and listened. The wind had dropped by now and it was a still, cool night. High in the sky a full moon was peering through broken cloud. Somewhere, perhaps a mile or so away across the fields, a fox was yipping; otherwise it was perfectly quiet. I put my seat right down and lay back. If they happened to come by on foot they shouldn't see me. I certainly hoped not anyway. I felt in my inside pocket to make quite sure I did have my police warrant card on me, just in case the occupants of the house came out to see who I was. I picked up the mobile again, and swore under my breath. Still no signal.

I sat there, listening to the gurgle of fluids and the tick-tick-ticking as the engine started to cool. I couldn't have been there more than three or four minutes, but that's a long time when you're on your own, waiting and wondering what's going to happen. As well as worrying about what the suspects were up to, I was frustrated that I couldn't relay the information back to Brian and update the troops. Then I heard a vehicle approaching. At the same time a tall cypress hedge opposite was illuminated by headlights. It was the yellow pick-up coming round the corner, followed by the other two cars.

Raising my head an inch or two so that I could see over the dashboard, I watched them all cruise slowly past, then eased myself upright, ready to start the engine and follow them. But they stopped in a line, right opposite the Blacksmiths Arms, not fifty yards from where I was parked. I suddenly felt very vulnerable. Had they spotted me? Had I inadvertently parked right next to the target premises? This was not a good situation. I was out of range and couldn't contact the control room, and if these people had seen me and decided to challenge me I had no means with which to protect myself. I could be in grave danger. I needed an exit strategy, and the only one that made any sense was the obvious one. Flight. I pressed my foot down on the clutch, eased the gear lever into first and closed my fingers on the ignition key. If they got out of their cars and approached me there was no doubt in my mind what I would do. Fire up and drive off, fast – and let them do the worrying. I wasn't going to attempt any heroics. Not with that lot.

Keeping my head as low as I could, I watched as the pickup doors opened and the three occupants got out. Would they be heading my way? My fingers tightened on the key, then relaxed a shade as I saw them approach the rearmost of the three vehicles, the Mondeo. What was puzzling me was, why the three-vehicle convoy? Was one going to be deployed as a look-out? A decoy? Or what?

The guy in the Mondeo just sat there, his window half open. He seemed nervous, pulling on a cigarette and flicking the ash onto the road with his forefinger more often than seemed necessary. I now saw that his car was fitted with a stout towbar.

The other four were clearly conferring, plotting their next move – but what had they got in mind? The pub? Maybe the antique shop further along the road. There had been a smash-and-grab there a few years earlier. I tried to make a mental note of each man's height, weight, clothing and so on, but they were all dressed in similar fashion: jeans, sweatshirts or loose jumpers, and trainers. They all had woollen hats pulled down low, so that it was hard to see their faces.

Whatever they had been discussing, they'd clearly made up their minds as to their next move. The three of them headed briskly back to the pick-up, got in and set off out of the village with the other two vehicles following.

I gave them a minute or so, then set off, my heart thumping. Once again, I broke the rules. It's something you just have to do from time to time. I'd already used my phone while at the wheel, and now I switched off my lights and drove by the light of the moon, which had now broken though properly. The landscape was brightly illuminated, and I could clearly see the convoy up ahead, their brake lights glowing red as they hit the bends. I was feeling a little less vulnerable now, and a broad grin broke across my face as I remembered similar surveillance jobs in my Met days. The thrill of the chase – although in those days I was always part of a team, with all-important backup. This was different.

I still hadn't a clue where the convoy was going. Up ahead was West Lilling, and beyond that Sheriff Hutton. I knew I'd get a signal there, if not earlier, and that was my second priority – to contact control as soon as possible and alert them to what was going on. The first, though, was not to lose contact with the three vehicles. They were now round the bends and out of sight. It was make-your-mind-up time. I switched the headlights on. My best strategy now was to act as an ordinary member of the public on his way home. I got my foot down and started to gain on them, picking up the phone as I did so. Thank God for that. The full five bars.

'Hello Mike, you all right? We were getting worried.'

'Bloody signal's hopeless round here, Brian. Listen, I've just left Flaxton, en route to Sheriff Hutton and – Whoa, hang on!'

I was just passing a gateway that led into a field of oilseed rape – and there was the pick-up, with nobody in it. I drove on by, maintaining a steady forty to fifty. Barely two hundred yards later I slowed on the approach to the crossing that takes you over the York-to-Scarborough line. On either side are a number of business premises, and on my right was the entrance to a small engineering works. And there, at the metal gates, and armed with a hefty set of bolt-cutters, were the three men from the pick-up. The Mondeo was tucked away just beside the gates, almost out of sight from the road. I might not have noticed it if the driver hadn't just blown a cloud of smoke out through his side window.

Bumping over the crossing I saw the other back-up vehicle. I drove on, looking straight ahead, keeping an eye out for some- where I could pull over and renew contact with control. But that's when Sod's Law kicked in. The road ran straight as a die for a mile or so and I had no choice but to keep going. When

I did finally get round a bend and out of sight, I picked up the phone to find I was out of credit.

It's at times like this that you thank your lucky stars for your backroom staff. I'd been sitting there less than a minute, cursing my luck and wondering what to do next when the phone rang.

'Mike, it's Brian.'

'You played a blinder there, mate. Bloody phone's out of credit.'

'Right, well, stay tuned. We don't wanna lose contact. Any developments?'

I filled him in on what I'd seen at the crossing, which was effectively a break-in in progress – and I reminded him I was still off duty, in civvies and unprotected. 'Well,' he said, 'I've got backup organised but you're looking at – at least ten, maybe fifteen minutes. There's an armed response vehicle en route from the York area, and a Malton car – but that's coming from Heslerton. Not even on the bypass yet.'

I needed to gather my thoughts. Because my problem is I'm inclined to get carried away. Overenthusiastic, you might say. Right now, above all, I needed to stay calm, which wasn't easy. I was sweating, and my heart was thumping. You very rarely come across villains in the act of committing a crime –and if these were the people who'd been plaguing us over the past few months, ripping off trailers and horseboxes, well, it could be a major clear-up. But what was I to do? Should I stay put and risk losing them completely, or go and see what they were up to? I had no way of knowing whether they were armed or not, but just the thought of those bolt-cutters was enough to make anyone think twice about approaching them.

I put the car into gear and let out the clutch. Bugger it, I thought. What's the worst that can happen? So long as I don't get out of the car.

'Brian, I'm heading back to see where they are. If I lose my signal again, just keep ringing, will you?'

'Mike, whatever you do, do not go jumping in. Keep your . . .' – he was fading again – 'distance and be care—' The signal was lost. Back over the railway crossing I found the gates to the works were closed, and the two vehicles that had been there earlier nowhere to be seen. The third one, the Cavalier, was still on the road side, with just the driver in it. Were the others inside the premises, or had they got what they were after and gone?

I barely had a few seconds to take all this in, maintaining my speed as I was. I drove on by, back towards Flaxton. There I looked ahead, checked my mirror, and pulled into the same driveway I'd used earlier, glancing up at the bedroom windows, hoping the occupants hadn't heard me. I crouched behind the dashboard and wound my window down a few inches, listening intently.

I'd only been there a couple of minutes when I heard the roar of the dodgy silencer. Moments later the Mondeo came hurtling through the village, swaying to left and right, its headlights dazzling me briefly. It was pulling a brand new Ifor Williams trailer – and looking as though it would part company with it at any moment. Hard on its heels was the pick-up, followed in turn by the Cavalier. These lads weren't hanging about now.

I started the engine, nosed forward towards the road, and watched as the convoy disappeared from sight before following on behind. Thirty seconds or so later my phone rang.

'Brian.'

'What's happening, Mike?'

'All three suspect vehicles leaving Flaxton and heading towards the A64. The Mondeo is pulling a bloody Ifor Williams trailer. Nicked. They'll hit the A64 any minute now.'

'Right, Mike. The good news is the back-up's not too far away. York car's just leaving the city centre. The Malton car's coming down Whitwell Hill.'

I'd got the tail-lights of all three vehicles in view now. At the junction with the A64 the lead car was straight out, barely seeming to slow down. It swerved, wobbled, and raised a puff of smoke as the driver hit the brakes at the last moment to avoid toppling it over. The pick-up followed, then the Cavalier, but as I followed him out into the main road the driver of this one swung to the left, braked hard and pulled over onto the verge to let me pass. I had a fair idea what he was up to. He reappeared in my rear-view mirror a moment later. Where the hell was my backup?

My hands were now slipping on the steering wheel, my palms sweating and my heart racing. We were fast approaching the Hopgrove roundabout, just on the outskirts of York. The car behind had now closed right up behind me. In my rear-view mirror I could see the driver's face lit up by his dashboard lights, flushed red as I put my foot on the brake. At first I thought he was just trying to get a closer look at me. His lights, reflected in my mirrors, were dazzling me. Was he planning to take me out?

'Brian, I've one on my tail – close up. Whoa, scrub that. He's turned off towards Stockton-on-the-Forest.' The question was, had he alerted the drivers in front on a mobile? They must have known that something was up. I was directly behind the pick-up, close enough now to give Brian the registration number – just as the driver pulled out, accelerated and passed the Mondeo.

'Yeah Mike, the pick-up has no registered keeper.'

'What's the backup situation, over?'

'Malton car'll be there in a minute or two. Just passing the Tanglewood. And you should see the York car any moment.'

'Hope you're right, mate. Hope you're right.'

I followed the pick-up onto the roundabout at speed. He didn't signal, just swung sharply off, taking the first exit.

'Brian, the pick-up's gone Leeds way. I'm following the Mondeo plus trailer. Into York, by the look of it, over.'

As we sped towards the outskirts of the city I saw the lights of the York ARV unit heading towards me – and speeding right by.

Surely they hadn't missed us? He hadn't. In my rear-view mirror I saw him execute a perfect 180-degree skid turn and race up behind me. Time for me to back and let him pass. To my surprise, he'd no sooner signalled the Mondeo to stop than the driver did just that, barely a hundred yards down the road.

I eased off and slowed down, drove on past the ARV guys and the Mondeo before pulling over a few hundred yards down the road. The last thing I wanted was to have my private car identified. If that got out on the bush telegraph I could look forward to all sorts of trouble. I left my car and walked the rest of the way back towards them.

They had the driver out on the verge and were taking his details. He was what I'd call gaunt. Sort of skinny, with narrow shoulders, lank hair and a thick lip. With his eyes narrowed and the blue lights flashing in his face he looked a pretty sorry figure. I now saw that his left eye was swollen and the cheek below it bruised and grazed. He was busy protesting his innocence. 'They made me do it,' he kept saying. 'They made me. They woulda killed me if I didn't.'

'Yeah well, you'll have plenty of time to explain everything back at the station,' the arresting officer said as they took him to their car. Then his partner turned to me. 'Pannett, isn't it?' he said.

'That's right.' I knew him vaguely, the way you do get to know a few faces from the beats that border your own. We'd met once or twice on various courses.

'Hardly recognised you in civvies,' he said. 'What was this, an undercover job or what?'

I shook my head, and watched his mate put the prisoner in the car. 'No,' I said, 'I was on my way home when I came across this lot.' He looked at me blankly. 'I'm off duty,' I said. 'I was just in the right place at the right time, and – well, call it a sixth sense.'

'What, and you gave chase in your own vehicle?'

'Nah, I followed them, that's all. And tipped off control. Not often you come across criminals in the act, is it?'

'S'pose not. Bloody good job mate. Well done.'

'Well,' I said, 'looks like you've got everything under control.' My only concern was that the Malton crew hadn't been able to find the pick-up, but circulations were out for both of the outstanding vehicles and another unit was on its way to Flaxton, to the premises that had been broken into, with the key-holder on his way. 'I'll meet you in York,' I said. 'I'll have to give a statement, I guess. See you there.' I lit a cigarette and made my way slowly back to my car.

As I drove into York I mused on the night's events with mixed feelings. It was brilliant that we'd made the arrest and recovered the property intact, but we hadn't managed to pick up the other members of the gang. The guy we'd got looked like the weakest link, someone they'd roped in under duress. The main gang seemed to have got away, and would doubtless be at it again before long.

Fifteen minutes later I was walking into York police station and making my way to the custody area when I heard a familiar voice behind me.

'Mike, what on earth's going on?'

Ann was standing there in the corridor, gaping at me. 'Has something happened?'

'No, it's all right. I was on my way back from my mum's and I came across a trailer theft.'

'You did what?'

'Well, I was on my way home and came across a team nicking a trailer, out Flaxton way. so I – well, I got after them. Your fellow officers from York collared them, and I've just come in to do my statement.' I looked at her and put on my most winning smile. 'Hey, any chance I can sit in your back office while I write it up?'

She shook her head and sighed. 'Can't let you out of my sight for two minutes, can I? You were supposed to be having a quiet night round at your mother's. Yeah, course you can use the office. Are you all right?'

'Yeah. Bit hairy at times, but – I'll tell you all about it later.'

'I'll put the kettle on. You'll find the statement forms in the drawers on the left. Hello – here they come.'

At that the door opened and the ARV crew appeared with the suspect. While Ann set about booking him in and sorting out a doctor to check his injuries, I went and started on my statement. I hadn't been writing long when I spotted Ann's familiar pack-up box on a side table. The thought of those cheese and tomato sandwiches I'd lovingly prepared for her several hours previously was too much for me. I had a little peek, and sure enough, there was one left. It would be a pity to see it go to waste.

'Don't even think about it!' Looking up, I saw Ann at the door. 'I was saving that for later. Here' – she threw me a half-empty packet of custard creams – 'have these.'

The moon was setting when I made my way down the wooded drive that led to Keeper's Cottage, and I was flagging. You burn a lot of mental and nervous energy on a job such as that. Yes, you have that glow of satisfaction when it comes right, but in the end your body reminds you of the resources you've used up. All I could think about now was bed. Henry, though, had other ideas. He'd been on his own since early evening and assumed I was going to take him out.

'Come on, then,' I sighed, threading Walter's rope through his collar. 'Just down the lane and back.'

It was half past three when I got into bed. I never heard Ann come in.

It was a few weeks after all this that a letter arrived from the chief superintendent, addressed to me. I looked at it for some time before opening it. I was thinking, Christ, now what? Letters from on high don't often land in your in-tray – and when they do they can spell trouble.

I needn't have worried. Our leader was writing to congratulate me on my display of initiative in chasing after the gang and whistling up support. A few days after that I got a second pat on the back, a congratulatory email from the chief constable. When I got home that night I couldn't wait to tell Ann about it. She listened patiently, then said, 'I've been thinking.'

'I thought you were listening.'

'I was. I have also been thinking. I am a girl and can multi-task, remember?'

'This sounds serious. Ominous, in fact.'

'Serious, yes. Ominous, no. Listen,' she said, putting her hand on mine, 'I think you're a fantastic copper.' She laughed. 'Unpredictable, slightly mad, but great at your job.'

'I like this. Is there more?'

'There is. I think you'd make a brilliant sergeant. I mean, look at some of the people you and I have seen promoted over the years. Some of them are fine and some—' She pulled a face. I knew what she meant. 'And when you think about the bad ones, you wonder how on earth they got where they are, am I right?'

'You can say that again.'

'And the good ones . . . '

'Cocksy, for example?'

'Yes, I'd rate him. But do you really think he brings anything to the job that you haven't got?'

I looked at her and thought for a moment. 'That's not for me to say.'

'I think it is, Mike. This is not the time for you to come over all modest,' she said. She smiled and looked me right in the eye. 'Come on, how do you rate yourself as a copper?'

'Blimey.' I had to think for a moment before answering. 'Well, now that you're asking I think I'm pretty bloody good at what I do. And I love the job.'

'That's more like it. And how about gelling with your fellow officers? Could you lead them into battle, take the initiative, lead by example?'

'Yeah, sure I could.'

'And would you stop and consider your options, before going in all guns blazing?' '

'Of course. You have to get people onside, don't you? All singing from the same hymn-sheet, as they say. Y'know, what you were saying about good supervisors and bad ones – I've always reckoned it's a matter of picking out the good characteristics and weeding out the bad. I mean, if you were modelling yourself on them.'

'Right, so what I'm saying, Mike, is why don't you set aside a couple of days and go through those books I gave you at Christmas, about the sergeants' exams?'

I groaned. 'I knew there was a catch. I hate studying. It reminds me of school. Remember what I always say? I left school with two qualifications: one in the study of motorcycles and— '

'Yeah, I know – and one in girls.' Ann sighed. 'You have mentioned it once or twice. But this time, surely you can see there's a payoff. There's the increase in salary, and in your pension. I mean, how much longer do we want to keep renting this place?'

'Keeper's Cottage? I love it here, don't you? I mean, it's a great place to live. Character cottage with a bit of land, fantastic location. Secluded.'

'Yes, I know all that. We both love it here. But it's like pouring money down the drain isn't it, paying rent month after month.'

'Costs a hell of a lot to buy a place like this,' I said. 'To be honest, we've been spoiled living here, haven't we? Any place we moved on to – that we could afford – it'd be a step down, wouldn't it?'

'Right, so why don't we hit Algy boy with a proposal? Why don't we ask him how much he wants for Keepers Cottage?'

'D'you reckon he'd sell it?'

'No idea. We'd need to ask him.'

'Well, Ann, that sounds like a plan. One that calls for a celebration.'

'We haven't bought it yet!'

'I know. But you've just agreed to get a mortgage with me. And that's a statement of intent, isn't it?'

'Only one trouble, Mike.'

'What's that?'

'You gave the last of the duty-free to Walter.'

Have you read the other tales from the Yorkshire bobby?

MIKE PANNETT

YOU'RE COMING WITH ME, LAD

Policing rural Yorkshire is a far cry from Mike's old job hunting
down drug gangs and knife crime in Central London. Settled back
in his native Yorkshire, however, Mike finds that life as a rural
beat bobby is no picnic.

After a crazed swordsman threatens to take his head off, he finds
himself confronting a knife-wielding couple bent on carving each
other up. When a stag night turns ugly he gets stuck with the
groom, the best man and the bride-to-be all banged up in the cells
– and the wedding just hours away. With record-breaking floods
and politicians to escort, will Mike find time to woo the woman
of his dreams?

Hodder & Stoughton paperback
www.hodder.co.uk